TRANSFORM WITH DESIGN

Transform with Design

Creating New Innovation Capabilities with Design Thinking

EDITED BY JOCHEN SCHWEITZER,
SIHEM BENMAHMOUD-JOUINI,
AND SEBASTIAN FIXSON

UNIVERSITY OF TORONTO PRESS
Toronto Buffalo London

Rotman-UTP Publishing
An imprint of University of Toronto Press
Toronto Buffalo London
utorontopress.com

© University of Toronto Press 2023

Library and Archives Canada Cataloguing in Publication

Title: Transform with design : creating new innovation capabilities with
    design thinking / edited by Jochen Schweitzer, Sihem BenMahmoud-Jouini,
    and Sebastian Fixson.
Names: Schweitzer, Jochen, editor. | Fixson, Sebastian K., editor. |
    BenMahmoud-Jouini, Sihem, editor.
Description: Includes bibliographical references.
Identifiers: Canadiana (print) 20230220827 | Canadiana (ebook) 20230220878 |
    ISBN 9781487506094 (cloth) | ISBN 9781487533298 (EPUB) |
    ISBN 9781487533281 (PDF)
Subjects: LCSH: Organizational change – Case studies. |
    LCSH: Organizational change – Psychological aspects – Case studies. |
    LCGFT: Case studies.
Classification: LCC HD58.8.T68 2023 | DDC 658.4/06–dc23

ISBN 978-1-4875-0609-4 (cloth)   ISBN 978-1-4875-3329-8 (EPUB)
                                        ISBN 978-1-4875-3328-1 (PDF)

Printed in the USA

Cover design: Michel Vrana
Cover image: danjazzia, envato

We wish to acknowledge the land on which the University of Toronto Press
operates. This land is the traditional territory of the Wendat, the Anishnaabeg, the
Haudenosaunee, the Métis, and the Mississaugas of the Credit First Nation.

University of Toronto Press acknowledges the financial support of the Government of
Canada and the Ontario Arts Council, an agency of the Government of Ontario, for its
publishing activities.

ONTARIO ARTS COUNCIL
CONSEIL DES ARTS DE L'ONTARIO
an Ontario government agency
un organisme du gouvernement de l'Ontario

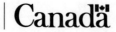

Funded by the   Financé par le
Government gouvernement   Canadä
of Canada   du Canada

Contents

Figures and Tables

Figures

Tables

CHAPTER ONE

Why Implementing Design Thinking Remains a Challenge

JOCHEN SCHWEITZER, SIHEM BENMAHMOUD-JOUINI, AND SEBASTIAN FIXSON

Why "Transform with Design"?

Design advocates like us argue that great new products and services do not simply arise from the uptake of a new technology or process but require a collective fit of the innovation with an organization's strategy and culture and integration with the whole innovation ecosystem.[1] More so, for an organization to adapt and strategically transform in the face of the ever-changing and more demanding market environments, it needs a way to engage with uncertainty and ambiguity and develop new business models and better strategies.

Only recently, managers have adopted design to *think like a designer* and solve *wicked problems*.[2] Over the last decade, design thinking has become an important method to draw on *designerly tools* to drive innovation, facilitate organizational change, and improve competitive performance.[3] Today, design thinking is recognized within large multinational and medium-sized companies across many industries as an alternative approach to innovating. Yet many organizations generally find the implementation of design thinking still very challenging.[4]

We wrote this book because we think the stories of why some succeed where others fail when it comes to employing design thinking to drive innovation and transformation in large organizations need telling. How have global players succeeded with product and service innovation and transformed entire organizations to become customer-focused? With this book, we attempt to answer these questions by presenting ten examples.

Why is the application of design thinking a challenge? Often design thinking finds itself in conflict with existing organizational structures, cultures, and processes.[5] More than with conventional approaches to innovation, design thinking calls for new mindsets and mental models that embrace user-centricity, ambiguity, risk-taking, and collaboration. Because design thinking challenges existing ways of thinking and working, it is often met with skepticism and resistance. It is these barriers that organizations must deal with before achieving success.

As management scholars, we are eager to understand better how barriers to implementing design thinking for innovation can be overcome and what processes and practices work best. Much of this research finds its way into academic journals. With this book, however, we aim to address a much more pragmatic objective, which is to feature the anecdotal experiences of professionals, who tell the story of implementing design thinking as it unfolded for them and how they navigated the many barriers and obstacles they encountered along the way.

This collection of ten stories is about how people in diverse settings and circumstances transformed their organizations with design and sustained the effort of implementing design thinking to achieve innovation outcomes. Our contributors review their experience from early beginnings to today, providing a personal perspective on the evolution of corporate innovation agendas and revealing some valuable lessons for everybody who finds themselves in a similar position.

Who Should Read This Book?

This book is written for design thinking practitioners, from novices interested in learning how design has played a role in transforming organizations to experienced consultants, managers, and innovation leaders who like to compare notes and get a fresh perspective on what others do. Each story illustrates the effectiveness – and sometimes limitations – of various design strategies and actions in particular environments.

In addition, we hope this book is also helpful for researchers, educators, and students of innovation, design thinking, and organizational transformation, as it provides a rich tapestry of examples and anecdotes that put into perspective design thinking methods and tools taught in education and training programs around the world.

What Is Design Thinking?

Design thinking is the application of design methods and tools to a broad range of innovation challenges; it is a way for organizations to balance feasibility, viability, and desirability of new product or service ideas, develop innovative offerings and capabilities, discover new business models and, if it all goes well, gain strategic advantage.

Design thinking engages multidisciplinary teams in iterative user research, idea generation, and prototype design and testing. However, the notion of design thinking as a *process* is paradoxical. There is a conflict between the iterative nature of design thinking tools and methods and the implied sequentially of a process. As a result, instead of referring to a "linear process," design thinking is often thought of as *navigating through various phases or modes*.

These phases are distinct from steps as they do not have specific boundaries or protocols as a scientific approach to problem-solving might have. As design thinkers, we go through these phases repeatedly, sometimes simultaneously and at different times in a nonlinear fashion to deal with the complexities of the problems we aim to solve.

Most of the writing on design thinking has focused on describing and evaluating the tools and methods people use. These include need-finding tools (e.g., ethnographic observations, in-depth contextual interviews, or customer journeys used to empathize with and understand the needs of end-users), idea-generation tools (e.g., brainstorming used to generate possible solutions to problems), and idea-testing tools (e.g., rapid prototyping and experimentation used to test ideas on a small scale for desirability, technical feasibility, and business viability).

The tools and methods are used across phases of exploration, ideation, and experimentation with the objective to either diverge (i.e., understand issues and needs, discover and explore opportunities, create options) or converge (i.e., analyze and synthesize information, define results, choose opportunities, options or solutions) toward an outcome.[6] The outcomes of design thinking are product or service prototypes, for which user desirability has been proven, and, at least partly, technical feasibility and business viability have been addressed as well.

Describing design thinking through tools, methods, and phases illustrates the various activities that design thinkers are engaged in. Nonetheless, these activities are guided by a set of mindsets or a "design state of mind" that recurs in any of these phases. A typical catalog of mindsets that are described in research and observed in practice include having empathy toward people's needs and contexts; embracing collaboration and diversity; being curious, social, and open to new perspectives; being open to the unexpected; embracing learning; being mindful, reflexive, and resilient; taking action; being creative; accepting uncertainty; and being playful and humoristic, optimistic and energetic.[7]

The *design thinking mindset* conceptualizes the enactment – or the *thinking* and *doing* – of design thinking. While people (and organizations) may adopt phases and learn new tools quickly, the mindset ultimately helps achieve innovation objectives at a deeper and more sustainable level. We believe that applying design thinking tools without forming the necessary mindset often leads to failure.

Some companies have been so fixated on processes and tools that they turned design thinking into a rigid plan, implemented like any other efficiency-based process that they know well, often with less than stellar results.

The ten cases presented in this book are aligned with our understanding of design thinking, even if some authors use different terminology. You will find references to human-centered design, design-driven innovation, design-led innovation, customer-centric innovation, and so on. While nuances differ regarding how these terms are defined, we think the core of each reflects what we have described broadly as design thinking above.

The differences in the terminology used by organizations also point at the importance of recognizing how people make sense of new ways of working, which often depends on how easily understood terms are and how accepted they are in their organizational context. More so, we do not want to dwell too much on methods, tools, and mindset – many other publications have already done that – but instead, explore and describe how the adaptation and the use of design thinking are managed in real life in large organizations.

How Did This Book Come About?

The idea for this book emerged from a discussion between Ingo Rauth and Jan Schmiedgen at a Design Thinking Exchange (DTX) conference,[8] a community-organized researcher-practitioner knowledge exchange. Reflecting on their experiences with design thinking, they saw a pattern: The challenges of and barriers to scaling and adapting design thinking in large organizations that participants of the conferences discussed were the same, year after year.

Typical questions included the following: How do we (the transformation team) get buy-in (from management and the rest of the organization)? How can we change the mindset or the culture of an organization? How do we best close the gap between design thinking efforts and early-stage product development? How do we address and include middle managers? Discussing these questions, they realized that it rarely is design thinking itself that poses a challenge for teams working with design thinking, but the context in which it is intended to work, that is, the often bureaucratic nature of large and established organizations.

Why is it that there is still such an overemphasized buzz in the design thinking community, both in academia and in practice, about "the process of design thinking," "the dissection of the design thinking mindset," or "how to apply it in project work" when the real problem seems to be "organizing the change for design by design"? In other words: Where is the book that describes how to manage the adaptation of design thinking and reap the benefits it promises?

Through their work, Ingo and Jan had seen many examples of successful organizational change toward innovation with the help of design thinking. They knew that the stories existed, but they had not been told widely. So, why not write a book that focuses on the critical aspects of design thinking implementation? A collection of case studies that allows people to learn from each other's efforts and see how different organizations adopted design thinking in different industry contexts. Not a "copy and paste" recipe or playbook but rather one that inspires and encourages by showcasing lessons learned, timelines and tactics, failures and ways in which other organizations started their transformation journey with design.

Eventually, this led to the editorial team forming with Jochen Schweitzer, Sihem BenMahmoud-Jouini, and Sebastian Fixson, who worked with nineteen contributors to produce the ten cases featured in this book. Author teams were made up of practitioners and scholars who jointly told the story of design thinking innovation they had been involved with.

What Makes This Book Different?

We asked authors to take a managerial- and strategic-level perspective on their experiences. You will not read much about the process or operations related to "how to do design thinking" but more about the activities and interventions, barriers and enablers that determine the adaptation of design thinking at the organizational level.

At the same time, we offer you a longitudinal perspective with cases that richly describe the activities, changing conditions, and outcomes over between four and sixteen years. With an average time of eight years per case, the data presented covers an extensive period. This data was collected in various ways. Interviews were conducted with a wide variety of people who were directly involved with or impacted by the design innovations initiatives. Researchers participated in internal meetings and had access to internal and external documents.

We think that the characteristics of these cases are important. There is much to learn from understanding how design has found its way into these organizations over such an extended period. There were quick wins here and there, but more importantly, we could document long-term strategic success, lasting cultural change, and individual development.

Any collection of cases on design thinking implementation must be biased. We don't usually hear much about the initiatives that failed or had no long-lasting impact on organizations, yet those would be the ones we could learn from most. Although the cases presented in this book can mainly be classified as successful and impactful design thinking implementations, they were not without failure. We tried to point out not only what worked but also what did not work. Even though the chapters were written generally by a researcher teaming with practitioners involved in the initiative, we paid particular attention to maintaining a critical perspective. Indeed, as the editorial team, we systematically reviewed all chapters to ensure that authors discuss both challenges and successes critically.

How to Read This Book?

We suggest reading the chapters of this book in any order. We have created a table (see table 1.1) that features key aspects of each case and gives a sense of the setting in which a case took place, including the industry, leadership involvement, scope, duration, and critical outcomes. We suggest using the table to identify the most compelling case and start there.

While it is tempting to see the cases in this collection as best practices, they are far from being recipes. Adaptation of design thinking is subject to organizational cultures, politics and governance structures, leadership dynamics and styles, industry settings, and competitive situations, to just name a few factors. So, even though we suggested earlier that people have similar questions and organizations encounter similar barriers when implementing and scaling design thinking, every case is different and points to unique lessons. These lessons, we suggest, serve as excellent starting points when discussing how to start (or continue) with the adaptation of design thinking in your organization.

About the Case Studies

The cases provide insights into design thinking implementations that vary across many factors, including strategic mission, size, scope, governance structure, organizational structuring, funding, and leadership support.

The case featuring **Blue Cross Blue Shield of Massachusetts (BCBSMA)** is about a health insurance company faced with two

Table 1.1. Case overview and comparison

Case	Country, Sector	Period, Scope	Approach	People Reached	Starting Point	Leadership Role	Type of Initiative	Team	Outcomes	Challenges
Blue Cross Blue Shield	USA, Health Insurance	4 years from 2015 to 2019, National	Top-down, but then pushed by a small team	Small innovation team became experts; 100s trained in methods and mindsets	Digitization and changed customer expectations	Initially highly supported	Strategic initiative targeted at developing innovation capability	Innovation team charged with helping the organization build innovation skills and mindset	Broad awareness of DT to work creatively	Despite widespread training with a focus on mindset, it is unclear how much of it will "stick"
Danone	France, Food	5 years from 2014 to 2020, International	Senior Leader Research and Innovation empowered one person	700+ people and 45 innovation projects	Missed strategic opportunities; need to speed up collaboration across functions and become more user-centric	Supported via funding early trials and a team of four	Strategic initiative, adoption via experimentation, first via external agencies then a small internal team	A senior leader at the corporate and division level and one designated person to launch and later lead a group of four	Diversity of projects; people-powered innovation via Innovation Academy; adoption of fast prototyping and user-centric approach; evolution to user experience team	Negotiating with marketing and experts representing the voice of users; convincing stakeholders; keeping design thinking principles alive in every project
Intuit	USA, Accounting Software	12 years from 2006 to 2018, International	Top-down and bottom-up	8000+ employees, 1000+ trained as Innovation Catalysts, core team up to 12	A focus on "ease of use" and "delight" was no longer supporting growth; inspired by the success of Procter & Gamble	Highly endorsed by the leadership team	Strategic but trial and error implementation	Central design team with influence throughout the organization	10x growth, innovation and cultural transformation, design thinking became how the firm expected work to happen	Keeping up momentum once design thinking was the new norm; as employee turnover occurred, new behaviors and mindsets faded
Kaiser Permanente	USA, Healthcare	13 years from 2003 to 2016, National	Approved by top, led by middle management with frontline support	Thousands reached across time; started by a small team	Alignment of interest with IDEO	Highly supported by part of the leadership team	Strategic, as a small, focused pilot test	A core team of three supported by VP Patient Care Services and COO	Multiple solutions spread across 40 hospitals and thousands of clinics: impact on patient outcomes and workforce capabilities	Continuing momentum through leadership changes, especially for more complex challenges

(Continued)

Table 1.1. Case overview and comparison (Continued)

Case	Country, Sector	Period, Scope	Approach	People Reached	Starting Point	Leadership Role	Type of Initiative	Team	Outcomes	Challenges
MindLab	Denmark, Public Services	16 years from 2002 to 2018, National	Small team co-sponsored by three government agencies	Employees of three ministries and public services in general	Business schools challenged the administration about innovation	Supported by Ministry of Business Affairs, later also Ministries of Taxation and Employment	Not strategic at first but later five strategic initiatives in policy and public services	A core team of five; approx. total of 15	Brought ethnography and design to government's decision-making and became an international thought leader in public sector innovation	Cost center where costs were evident but outcomes difficult to measure; replaced by a digitization initiative
Mirvac	Australia, Real Estate and Construction	7 years, from 2014 to 2020, National	Top-down initiated by CEO, then driven by middle management	100s trained and involved, a small team of innovation champions	Global financial crisis, strategic need for innovation	Highly supported	Strategic from the beginning	Two middle managers oversaw the initiative	It increased innovation capability across the organization; changed culture that enabled both incremental and disruptive innovation	Achieving business unit buy-in, creating measurable short-term success and long-term strategic impact at the same time
Swisscom	Switzerland, Telecommunications	6 years, National	Top-down empowered by CEPO, initiated by middle management	Team of 4 grew to 70; 100s of projects, 60+ professional inventors, 7000+ people trained	Desire to bring agile human-centered work methods to the organization and foster innovation in a 150-year-old firm	Supported after some time	Not strategic at the beginning	One manager working with a design team and stakeholders from across the firm	Embedding human-centered ways of working alongside an established innovation culture; becoming an experience-driven firm and having an impact on customers; measuring and tracking innovation	Achieving disruptive innovation through building external capabilities to foster disruptive innovation from the outside

(Continued)

Table 1.1. Case overview and comparison (*Continued*)

Case	Country, Sector	Period, Scope	Approach	People Reached	Starting Point	Leadership Role	Type of Initiative	Team	Outcomes	Challenges
Thales	France, Aeronautics, Defense, and Security	9 years from 2012 to 2021, International	Bottom-up, empowered by Vice President HR	3000+ trained, 1000+ workshops and 80+ projects supported	A learning expedition and projects with d.school at Stanford University	Highly supported in one area of the organization	Not strategic and *under the radar*, encouraged by Head of Corporate University	A core team of six and 60+ professionals across the firm	Establishing 13 design centers globally	Growing the initiative and adapting the method to the variety of project needs
US Dept. of Labor	USA, Government	4 years from 2014 to 2017, National	Bottom-up	1000s	Not knowing how to create services that meet unique customer needs	Supported after a while	Not strategic and improvised, yet building on other initiatives that happened at the same time	One senior executive who had been working on large-scale system change in government	Government-wide exposure to design thinking for the public workforce development system; training and inspiration to move from *compliance-focus* to *customer-focus*	Convincing people that experimenting with improving customer service would not get them *in trouble*
US Dept. of Veterans Affairs	USA, Government	6 years from 2011 to 2017, National	Small exploratory activities and top-down, then spread throughout the organization	1000s	First strategic, then crisis due to faded veterans' trust; replacing *system-centered* with *human-centered* perspective	Initially very supportive, but then attention shifted to other topics	An idea that gathered momentum then waxed and waned; over the years, several restarts	Various design teams, sanctioned by executives, albeit shifting priorities	Human-centered perspective changed the conversation in large parts of the organization, and prototypes demonstrated their value	Shifting strategic priorities created larger forces that a small team struggled to navigate

powerful forces beyond its control: rising customer expectations and increasing cost pressures. In response, the leadership team launched a project to improve the organization's competitiveness through innovation. It became apparent quickly that to build innovation capabilities throughout, the company required a dedicated organizational innovation unit. Design thinking became the central innovation method, and numerous training events for the company's employees were created, ranging from short, two-hour to two-day design thinking boot camps to week-long design thinking sprints that involved all layers of the organization. The team worked on projects together with line units, guiding them in the application of design thinking. Later, an internal innovation center was created to house project teams, provide space for incubation, and plan programming events.

In this case, three factors were critical and are worth pointing out: First, from the start, the team communicated to all parties involved that the initiative was a long process that needed time to develop. Second, the team's focus on capability building and using real projects helped spread design thinking throughout the organization. And finally, the appropriate adaptation of design thinking to the company's culture was reflected by applying labels to activities and processes that matched the organization's worldview.

The **Danone** case describes the implementation of design thinking in a global food company for six years. Like many other firms, this initiative started with a learning expedition to get inspired that resulted in a mission to speed up an existing but not very effective corporate innovation process. Senior leaders funded five strategic projects following a design thinking approach involving external consultants and a small internal team who learned from these early projects and developed the Danone design thinking recipe for innovation.

What makes this case interesting is that it reports on introducing a human-centered approach to a firm where the *voice of the customer* was already strongly represented through marketing experts and a sensory and behavioral sciences team. Furthermore, employees were also used for *consumer testing*, which is common in the food sector. However, the projects revealed how complementary design thinking (mainly fast discovery, rapid prototyping, and cross-functional teams) coexists with the existing approaches practiced for decades. Another interesting dimension is the international and decentralized context. The diffusion of design thinking on a global scale required complex and not always successful negotiations between corporate where design thinking has been initiated and local subsidiaries where projects were developed. However, after six years, more than forty-five innovation projects, including product and process innovation, rebranding, and new product development, adopted design thinking, involving almost 700 people. Today, the former design thinking team has been renamed the User Experience team and comprises more than 100 people across the globe.

The **Intuit** case features the implementation of design thinking covering thirteen years, the third-longest period documented in this book. Such a longitudinal perspective is valuable and uncommon. It shows that successful execution of design thinking often is a long-term endeavor. Indeed, the case describes how seven years after the first adoption of design thinking, and while design thinking had already been ingrained in the daily work of many employees, it began to fade from the skillset. It became necessary to generate a second momentum.

The case also shows how design thinking is much more than understanding customers and integrating ease of use (which was at the core of Intuit's strategy). At Intuit, design thinking combines emotion with a crafted iterative problem-solving approach (designated as Design for Delight) used in a wide range of situations. The diffusion of this approach was based on two strategies: First, hands-on experiential workshops involving leaders to have them experience the approach's potential and, second, a core team of ten people who animate a community of active catalysts. Another noteworthy feature of the Intuit case is the openness of Intuit staff toward learning from other firms and approaches.

With **Kaiser Permanente,** we documented the implementation of design thinking at a decentralized healthcare non-for-profit organization, characterized as risk-averse and data and evidence driven. Yet this case features a remarkably pragmatic approach based on a small enthusiastic team working on projects addressing non-incremental improvements. The initiative's objective was to prove the value of a human-centered design approach and build capability using storytelling and training. Consequently, the choice of projects and the people involved were critical and deliberate. Kaiser Permanente chose projects that feature diversity in locations and units (patient care, IT, etc.), direct impact on customers or front-line staff, and a possibility to share results within and outside the organization.

Progressively, projects were run by front-line staff trained in design thinking. Notably, the small team in charge of design thinking implementation considered the scale-up of the initiative as a design challenge in its own right. The team was open to adopting other methodologies, including behavior design and behavioral economics, and Lean Six Sigma. From this case, we also learn about the importance of using external communication to fuel the internal fire and gain legitimacy. Finally, this case highlights the central role of leadership for design thinking implementations in two surprising ways.

The case of **MindLab** describes the development, growth, and ultimate demise of a lab created by the Danish Ministry of Business Affairs to diffuse and apply user-centered design methods to public services and beyond to influence and establish these different ways of thinking in government. The objective was to disrupt the bureaucracy. The case shows how it morphed over the sixteen years of its existence. It started small in 2002 and, in its heyday, became an international thought leader in public service innovation. In 2018, it was shut down and replaced by the Ministry of Business' Disruption Task Force.

The case offers lessons for design labs everywhere. Indeed, despite the facilitation of over 280 workshops in its first four years, showing a real value as a process catalyst and a project initiator, the impact of the lab more generally remained limited. Therefore, the scope was extended, and five axes were defined: (1) impacting policy-making across ministries, (2) impacting the design of services, (3) impacting the culture, (4) building capacity, tools, and methods, and (5) sharing, expanding, and disseminating MindLab's work. Adjusting the lab's strategy resulted in moving from an idea lab to a lab that brings about lasting change and thought leadership in public sector innovation.

The **Mirvac** case is an example of how a publicly listed company, which was lacking any formal structure and process for innovation, successfully built an internal innovation capability within the short period of four years. For Mirvac, the journey started with a change in the top leadership of the firm. A new CEO set the innovation agenda, brought along the leadership team, and resourced an initiative initially supported by external consultants. To achieve both incremental innovation and disruptive innovation outcomes, the small corporate innovation team started to engage with key business units and central departments.

However, balancing the need for tangible outcomes and successes that would satisfy the business unit managers and secure further buy-in with achieving long-term strategic and possibly disruptive innovation outcomes proved difficult – if not impossible. The team leveraged design thinking, tried out different and clever ways of engaging with various stakeholder groups, introduced new methods, including open innovation, agile management, and design sprints, to ultimately succeed.

What is of interest in this case is how the small, centralized innovation team managed over time to pursue explorative and exploitative types of innovation by leveraging design thinking, which did not occur at the same time but was achieved successively. At Mirvac, design thinking was key in making innovation a priority. It contributed to a significant shift in the company's culture with positive follow-on effects on various other aspects of the company.

The **Swisscom** case is about the development of a human-centered design capability at Switzerland's leading telecom company. Here the initiative did not start at the top. To obtain buy-in, create awareness, and attract the attention of top management, a group of managers started by creating an open and visible creative workspace in a central location. The space embodied human-centered design methods, featuring interdisciplinarity, prototyping, co-design with customers, and so on. In addition, the team started teaching people human-centered design methods, which resulted in the development of a community of facilitators who were determined to develop a design-driven innovation culture and diffuse its practices. Over time, other roles were created, so that human-centered design could play a more active role in business projects and its value could be demonstrated.

The case highlights the critical role of measuring the value of design thinking. At Swisscom, new KPIs with a focus on customer-centricity were implemented. Another exciting aspect of this case is the role and involvement of an external consultancy, which enabled Swisscom's team to learn from external clients and projects and gain internal legitimacy. Finally, a strategic partnership with the consulting partner allowed mixing employees and gaining access to complementary resources and competencies, which enabled Swisscom to address larger innovation projects faster.

With **Thales,** we report implementing design thinking at a high-tech company in the global Aeronautics and Defense industry over nine years. The initiative started following a partnership with the Stanford d.school, which convinced top managers at Thales of the great potential design thinking has for innovation.

However, unusual in this case is that the first internal supporter was the manager of Thales's corporate university. While the corporate university hosted the first design center – a space for learning about and applying design thinking – it escaped the attention of the research and technology unit, which in high-tech firms is usually in charge of innovation. The way design thinking took hold at Thales can best be described as an *underdog strategy*. It started with training and facilitation of creative workshops, which gradually turned into more and more innovation projects involving various business units of the firm. To preserve the integrity and independence of the design center, the creation of an internal consultancy business model was critical. Furthermore, this led to the widespread adaptation of design thinking as it accommodated different briefs from internal customers. The consulting model enabled the delivery of results and outcomes rather than evangelizing and advocating for a method. Innovation projects were co-designed and involved business unit staff throughout all phases, which ultimately resulted in business unit staff taking responsibility for the destiny and outcomes of innovation projects. Thales developed a "franchise" model that enabled the global diffusion of design thinking via thirteen Design Centers and allowed other innovation teams to leverage the approach and to benefit from network effects.

The following case features the **US Department of Labor** (DOL), which in 2014 was tasked with implementing a new law called the Workforce Innovation and Opportunity Act (WIOA). At that time, DOL was widely perceived as an agency focused on ensuring compliance with laws but not creating innovative services. When implementing a new law, the usual practice is to work with lawyers and experts to write, issue regulations, and provide guidance and training. But this time, people believed a new approach was needed. This case shows how a human-centered design (HCD) movement was built from the bottom up, starting as a zero-budget one-person band. Human centricity became part of the fabric of the new law through guidelines, deliberate communication and working with internal stakeholders. Other critical factors, in this case, include building relationships with the *right* people, communicating wisely, and being somewhat shielded from Washington's bureaucracy. Today, over 2,000 workforce development professionals have participated in HCD training. Many of them have used new methods and tools to improve government services. The WIOA now requires government agencies to collaborate, where previously they had been siloed and did not work together. HCD also gave the government and not-for-profit workers a renewed sense of purpose, connection with the government's mission, joy in the workplace, and appreciation for their work.

Finally, the **US Department of Veterans Affairs** case displays a design thinking initiative's journey in a huge governmental healthcare organization. Started by an innovation initiative and the insight that the department had to shift from a system-centered to a human-centered approach to innovation, the Veterans Affairs Center for Innovation and the Veterans Experience Office were created. Both units invested substantial time in user research to develop a deep understanding of the gaps and shortcomings of Veterans' experiences with the current system. The user research proved invaluable when working on issues that were difficult to articulate, such as the need for mental health services. Other creative tactics that the teams employed to increase their impact included new forms of collaboration with the Office of Personnel and Management. In addition to overcoming the inertia typical for large government organizations, developing a human-centered approach in an environment where substantial high-level political forces are at work was particularly challenging. The forces that direct attention, and ultimately resources, needed to be navigated – sometimes it was like paddling across a calm lake and sometimes like running white-water rapids.

About the Contributors

People across the globe are engaging with design thinking and applying it passionately to address their organizational needs. There is a broad and deep application of design thinking and some fantastic work being carried out in our community. As an editorial team (and we think we can speak for the nineteen co-authors in this book), we found that writing this book was a great way to reflect and discuss, learn from each other, and inspire new and different ways of working with design thinking.

Here is a brief overview of the people who contributed to this book. Each co-author is an expert in their field and industry with deep knowledge and broad experiences working with design thinking. We list the authors to follow the order of the cases presented in the book.

Matt Templeton is an artist, designer, and educator. His work has been exhibited internationally, has received critical acclaim, and has been included in various collections and publications. He has worked as a designer with businesses of all shapes and sizes. He is currently working as Principal Design Strategist, HealthSuite Labs Engagement Lead NA, Philips Experience Design. He has been a professor of art and design at many different schools, including the School of the Museum of Fine Arts, RISD, and Wentworth Institute of Technology. The thread through all of Matt's work is human-centered design, creative confidence, and helping people work with more skillfulness, effectiveness, and delight. In his free time, Matt enjoys surfing the cold waters of New England and making music with his daughter. He plays well with others and always cleans up after himself.

Sebastian Fixson is Professor of Innovation and Design and Associate Dean of Graduate Programs and Innovation at the Graduate School of Business at Babson College. Trained as both an engineer and a social scientist, Sebastian concentrates his work on helping people and organizations build innovation capabilities. In his research, he investigates how innovation performance is impacted through choices in process governance (open vs. closed innovation), using digital design tools, and using innovation practices such as design thinking. His research and consulting work stretch across large enterprises and entrepreneurial firms. In addition, he teaches innovation, design, and operations management at Babson and at universities and companies around the world. From 2014 to 2017, he served as the founding Faculty Director of Babson's Master of Science in Management in Entrepreneurial Leadership (MSEL) program.

Molly Mazzaferro is Senior Director on the Innovation team at Blue Cross Blue Shield of Massachusetts. In 2015, Molly led the effort to evaluate and define the path forward for innovation at Blue Cross, which resulted in the formation of the dedicated team she now helps to lead. Her innovation work has ranged from standing up a 30,000-square-foot innovation center to driving projects that improve quality outcomes in care, reduce system costs, and create an unparalleled consumer healthcare experience. Molly holds a Master of Business Administration from Babson College, a Bachelor of Arts in English and History from Lafayette College, and is trained in lean and human-centered design innovation methodologies. In her spare time, Molly enjoys figuring out life as a new mom.

Sabine Gourmain spent twenty-five years in innovation management at Group Danone, from food scientist to executive. She led the experimentation and adoption of user-centric innovation and has a proven record of engaging with decision-makers and teams, creating a shared vision by working collaboratively, and combining rigor, creativity, and compassion. Sabine believes that the practice of mindfulness is essential to innovation management and leadership. Since human capital has always been at the heart of her attention, she decided to devote herself to it by becoming a Senior Consultant and Facilitator at Potential Project. Today, she is passionate about sharing her experience and knowledge, contributing to a better world and workplace, helping organizations and leaders develop more focus and clarity, and leading to sustainable performance and innovation.

Julie Deschamps specializes in innovation management. She worked at Danone, combining her business background with research and innovation expert knowledge, researching innovation practices. Convinced by the company's mission, she initiated several breakthrough projects by designing new business models focused on the mission of hydration and building engaging storytelling. Generally, she contributed to implementing design thinking throughout the company. Julie is driven by expanding businesses toward opportunities in adjacent categories. Her multi-disciplinary background creates surprising and unusual connections for business and technology. She recently joined Tilt Ideas, a consultancy company specializing in foresight and innovation. At Tilt, she is putting her strategic thinking in the service of clients from all sectors. Passionate about people development, Julie coaches entrepreneurs and intrapreneurs, helping them to leverage innovation approaches, mindsets, and behaviors.

Sihem BenMahmoud-Jouini is Associate Professor at HEC (Paris, France). She is the Director of the Masters in Project, Innovation & Design and in Entrepreneurship and of a Major in Innovation and Entrepreneurship (Executive MBA). She is an engineer by training and has a PhD in Strategy and Innovation Management from Paris-Dauphine University, France. Sihem has been a Visiting Scholar at Babson College and at the Stern Business School of New York University. Her research addresses how large companies manage and renew their innovation processes, especially exploring new domains and methods such as design thinking. She adopts an action research approach within firms from several sectors. Prior to becoming an academic, she worked on projects in engineering firms. Her work has been published in books such as *Le management* *des innovations de rupture* and academic journals such as *Creativity Innovation Management, International Journal of Project Management, Journal of Product Innovation Management*, and *Research Technology Management*.

Wendy Castleman is a consultant, coach, and MasterCatalyst® focused on the mechanisms for creating and spreading sustaining change across organizations. Wendy is the founder of Developeople UX, LLC, which concentrates on helping design leaders spread and elevate the influence of design. She was one of the founders of Intuit's Design for Delight program, leader of the Intuit Innovation Catalysts, and was a Design Research Strategist at Intuit for fourteen years. Earlier in her career, she worked in experience design at Remedy, Motorola, Philips, and Lucent. She has a PhD in Cognitive and Perceptual Psychology from University of Texas at Austin and over twenty years of experience helping teams create awesome experiences. In her spare time, she drinks wine, runs half-marathons, and plays with her daughter.

Christi Zuber, RN, MHA, PhD, is recognized for her trail-blazing work in innovation and human-centered design in healthcare. She is the Founder and Managing Director of Aspen Labs consulting practice in Denver, CO. This follows a fourteen-year career as the Founder and Director of the first design and innovation practice in Kaiser Permanente; the work she and her teams accomplished have been featured in the *Harvard Business Review, Fast Company*, and the *New York Times*. Zuber is the Executive Director of the non-profit Innovation Learning Network, which includes over forty healthcare organizations that share user and community-centered workforce practices, space designs, and technology solutions. She also serves on the faculty at Northwestern University, teaching Service Design. Zuber's research focuses on bringing human-centered design into large complex organizations that may not be so keen to change.

Lisa Carlgren holds a PhD in innovation management and works as a Senior Researcher at the Research Institutes of Sweden (RISE).

She is affiliated with the Chalmers University of Technology, where she teaches design thinking at the master's level. Her research is primarily about the implementation and use of design thinking in large organizations, focusing on the role of design thinking in building organizational innovation capabilities. She is a firm believer in action research as a democratic way of creating knowledge and contributing to positive societal change, and she is now working with policy innovation in mobility transformation and gender diversity in the maritime sector. Lisa was a visiting scholar at the Potsdam University, has worked in Tetra Pak and Ericsson, and has long experience teaching and facilitating design thinking at the university and in organizations.

David Dunne, PhD, is Professor at the Gustavson School of Business, University of Victoria. His research and teaching focus on design thinking and how design thinkers deal with organizational barriers. He has published in many academic and practitioner journals on this topic, and is the author of *Design Thinking at Work: How Innovative Organizations Are Embracing Design* (University of Toronto Press, 2018), which explores the successes and challenges of applying design thinking in organizations. He is currently working on a second book on design and managerial mindsets. He has received several awards for teaching and innovation; he has held visiting positions at several design schools, including TU Delft and IIT Institute of Design. He is past Board Chair of Academics Without Borders and regularly volunteers to support higher education in Nepal.

Natalia Nikolova, PhD, is Professor in Organization Studies and the Academic Director of Plus UTS Business Futures at the University of Technology Sydney (UTS) Business School. Natalia's research interests are diverse, including organizational practices, strategy, innovation, and leadership. Natalia has published in academic journals and books, and her work has been presented and recognized at several international conferences. She has developed extensive experience as an innovative educator and facilitator in business strategy, innovation, and leadership.

Jochen Schweitzer, PhD, is Professor of Strategy and Innovation and Director of Entrepreneurship at the University of Technology Sydney (UTS) Business School. As a social scientist and engineer, he advocates innovation and entrepreneurship with a particular interest in design thinking, emerging technologies, and the future of work. Jochen also serves as the Director of UTS's Executive MBA and Bachelor in Entrepreneurship (Hons) programs. As a researcher, educator and advisor, he is dedicated to solving social complexities with humanity, creativity, and technology (in that order). He provides insights into emerging trends, alternate perspectives, and fresh ideas to several private and government organizations. Before becoming an academic, he was a Principal at PwC's Central American and European strategy consulting practice. Jochen lives in Sydney, Australia, but enjoys regular visits to other favorite places, including Berlin, Vancouver, and New York.

Christine Gilroy is an experienced business professional with over seventeen years of experience in real estate. From 2014 to 2019, Christine was Group General Manager of Innovation for Mirvac Group (a Top 50 ASX listed company), creating the award-winning Hatch innovation program. Passionate about delivering tangible outcomes rather than "innovation theater," Hatch drove a strong culture of innovation and spun out several industry-disrupting startups. In 2019, Christine became the co-founder of a startup backed by Mirvac, focused on solving housing affordability for young Australians. Christine started her career as a Chartered Accountant at PwC and spent three years in banking in the UK and Sydney before commencing with Mirvac in 2006. Before following her passion for innovation and entrepreneurship, she held several roles in strategy, mergers and acquisitions, and funds management.

Katja Bürki is Partner at Creaholic and has worked as a professional inventor since 2017. She leads projects for companies in various industries in Switzerland and abroad and spreads the innovation spark further. Katja develops innovative products, services, and processes from a customer perspective and flourishes an innovation culture at the team and company level. Through her holistic thinking, she understands critical dependencies and creates unique end-to-end experiences. Her background in business administration, innovation, and creativity enables her to bridge the gap between these often contradictory topics. As a human-centered design expert, Katja has driven the cultural transformation within Swisscom and implemented an open innovation platform, "Customer Experience Day," which created awareness beyond Swiss borders. Previously she has worked in business development at Swisscom, developing new growth areas such as eHealth.

Didier Boulet is leading the group-wide design transformation at Thales, aiming to transform the company into a world-class design organization. In early 2020, he was appointed as the first Chief Design Officer in Thales. Didier is the founder of the first Thales Design Center. Its mission is to leverage design-driven innovation or design thinking throughout the company. The Design Center Network is currently present in thirteen locations across the world. Since joining Thales, Didier has held multiple roles in business, innovation, and design. He is also serving on several boards, including the Digital Transformation Steering Board, the Design Center Network, the Digital Marketing Board, and the Thales Belgium Board of Directors. He is a Belgian national and a graduate of the Haute École de Bruxelles.

Virginia Hamilton is a Public Sector Innovation Catalyst. She practices and teaches human-centered design (HCD) and insights from behavioral science as levers for innovation. She has led HCD projects for adult education, early childhood education, workforce development, and healthcare. She has extensive public policy experience in skills, jobs, unemployment, job training, youth unemployment, economic development, poverty, access, equity, and the future of work. She has extensive experience in large-scale systems change and improving government services through participatory leadership and design thinking. Hamilton is a Strategic Advisor for the Partnership for Public Service, where she teaches public servants who are committed to improving services and policies for the public good. Previously, Hamilton worked for the US Department of Labor and founded an NGO, the California Workforce Association.

Aaron Stienstra is Senior Design Strategist with the Office of Customer Experience at the US General Services Administration (GSA). He previously served as a Human Innovation Fellow and Designer with the Lab at the US Office of Personnel Management (OPM). In that role, he worked extensively with the Veterans Experience Office at the US Department of Veterans Affairs (VA). Aaron is based in Washington, DC.

Amber Schleuning (pr. Slyning) is the former Executive Director of the Center for Innovation at the US Department of Veterans Affairs, where she and her team grew the organization from a "startup" within the federal government, scaling design and innovation capacity across the largest integrated health system in the United States. She currently leads her consulting practice, partnering with organizations pursuing world-changing missions. She has led teams at the US Department of Defense and the US Army as a combat engineer. Amber holds a Master of Public Health (MPH) from Emory University. She serves on advisory boards at Everytown for Gun Safety and the Commit Foundation. She writes and speaks on design, healthcare, and impact for groups like American Institute for Graphic Arts (AIGA) and the Service Design Network (SDN). She lives in Austin, Texas, with her old dog, Max.

Veronica X. Vela, PhD, is a designer and innovation leader focused on improving the health and well-being of communities. She is interested in projects that help people lead full and vibrant lives. She is currently the Director of Community Health Design and Innovation at Sibley Memorial Hospital and Johns Hopkins Health

System. She leads system-wide efforts to improve health outcomes for DC's most vulnerable communities. Previously, she served as a Human Innovation Fellow with The Lab at OPM, assigned to the Department of Veterans Affairs. In this capacity, Vela led discovery research and design to improve the patient experience of veterans and paid particular attention to the unique needs of women. She is a former Teach For America corps member and lives in Washington, DC, with her puppy, Caramelo.

Jaryn Miller is a designer and researcher who works with communities to improve services. His focus is to bring equity and community-driven approaches to design. As a Senior Service Designer for Kaiser Permanente, Jaryn works at the intersection of technology and community health. Previously, he led design efforts within the federal government and the Department of Veterans Affairs. He also served as a T-Lab Fellow for the San Francisco–based non-profit Tipping Point Community. Jaryn lives in Oakland, CA, with his wife and young child.

Before You Start

Books like this one are not possible without the support and contribution of many people. We would like to acknowledge and thank especially Ingo Rauth and Jan Schmiedgen for co-initiating this book project and not losing the confidence that it would get finished. Ingo is a great advocate for innovation as human-made evolution; he is passionate about supporting those that seek to shape the future through innovation. Ingo lives near Toronto and serves as an Adjunct Professor at IE Business School in Madrid, teaching and coaching current and future innovation leaders and entrepreneurs in innovation leadership. Jan is a designerly social scientist and economist by training; he works as an innovation strategist and is a founding partner at the Berlin-based innovation consultancy co:dify

Group. Ingo and Jan were instrumental in reaching out to authors, finding collaborators, and getting the ball rolling. Without Ingo and Jan, this book project would have never started.

We would also like to extend a profound "thank you" to every team of authors who wrote a chapter for this book. We are very grateful for the hard work everyone has put into drafting their manuscript, listening to feedback from us, and then revising and rewriting their cases, all of which was done in addition to their demanding day jobs and busy personal lives. We thank them for their patience, working with us through all of this during the global COVID-19 pandemic. What was planned to be an eighteen-month project has stretched over four years. We also thank the anonymous reviewers for their insightful feedback and the University of Toronto Press editorial team for their expert support and considerable patience.

Many connections with case authors and case organizations were made possible through the research and teaching activities of the editorial team and academics involved. We are grateful for these interactions and think that such collaborations are tremendously beneficial for all parties involved. Our students learned from this work, were inspired, and made career choices as a result of their exposure to the innovative work. Some even joined the innovation initiatives of these organizations as interns or graduates. Likewise, practitioners working at the case organizations appreciated the opportunity to reflect on and share their valuable experiences. The resulting trust, partnership, and interactions between practitioners, scholars and students of innovation are the highlight of our scholarly work.

Now we hope you enjoy reading the result of this collaborative effort.

CHAPTER TWO

Reimagining Healthcare – Implementing Design Thinking in a Health Insurance Company

MATT TEMPLETON, SEBASTIAN FIXSON,
AND MOLLY MAZZAFERRO

Blue Cross Blue Shield of Massachusetts (BCBSMA) is a health insurance company faced with two powerful forces beyond its control: rising customer expectations and increasing cost pressures. In response, the leadership team launched a project to increase the organization's competitiveness through innovation. It became clear quickly that to build innovation capabilities throughout, the company required a dedicated organizational innovation unit. Design thinking became the central innovation method, and numerous training events for the company's employees were created, ranging from short two-hour crash courses to two-day design thinking boot camps to week-long design thinking sprints involving all layers of the organization. The team worked on projects together with line units, guiding them in the application of design thinking. Later, an internal innovation center was created to house project teams, provide space for incubation, and provide space for programming events. In this case, three factors were critical: First, from the start, the team communicated to all parties involved that the initiative was a long process that needed time to develop. Second, the team's focus on capability building, and using real projects in doing so, helped spread design thinking throughout the organization. And finally, the appropriate adaptation of design thinking to the company's culture was reflected in applying labels to activities and processes that matched the organization's worldview.

Compared to countries like Canada and many in Europe, in which a substantial portion of the health system is funded by taxpayers and administered by the government, the United States, by and large, maintains a privately managed healthcare system.[1] These non-governmental players include hospitals, doctors, pharmaceutical companies, and health insurers. One of the largest health insurance organizations is Blue Cross Blue Shield, a national association of thirty-six independent community-based and locally operated companies that collectively provide coverage for over 100 million members in all fifty states, Washington, DC, and Puerto Rico.[2] Blue Cross Blue Shield of Massachusetts (BCBSMA) is one company under that umbrella, operating as a not-for-profit organization and as an independent licensee of the Blue Cross Blue Shield Association (BCBSA).

Over eighty years ago, two separate companies began to offer health insurance products in Massachusetts: Blue Cross began offering insurance for hospital stays in 1937, and Blue Shield started coverage for doctor's visits in 1941. For most of the twentieth century, both companies operated independently before merging in 1988 to form Blue Cross Blue Shield of Massachusetts.

In 2019, **Blue Cross Blue Shield of Massachusetts** covered about 2.9 million members.[3] It employed about 3,800 people, internally called associates. BCBSMA's provider network included over 60,000 providers and 74 hospitals. In 2019, BCBSMA processed 50 million claims and handled over 3 million phone calls. Annual premium revenue was US$8.3 billion, 90 per cent of which covered medical care for its members. In addition to medical insurance, BCBSMA also offers dental and vision plans, disability insurance, term and dependent life insurance, and workers' compensation.[4]

The Rising Cost of Health Insurance in America

From 1960 onwards, when US healthcare costs represented about 5 per cent of the gross domestic product (GDP), healthcare costs increased faster than most other expenditures: the annual growth rate was almost always above 5 per cent, in the 1970s, and for parts of the 1980s even above 10 per cent. As a result, in 2017, US healthcare costs topped US$3.5 trillion, which is almost 18 per cent of the GDP.[5] This significant cost increase is typically attributed to a range of causes, including a substantial increase in coverage, the high cost of treating chronic diseases, inefficiencies in administration, heavy use of emergency rooms, and high prescription drug prices.[6]

The Innovation Unit Genesis at BCBSMA

Blue Cross Blue Shield of Massachusetts has a deep history of innovation, from being among the first insurers to cover life-saving heart and lung transplants over fifty years ago to pioneering the Alternative Quality Contract (AQC) model for value-based care and paving the way for local and national healthcare reform in recent years. Still, in addition to steadily increasing costs, a variety of other factors in the 2010s sparked a rapid and dramatic transformation of the healthcare landscape and demanded new attention to innovation. From provider and payer consolidation to Affordable Care Act (ACA)–driven changes around cost and transparency requirements, to heightened consumer expectations for fast, reliable, personalized services and increased involvement in the buying process, to shifting channels through which care was provided (e.g., retail clinics, telemedicine), the healthcare system was fundamentally changing.

The combination of these and other market dynamics propelled several Blue Cross Blue Shield plans to stand up dedicated innovation units inside their own organizations to address and drive change. These units spanned a variety of innovation models, ranging from internal accelerators to investment arms to centers of excellence and culture change agents. The Blue Cross Blue Shield Association established an innovation workgroup with representation across Blue Cross companies to enable knowledge sharing and accelerate the growth of these new units. BCBSMA, with a leadership team invested in upholding the company's long-standing commitment to innovation, was an early and active participant in the cross-plan innovation conversation.

One of the initial steps taken by BCBSMA leadership was sponsoring a project in 2015 that paired the company's internal consulting group with an external consulting firm to jointly define the path forward for innovation at BCBSMA. The project was initiated under the umbrella of a vast array of consumer engagement work that was underway at the company and was co-sponsored by executive leaders from the strategy and consumer and provider solutions business areas. Leadership commitment at the Board of Director, C-suite, and

VP levels was crucial to gaining initial momentum and has continued to be an essential factor in driving sustained innovation.

One of the co-authors, Molly Mazzaferro – at the time, a principal in the internal consulting group – led the initiative; for eight months from March 2015 to October 2015, Mazzaferro partnered with the external consulting team on two parallel tracks of work. One track focused on populating an initial innovation pipeline, identifying and addressing three priority challenges, introducing new innovative approaches to the organization to tackle those challenges, and extracting lessons learned about innovating at the company along the way. The second track included recommending a strategy, structure, and process for a dedicated innovation function at BCBSMA (based on the lessons learned from track one).

Mazzaferro tested various innovation tools and tactics for the project, including running an associate innovation challenge/hackathon, leading customer journey mapping sessions, hosting focus groups with target-customer recruits, and collaborating directly with provider partners to solve for shared pain points. In doing so, she learned firsthand about the benefits and challenges of different methodologies as applied in a corporate environment; equally as important, by collaborating with stakeholders in pockets across the organization, she learned that for innovation to have a long-term, meaningful impact, it would require a dedicated group to drive the work forward. Based on these and other findings, the team recommended that BCBSMA establish a corporate innovation function under the umbrella of the Strategic Services Division and the leadership of the chief strategy officer. This team was initially established to achieve three primary goals:

1. Identify opportunities "at the edge of the business" and develop new products and services based on priority opportunities,
2. Develop internal innovations for high priority cross-organizational problems and challenges, and

3. Equip the broader organization with innovation strategies, methodologies, and skillsets.

As a result of these recommendations, in late 2015, BCBSMA launched its own innovation function and hired a chief innovation officer (CIO) to lead the function. Having spent the last nine months laying the groundwork, Mazzaferro also transferred into the innovation group to help establish the function's initial infrastructure. One of the core components of that initial work was identifying an innovation methodology. Mazzaferro began exploring design thinking, which she was first introduced to as a student in a Babson College graduate course taught by the second co-author, Sebastian Fixson, professor of innovation and design. Given BCBSMA's focus on consumer engagement, Mazzaferro recognized the potential of design thinking (a relatable and customer-centric approach) to become part of the innovation team's methodology. As she networked with local experts to learn more about the methodology and its application to corporate innovation, she was introduced to Matt Templeton, the third co-author of this chapter. At the time, Templeton was working simultaneously at the financial investment firm Fidelity as a designer and at the Wentworth Institute of Technology as a professor of industrial design. Talking to Templeton, Mazzaferro realized that his profile, expertise, and the possibility to collaborate with a university made him a perfect addition to the innovation group. Templeton, and two additional team members, joined the innovation team in January 2016.

The Early Days

Initially, the innovation team operated out of a small, glass-walled conference room within BCBSMA's corporate headquarters in Boston and leveraged a "see one, do one, teach one" approach to design thinking skill development. The model the team selected was a variation of the four stages of competence, sometimes called the "conscious competence" learning model.[7]

According to this model, individuals learning a new skill first move from unconscious incompetence (UI), where they don't know what they don't know, to conscious incompetence (CI) by realizing what they don't know. Next, they learn the skill, but executing it initially requires focused attention, that is, they have achieved conscious competence (CC). Finally, the skill becomes second nature with good practice, and the individual develops mindful competence (MC). This model of successive levels helped to explain that design thinking is not a quick fix and that it would take time to train people internally. To move various parts of the organization from one level to the next along this development path, the team used various channels for engagement. The team started with shorter activities and subsequently added other building blocks to engage and collaborate with associates across BCBSMA.

The earliest activities aimed to expose BCBSMA associates to the process and mindset of design thinking. The smallest unit that the team employed was a two-hour crash course, modeled after the Stanford d.school crash course, to redesign the gift-giving experience.[8] The team experimented with different venues and group sizes to create this form of exposure to and awareness of design thinking – what it was and how it could be applied to healthcare. Approximately half of BCBSMA's approximately 3,800 employees were exposed to design thinking through this channel within the first two years.

For about 5 per cent of BCBSMA associates, who were strategically selected, the innovation team designed as a next step a two-day design thinking boot camp. In addition to the crash course, the boot camp allowed the participants to dive deeper into the mindsets and processes of design thinking. For example, in addition to teaching associates the definition of empathy and its importance in the innovation process, each boot camp included experiential empathy with real customers. While empathizing with members had long been a principle upheld by BCBSMA's service arm, bringing customers directly into the problem-solving process was new for the company. Every boot camp ended with a small ceremony, celebrating the participants graduating to the level of "innovation catalyst," which meant they were now equipped to apply the design thinking practice to their respective business challenges. In the conceptual model of the team, it moved participants from UI to CI.

A couple of the first boot camps were co-created and co-run with Sebastian Fixson from Babson College. Templeton and Fixson met originally at the Design Thinking Exchange (DTX) gathering, a North American group of design thinking practitioners and academics that meets once a year. Sharing their experiences, they realized their shared interest in bridging practice and academia. As a result, the project teams in these early boot camps were composed of BCBSMA associates and Babson students. The students were also BCBSMA customers (as Babson provided employer-based health insurance through BCBSMA), enabling boot camp participants to gain an unusually close view of the customer experience.

This is one example of how the innovation team began leveraging the design thinking methodology to craft projects and learning experiences to make it easy and normal for BCBSMA associates to go beyond the organization's boundaries to gain new perspectives and input. This attitude is captured by a senior executive who said soliciting outside perspective is a necessary ingredient to driving corporate innovation. These experiences made it clear to the innovation team that a focus on mindset was at least as important as a focus on process, an insight that is familiar to many design thinking experts.[9] This, in turn led, to the important decision to include senior leadership in design thinking training, at least to the level of CI. A new mindset can be established in an organization only if it is shared; senior leaders did not have to become innovators themselves, but they needed to understand the basics about the design thinking mindset as well as its application to healthcare and, specifically, health insurance, so that they could effectively support and advocate for this new approach to problem-solving.

To allow a broader sharing of the design thinking mindset, the innovation team began to increase the frequency and size of the boot camps (from initially 20 participants, scaling to about 100) but kept the coach/participant ratio constant. To cover this increased need for coaches, the team involved Wentworth design students, where Templeton still taught, and other external partners. As an added benefit, Wentworth design students' hands-on participation in these boot camps allowed the innovation team to identify and recruit top talent in the form of internships and full-time positions down the line.

The team strove to involve other BCBSMA business areas in identifying problems and opportunities to explore in a boot camp. In particular, the team made sure that senior leaders were part of the topic selection process. This strategy ensured that the boot camp participants always worked on real challenges relevant to the organization. However, while this made the projects more relevant, it also opened doors for strong opinions regarding what should be worked on and sometimes made it challenging to prioritize projects and execute the new design thinking approach. The CIO played a critical role in navigating effectively within this environment; with her strategy background, she helped communicate, align, lead, and form the necessary relationships to support the team's work, which was especially critical in an organization that historically had not been design-driven.

Picking Up Steam

Whereas boot camps started as stand-alone service offerings for the innovation team, they increasingly evolved into springboards for other innovation efforts, such as "partnering" and "projects."[10] With "partnering," the innovation team provided low-hurdle opportunities for boot camp participants to continue working on some of their challenges via a design thinking tool called "user-testing parties."

User-testing parties began in 2017 to test ideas with end-users. The subject matter for testing ranged from new health insurance product offerings to a game that teaches kids the basics of health insurance (with the hope that establishing a fundamental understanding in youth would lead to smarter utilization in later years). Testing concepts for desirability with early-stage ideas proved beneficial on several fronts: it saved time and money and allowed associates to gain insights into the consumers' perspective, which they could then apply to future projects. One example in which user-testing parties helped accelerate the path forward for a project was the development of ideas for next-generation engagement products for a significant market segment. After several concepts had been developed, the innovation team – in partnership with several other cross-functional teams – held two user-testing parties to gather additional consumer input on the product ideas. The consumers shared what they liked, disliked, and what was confusing to them, which was then synthesized and used to drive strategy and product bundling efforts. Additional consumer testing followed, and the value of user-testing as an early tactic to develop better products began to take hold. Testing concepts with end-users early and often is a design thinking pillar that continues as an important foundation for the innovation team's work even today.

Another variant of partnering was to reach out into the broader community of design-interested individuals via Meetup (a platform for bringing people together with shared interests). BCBSMA's innovation team hosted meetups monthly for the entire design thinking community in Boston, including BCBSMA associates, to test innovation frameworks, allow associates to sharpen their design thinking skills, and enable networking with like-minded individuals. Associates were made aware of these opportunities through various mechanisms, including stories on BCBSMA's intranet, innovation email blasts to catalysts, social media, and the innovation team's website.

Lastly, the innovation team also used outsider-in partnering to explore and build early ideas with external organizations – some healthcare companies, but equally as important, some companies from other industries. Radical collaboration – the design thinking principle that diversity of thought enables better problem-solving – helped the team continuously apply an outside-in perspective and strive toward breakthrough innovation. One example of an initiative that stemmed from this outside-in partnering involved reimagining, through prototyping, the way that members understand and pay for their healthcare at the time they receive it, which could potentially reduce or eliminate high administrative cost and burden of bills, explanation of benefits (EOBs), calls to member service, collections, and bad debt. Cost surprises are one example of a significant, relatable consumer pain point that continues to benefit greatly from external perspectives. This initiative is still underway at the time of publication.

A second method to carry some of the boot camp work forward was "projects." They could take various forms, but the most common forms were design thinking sprints and sessions. Most of the sprints were run Google-style over a timeframe of five days, usually with a dedicated, co-located, and cross-functional team bringing all required skills and decision-making authority together. In comparison, sessions were typically run over a shorter time frame – ranging from several hours to several days – and often involved applying the design-thinking process to a current challenge faced by a single business area or team.

One example of a successful sprint included participation from senior leadership and resulted in a new pilot with a local hospital, in which the parties agreed to switch from a fee-for-service payment model to a fee-for-value model.[11] Senior leaders were impressed with the speed of the sprint model, noting that by using design thinking versus traditional methods, more was accomplished in a much shorter time. A side benefit of sprints with senior leadership was that it allowed leaders to experience the value of the innovation process firsthand and allowed for subsequent, related conversations around key skill sets and resources required for innovation to be successful. In one instance, this deeper understanding even led to the funding of a new hire.

In general, the shift toward quickly prototyping and testing solution ideas coming out of the boot camps helped the innovation team generate more buy-in from the boot camp participants and their leaders, as it signaled applicability and real results of the design thinking method. In response, business area leaders agreed to dedicate some of their staff to a twelve-week incubator (i.e., several rounds of sprints). Sprints and rapid prototyping also helped make a case for why purposefully dedicated space matters as an enabler of innovation activities and ultimately led to the creation of a dedicated, state-of-the-art innovation center in 2019, led again by Mazzaferro. More broadly, the innovation team noticed that prototyping and testing and consumer focus and input became a habit for many teams in the organization. Working collaboratively after the boot camp allowed the participants to develop new ways to work with each other and with end-users. With the innovation team continuing to provide support, an important aspect was that the innovation team did not act as an external agency but rather made every effort for BCBSMA business areas to take ownership of the design and innovation work. The key to achieving this outcome was the collaborative nature of all projects; in contrast to earlier experiences where business areas were merely recipients of consultant recommendations handed off for implementation, innovation projects became end-to-end partnerships between cross-functional teams with shared goals.

Another move to help various constituents carry back the design thinking mindset and tools into their business area was a switch in labeling from design thinking to human-centered design that the innovation team orchestrated. The focus on the person in the method's name helped make it easier for many customer-facing roles to immediately see value in this new way of working.

In parallel to all internal design thinking efforts, Templeton embedded one of his studio courses at Wentworth with the innovation team at BCBSMA. The students spent a substantial amount of their studio time working with the innovation team. One project born out of the collaboration with the embedded class[12] was an opioid tool kit in the summer semester of 2018.[13] Drug poisoning via overdose has become one of the leading causes of unintentional death in the United States. Because overdoses often occur at home, at work, and in public places, they have put more and more people with no medical training in the role of first responders. Inspired and supported by a behavioral health medical director at BCBSMA, an opioid overdose response kit – which included two doses of Narcan and simple use instructions – was created to address this issue. Applying tools and techniques from design thinking, Alex Connor (a Wentworth student who later interned and ultimately worked full-time with the BCBSMA innovation team) built trust with internal stakeholders. He completed the project in under seven months, much faster than comparable projects. In addition to providing a powerful resource to BCBSMA members and associates, the tool kit's development story became an internal case study on how co-creation, rapid prototyping, and design thinking in general, can accelerate the innovation process and positively impact community health. The team also shared the project's story as a best practice for other plans to adopt at the Blue Cross Blue Shield Association's National Summit, a large annual conference hosted for all BCBS plans.

Additional internal case studies were generated from the innovation team's early work with the member service arm of the organization. When the innovation team was small, it made the strategic decision to work with this group – not only were the consumer-centric methods of design thinking highly relevant for this group but they also aligned with the empathy-focused approach the group already practiced. As a result, many leaders and associates from this area took to the work and became highly competent innovation catalysts. By year two, this group was running projects on their own using design thinking and achieving tangible results, ranging from reduced cost for the organization to increased member and associate satisfaction.

Today, the innovation team remains small but mighty. With limited resources, they focus on incubating and accelerating select, priority projects that will drive value for consumers, accounts, partners, and BCBSMA. Several recent project examples include creating a data-driven, personalized experience for consumers trying to navigate their health plan and benefits; reimagining the prior authorization process – currently a major pain point for providers, payers, and consumers alike; and developing new models for virtual care to ensure members have flexible options that meet their lifestyle needs. The team continues to leverage design thinking as an important foundation for the innovation process – bringing consumer insights into the problem-solving process early and often and rapidly building, testing, and iterating ideas. In addition, the team proactively engages with senior leadership to identify top priority projects, strives for strong business participation embedded throughout the process, and incorporates business cases and value projections into every pitch, increasing the likelihood that ideas will make it to market.

Lessons Learned

At the time of writing, the story of the implementation of design thinking at BCBSMA is still evolving; however, the methodology continues to serve as an important foundation for the company's innovation efforts. Although the journey started only a little over four years ago, and it is too early to report large-scale downstream impacts, several key lessons can be shared:

- Innovation has long been a core tenet for BCBSMA. As such, support from the very top of the leadership chain (e.g., Board of Directors, CEO) was an important catalyst for the team's early work and continues to be a critical factor in the team's continued existence and success.
- Don't underestimate the time it takes to make an entire organization more innovative. Although intuitive for everyone who has worked in a large organization, it needs to be stressed that inertia is the standard modus operandi of existing structures, systems, and organizations. Articulating from the start that changing mindsets and helping people to develop new competencies takes time is critical.
- Understand who the key people are that represent leverage to convince others. As the purposeful involvement of senior leadership in the decisions of the innovation team illustrates, this consideration must be part of the larger change efforts. Knowing who the influencers are and how to make them a partner is an important skill for the leader of any innovation effort. Proactive engagement with senior leaders to align innovation projects with business priorities has recently become an even more prominent part of the innovation team's strategy.
- A critical role for innovation leaders is to provide air cover for design thinking activities and lobby for resources. Within the leadership team, someone like the chief innovation officer needs to have the clout to provide support for activities of the innovation team that might otherwise be seen as foreign to the organization's standard practices. Every organizational change includes violations of established norms, and consequently, someone to explain why the violations need to be tolerated.

- Align innovation efforts to corporate strategy and other internal groups doing similar work at the more incremental end of innovation (consumer experience, marketing, IT, etc.). One crucial decision in this effort was replacing the label of design thinking with human-centered design. Other newly established roles focusing on consumer experience within BCBSMA were much better represented by including the human in the approach's name. Projects that are aligned to core business functions and that demonstrate clear value to the organization continue to be more broadly embraced than projects deemed more disruptive and less immediately relevant.
- Challenges to convince middle management often hinge on established cultural norms. For example, past experiences working with consulting groups created a client attitude of passively receiving recommendations, whereas working with the innovation team on design-thinking projects required commitment to collaboratively working in the new process. To increase the likelihood that ideas are realized, the innovation team also stayed involved after the point of typical consulting recommendation handoff.
- Naming and labeling matter! For example, the team used the term design-thinking primarily for early exposure activities but added the term "design doing"[14] for project work to message that these are not just thought experiments. In other cases, the team chose names based on this organization's history. For example, the term "consultant" was initially avoided because it conjured mental models of past consulting engagements. Similarly, the term "facilitating" was avoided to ensure an understanding that the projects were all "real," that is, not toy or training projects, and the shift from design-thinking to human-centered design made the method more immediately relevant for all consumer-facing activities and roles.

- Space is an essential enabler to innovation and hands-on design thinking activities. Having a few small, dedicated rooms, purposefully built to foster collaboration and innovation, enabled sprint and incubator teams to work more efficiently and effectively, which in turn helped convince leadership to invest the resources to create the innovation center that now houses BCBSMA's innovation efforts.

Timeline

- 2014–15: BCBSMA leadership sponsors a project involving the internal consulting group with an external consulting firm to define the path forward for innovation; outcomes include that for innovation to have a long-term, meaningful impact, it would require a dedicated group to drive the work; launch of an innovation function and hiring of a chief innovation officer.
- 2016: The innovation team operates out of a small conference room; the team starts with shorter activities and subsequently added other building blocks to engage and collaborate with associates across BCBSMA; the innovation team understands that a focus on mindset is as important as a focus on process; further inclusion of senior leadership in design thinking training.
- 2017–18: Approximately half of BCBSMA's approximately 3,800 employees are exposed to design thinking; user testing parties begin to test ideas with end-users; engagement of the broader community of design-interested individuals in Boston, collaboration with external organizations to explore and build early ideas.
- 2019: Facilitation of innovation sprints and rapid prototyping help make a case for a purposefully dedicated space to enable innovation activities; creation of a dedicated, state-of-the-art

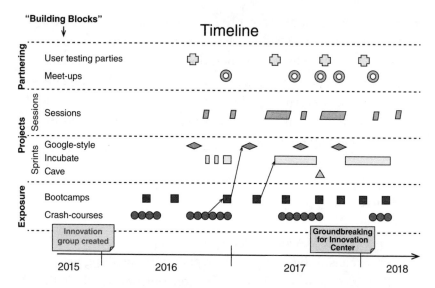

Figure 2.1. Channels in which BCBSMA's innovation team worked

innovation center; shift in labeling from *design thinking* to *human-centered design* to help constituents carry back the design thinking mindset and tools into their business areas.

- 2020: The innovation team is small but mighty; with limited resources, it maintains its focus on incubating and accelerating select, priority projects that drive value for consumers, accounts, partners, and BCBSMA; the team continues to leverage design thinking as an important foundation for the innovation process; the team engages with senior leadership to identify top priority projects.

CHAPTER THREE

Design Thinking Recipe in a Food Company – The Case of Danone

SABINE GOURMAIN, JULIE DESCHAMPS, AND SIHEM BENMAHMOUD-JOUINI

Design thinking at **Danone** started with a learning expedition where senior leaders discovered their potential. They backed several projects following a design thinking approach, involving consultants and a small team of employees. At Danone, the voice of the customer was already a very well-known concept, hence, introducing design thinking with its fast discovery, rapid prototyping, and cross-functional teams was relatively straightforward. Remarkable, however, was the multinational and decentralized context of the initiative. Scaling design thinking globally required difficult and not always successful negotiations between corporate headquarters and local subsidiaries. However, after six years, more than forty-five innovation projects involving 700 people had adopted design thinking to innovate on products and processes as well as for rebranding. Six years after the launch of the initiative, the user experience team included more than 100 people across the globe.

Danone is a multinational food-products corporation based in Paris, France, with three business divisions: Waters, which includes the famous Evian brand; Dairy and Plant-based Products, which include Activia and Alpro; and Specialized Nutrition, which includes early life or medical nutrition products. In the early 2010s, Danone was faced with a great challenge. While it had a track record and a strong portfolio of incremental product innovation and renovation of the brand, it lacked the ability to bring truly disruptive or breakthrough innovations to market.

Danone's product development managers were missing out on potential business opportunities for several reasons: They too often leaped too quickly from an idea stage to product realization. At the same time, projects often needed to be reworked as every function joined the project successively without a transversal approach leading to extended duration and delays. In the end, often only a weathered-down version of the original idea was developed, and sometimes no product was ready to go to market in a reasonable amount of time. There was a clear need to bring more discipline to the innovation process and to improve the innovation management system with the objective of making it cross-functional, iterative, and much more consumer centric.

It was in this context that "top-chef" leaders Jean-Philippe Paré and Christophe Perthuisot organized a learning expedition in June 2014. Jean-Philippe was a member of Danone Comex,[1] leading its Research and Innovation (R&I) unit with more than 1,000 researchers and engineers around the globe. Christophe was the vice president of the research and innovation department for Danone's Waters Division.

Danone S.A. is a multinational food-products corporation based in Paris. Danone's portfolio includes leading international brands like Actimel, Activia, Alpro, Aptamil, Danette, Danio, Danonino, Evian, Nutricia, Nutrilon, and

Volvic. Danone also owns a range of strong local and regional brands around the world. As of 2020, Danone sold
products in 120 markets, with combined revenues of almost EUR 23.6 billion; 55 per cent of the markets were in
Europe, the United States, and Canada, and 45 per cent
were in the rest of the world. Key markets are the United
States, China, and France. Its 100,000 employees work in
120 countries.

Looking for the Recipe

Danone's twenty-two leaders who participated in the expedition
came from various parts of the global organization, including research and innovation, marketing, purchasing, manufacturing,
and general managers of business units. The expedition included
thirty-three visits to best-in-class innovative companies in New
York, Shanghai, Paris, Tel Aviv, and San Francisco. The group
met with passionate innovation directors, R&I and marketing
directors, general managers, and designers who were willing to
share their learnings and discoveries of their organizations and
personal innovation journeys. They visited firms such as IDEO,
Awaken Group, RebelMouse, Procter & Gamble, Hyundai, Pfizer,
3M, Jansen, SAB Miller, L'Oréal, and several startups, including
Hampton Creek.

   This learning expedition inspired the R&I executive team with
new ways of managing innovation at Danone and especially how to
develop a customer-centric approach to innovation. Following the
trip, Jean-Philippe decided to include design thinking exploration
in the five-year R&I strategic plan. He wanted to experiment with
design thinking in Danone's product innovation projects to learn

how it could be applied more broadly. Christophe presented the plan to the Executive Committee and gained full support (i.e., resources and consent).

The expectations were to make innovation management faster, bolder, and more consumer-centric. Until then, the usual process for innovation was to spend several months and even years on the front-end innovation phase for breakthrough innovation. It was time to speed up this phase. Furthermore, at the start of the project, only marketing was involved for dairy products and R&I for specialized nutrition. Moreover, project teams were hardly in direct contact with consumers. User research was done through focus groups, mostly to validate a product mix or finished prototypes rather than exploring user needs. In the medical nutrition business, innovation teams would interact much more with doctors and medical staff as prescribers and rarely with consumers or patients directly. Consumer research was commonly shared via long-lasting data-heavy PowerPoint presentations with limited insights into user's real experiences or emotional associations with Danone's products.

After the expedition, in September 2014, Sabine Gourmain, who worked with Christophe in the R&I department of Danone's Waters Division, was appointed to lead the design thinking experimentation projects. Sabine was a business process organization director and, in this role, she was responsible for maintaining existing innovation processes, like project and portfolio management, aiming at efficiency and performance but also trying out new approaches, including open innovation. Sabine knew a lot about Danone's innovation management due to the many years she had worked in product development as a food scientist. She had been working with many individuals across the organization, which gives her credibility and strong networks. Sabine's peers and managers trusted her to lead teams into the unknown. While all of these were great qualities needed to become Danone's first design thinking cook, at this stage, Sabine had never heard about design thinking.

Searching "design thinking" on the Internet returned hundreds of thousands of references, too many to read. Hence, she decided to meet and learn. Over the three following months, Sabine visited numerous innovation events and had many one-on-one meetings with experts. She spoke to peers working in other industries that had already worked with design thinking, including people at GE, Airbus, Thales, and Dim. She understood that each of these companies had developed its own approach to implementing design thinking. She participated in a three-day training at the Hasso Plattner Institute (HPI) d.school in Potsdam, Germany,[2] which turned out to become her "aha moment." She realized that during previous years as a food scientist and product developer, she had been urged to somehow become consumer-centered, but with no practical instruction as to how one can become consumer-centered. It was like an incantation with limited application on her day-to-day job.

After the training, Sabine was enthused to experiment and adopt the newly learned methods right away, like time-boxing meetings. She would be seen carrying a timer everywhere and using it in every meeting. She needed to identify suitable internal projects to start with and external agencies that could help facilitate the design thinking process.

Going for Experimentation: Fast&Furious

When Jean-Philippe decided to allocate a budget to pursue one experimentation per division,[3] he found there were many candidates.

It was important to choose carefully which project could benefit the most from applying design thinking. With Christophe, Sabine had sought discussions with general managers[4] to ensure that the scope of the projects was open enough to allow innovation to happen. It was difficult to explain the design thinking approach since very few leaders were aware of it, and there was no iconic project dealing with food products similar to the General Electric magnetic resonance imaging machine (MRI) for kids promoted by design thinker David Kelley, for example. Danone leaders were hoping to speed up their projects, mainly since Jean-Philippe chose to call the sponsored projects Fast&Furious. They chose projects according to the following criteria:

- Select an ambitious goal that goes beyond current brand positioning that focuses on an adjacent category from existing product ranges and that targets a pre-defined community.
- Secure the sponsorship of the R&I VP from the division involved.
- Appoint a full-time project leader with a dedicated team (full-time or part-time).

Five projects were initiated. One focused on the Dairy Division: Jerry focused on the creation of a new healthy snack based on the benefits from ferments in the United States. The second was in the Waters Division: Donald dedicated to designing healthy energy beverages in the UK. The third happened in the African Division: Daisy aimed at imagining healthier snacks for middle-class kids in Morocco and Ivory Coast.

To drive project teams, Sabine contracted with external agencies. She chose to have different settings to maximize learning from the experimentation. She partnered with big agencies like McKinsey-Lunar and Veryday, and smaller ones like Furious Intent and Wood for Trees. At that time, Wood for Trees was the only one with experience in food design. These agencies oversaw the leadership of the projects as well as formalizing the story of each project in a book. They pushed for new kinds of iterations with consumers and for new ways to develop fast and rough prototypes. Moreover, they ensured a truly cross-functional collaboration ensuring psychological and emotional safety for the members involved.

On top of her involvement in a project, Sabine decided to have a special person (i.e., a reporter) in every project who would be responsible for gathering the learnings generated; these learnings would be used to build the Danone design thinking recipe progressively. She integrated Alexandre, who was working for Jean-Philippe on an innovation mission as marketing manager, and Julie, who was already working with Sabine as an intern on a project portfolio management tool. They worked part-time, attending parts of the workshops in each project either as observers or as participants, which allowed them to have the same experiences as the team members.

In addition to consolidating the learnings from each of the experimentations and starting to develop the Danone design thinking, the role of Sabine, Julie, and Alexandre also included managing the personal relationships between the agencies and the Danone teams.

The projects lasted from three to eight months during 2015 and 2016. Jerry in the United States managed to move on to the development phase. After several pivots due to technological pitfalls, the healthy snack bar reached the market under the Cultured Snack Company©[5] brand in 2018. Donald stopped in 2016, and the learnings were used in another project that delivered the first natural energy drink, Flyte,[6] in the UK market at the end of 2017.

In 2017, Daisy delivered a portfolio of product mixes illustrated with prototypes that fueled the strategic thinking around the category.

As a team and with the help of the agencies, Sabine, Alexandre, and Julie synthesized a story for each project. They gathered the stories in a dedicated book, each story highlighting the team dynamic, the iterations with consumers, the outputs, and the tools that significantly impacted the project. The book had two objectives: it helped convince the management of each of the divisions to finance another project, and it served as a source of inspiration and a reference tool that helped Julie and Sabine build the Danone design thinking recipe. Thanks to the diversity of agencies and contexts, and with parallel projects being set up simultaneously, they managed to learn fast by observing several ways of applying design thinking. It drove their decisions on what was essential to keep and apply later. Following are some examples of what would become the cornerstones of the Danone design thinking recipe:

- Include an "intent" phase at the start. While they noted similar stages of empathize, define, ideate, prototype, and test in all projects, they saw the value from one agency of the "intent" phase at the start to make sure the team and internal stakeholders took enough time to align on the scope, the intention of the project, and the fixed and open parameters.
- Organize the team in three streams: desirability, viability, feasibility. While all agencies were able to settle on the right mindset for collaboration among the team, when the team was organized by these three streams, the psychological frontiers between functions were fading and the team was more focused on the goal of designing a desirable, viable, and feasible solution.
- Include external people in the project team to boost the creativity of fast prototyping. They saw different ways to partner with

chefs, suppliers, and design agencies to produce in a very fast mode rough but appealing prototypes to test with consumers.
- Organize the teamwork through a series of two-to-three-day workshops: it was easier to plan.

Design Thinking Impact on the Project and on the Corporate Level

In all projects, design thinking shook the existing relations and power games between the players. The voice of consumers used to be the territory of marketing and consumer expert (SBS: Sensorial and Behavioral Sciences) teams within R&I. The design thinking agencies invited all the teams' members to spot insights about the consumers and insisted on speeding up consumer testing; all of this questioned the existing consumer study practices and has been moderately accepted by these teams. Design thinking agencies created a new way of working, where cross-functional teams interact and collaborate. Beyond personalities, it meant that the boundaries between function-associated responsibilities got blurred: project briefs were written by the group (and not by marketing only), for example. Danone teams used to only present perfect and almost finished products to consumers. Through the projects, they experienced how rough prototypes can uncover insights and create reactions from consumers. R&I and quality departments needed to develop new ways of developing rough prototypes and validating safety issues to allow testing with consumers. All these frictions had to be managed alongside the projects. From that perspective, the "reporters" were vital. They were used by the agencies as translators of Danone culture, making it easier for the agencies to understand reactions. On the other hand, they captured team members' struggles and addressed them later on through the Danone design thinking recipe. Eight months later, Jean-Philippe decided to present the learnings to the Executive Committee at the Strategic Danone Yearly Committee. Fast&Furious outputs were as bold as expected: the front-end innovation phase had been accelerated (from one year to three to six months); the teams learned how to be consumer-centered and build persona points of view and collaborate iteratively. But these benefits came at a cost:

- Relying on an external agency made it too expensive. This cost was supported by Jean-Philippe's central budget for the experiments, but it was illusory to think that a local business unit could afford it for further projects.
- The projects involved a new brand, but could it work for existing brand innovation or renovation?
- The designed solutions came with technological challenges; therefore, more time and money were needed for the next development stage. Beyond accelerating the front-end, the issue was to address the next phase that must not last for long, making the total project's lifespan look long.
- Fast and rough prototypes required a new set of partners around the R&I teams.
- Fast&Furious projects mobilized the whole project team from the start (vs. existing process where only marketing was in charge), making it look demanding in terms of human resources.
- The approach demanded new behaviors from all individuals involved in the projects. Emotional and psychological safety had to be ensured along with the ups and downs of the project. Internal expertise was needed to drive this change.

Jean-Philippe let each R&I director decide how to pursue design thinking going forward.

Implementation at the Waters Division

In mid-2016, it became clear to Christophe that it would be best to master design thinking internally rather than relying on the external agency. As Sabine had gained experience with Fast&Furious projects and had embedded it in her daily ways of working, Christophe turned Sabine's mandate from *business process and organization* to *innovation and organization*. In addition to her current mission, Sabine was given the mandate to develop the capabilities around design thinking for R&I in the Waters Division. She was also given the budget to offer Julie a permanent position and recruit Damien, who was responsible for open innovation, as part of the innovation and organization scope. Indeed, Sabine thought that some benefit could be found in mixing open innovation with design thinking.

From that moment, the design thinking story was written by four permanent staff. Julie, Damien, and Sabine were trained following the professional track of design thinking education at the HPI, Potsdam. As the HPI program combined theoretical learning with practice through business projects, it was very helpful to put theory behind what they had lived and experienced with the agencies. Being trained by the d.school helped give them confidence and, most and foremost, increased their internal credibility.

In September 2016, at an innovation committee meeting of the Waters Division, Sabine convinced participants to bring design thinking to an open innovation project. Julie and Damien used this project within their ten weeks training at HPI. They experimented with a new way to make open innovation technology become a real business opportunity for a specific user target. As well, they convinced the Spain's Country Business Unit about the value of this new way of working.

An Example: Developing a Hydration Coaching Device

This project was about turning an open innovation technology in Smart Hydration into a business opportunity. Design thinking was helpful in the first phase as it could help the team step back on the technology and refocus their attention on framing the usage. The initial idea was to sell an overcap with a light reminder to drink water.

In the summer of 2016, after meeting the founders of the startup Water.io, Damien started to analyze which business unit would be the best candidate for such a project. One year before, Spain's business unit had identified seven innovation priorities, including Smart Hydration. Besides, the general manager of this business unit was quite open to breakthrough innovation. So, it became clear that it would be a good context for a collaboration with the startup. Yet the Innovation and Organization team decided not to present the startup idea right away to the general manager.

The team chose to do some preliminary research on who could use the technology. The first hypothesis included parents of young kids, older people, sport-addicted people, and HR departments. They then interviewed some representatives of these target groups. In addition, they designed a first project approach dedicated to answering the question, who is it for? With the first intuitions from interviews and a recommendation on the process, they could present the opportunity to the general manager and the marketing director. The project required Spain's Country Business Unit (CBU) to dedicate two people (approximately 25 per cent of their time over ten weeks; one digital marketing manager and one packaging developer) to the project. In return, the Innovation and Organization team would dedicate two people and donate Euros 35,000 for the first step. Those conditions made the deal easy to accept as Spain's CBU had no other project fueling its priority around Smart Hydration.

The suggested process was inspired by the Danone design thinking recipe and integrated into the HPI program over ten weeks. The first phase was about exploring the hypothetical targets and understanding their relationship with hydration. The second phase was dedicated to creating, prototyping, and testing ideas. To focus the effort, the project team, with Spain's CBU approval, focused the exploration stage on three targets they interviewed: parents of young kids, sport-addicted people, and HR departments.

After this inspiration phase, the four-person team turned to more people for ideation, from inside and outside Danone. They prototyped those ideas with the help of some external designers and tested them. The results were easy to interpret. Parents were afraid of using an object paired with an app that would give their kids another excuse to be in front of a screen; employees wanted to have their office chair fixed before receiving hydration advice; sport-addicted people wanted to know when it will be available. The project team paused for a moment and framed the next phase before presenting the results to the general manager and marketing director. Applying the same trick, they suggested a deal easy to accept: another four months to explore the question on usability – would people transfer the overcap from bottle to bottle?

For this second step, the startup joined the team in early 2017. They designed a real-life test with the prototype produced by the startup in the shape of a cap. After five weeks of real-life tests with forty respondents, the team knew what the specifications should be. They chose to go for an overcap to decrease the risk for certification even though that implied a change in the technology used. The development could start. The launch had to be postponed four times as the new technology proved hard to control, and the certification process was not compatible with iterations. All in all, the development lasted more than one and a half years. The overcap worked by being clipped onto the existing lid on a water bottle and instantly tracked how much water the consumer was drinking daily. The overcap also reminded them to take sips continuously.

The project team managed internal expectations with regular updates on the project. They even suggested starting external communications around the project in February 2019. The Spanish brand communicated to its networks, and the Danone group did the same. On the one hand, the innovation won two design awards. On the other hand, the reactions on different channels helped discover more about the audience for the innovation. For example, LinkedIn happened to be a terrible channel as the audience was too sensitive to plastic bottles. In September 2019, the team was finally happy to launch a limited edition of Coach2o. The launch itself had been designed to continuously learn about the audience and plan further iterations. This project showed that even with technology as a starting point, a design thinking approach was helpful because it allowed the first critical step to focus on identifying quickly and at a low cost the cohort with the unmet need/hot pain point that wanted this product.

Evangelization Starts Now

From that experience, the Innovation and Organization team of the R&I in the Waters Division gained confidence in catalyzing projects using design thinking and thus began their journey of evangelization. Two years after the expedition, they started giving conferences inside the Danone R&I center to the cross-division public and to the public outside Danone. They communicated internally on the new Danone internal social network and animated one-hour design thinking discovery (Stanford model) three times to around fifty people, each involving staff from R&I and regulation and quality. Julie and Sabine became the internal references for design thinking, and other innovation teams across divisions and functions came for advice asking how to lead projects, how to choose the external agency, where to be trained, and so on. Damien showed how Danone had mixed design thinking and open innovation during innovation days in the startup ecosystem in Tel Aviv and the startup boot camp tour.

In 2017, they organized a three-day training workshop for twenty innovation managers from the Waters Division, hoping they would spread the word in other CBUs. These were managers from local CBUs with either formulation, packaging, or consumer expertise involved in innovation projects and appealing to new ways of managing innovation. Although it was a learning-by-doing training, it was not enough to equip them to make the change. They were middle management. They acquired the required knowledge and practice to understand consumer-centricity, but they lacked local power to decide the change. That was a failure in terms of impact since no significant change happened. However, the team learned from that experience.

A First Opportunity to Have a Direct Impact on Business Needs

The opportunity to make a step-change for using design thinking came from the Philippines. In January 2017, the VP of the Waters Division challenged the general manager of the Philippines subsidiary to launch a new beverage brand within one year. Danone had launched the brand Blue a few years back, and it took around three years to reach the market. So, the challenge called for new ways of innovating. The head of Waters R&I Asia convinced the general manager to try design thinking and called the Innovation and Organization team for support. Because of the distance between Paris and Manila, they could not replicate the Design Thinking@Danone (figure 3.1) recipe using a sequence of short workshops, so they tried something new inspired by the one-week Google Design Sprint methodology. They allied with Jacinthe, Global VP of Waters Marketing, to support

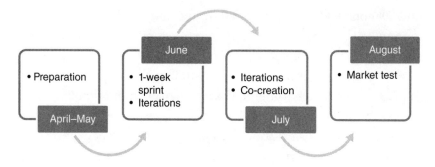

Figure 3.1. Design Sprint with a business mandate

the local marketing team change. Julie and Sabine guided the local team on how to organize the viability, desirability, and feasibility streams, and on what to do during the nine-week preparation. The local team gathered eighteen people in different fields of expertise: marketing, consumer studies, product formulation, packaging development, anthropology, mixology, and design.

The project leadership remained local so that they had full ownership of the experience and output. During the preparation time, Julie, Jacinthe, and Sabine managed the project team and work streams through weekly conferences, going from the intent (i.e., framing the project as a user-challenge) to the point of view (i.e., summarizing the findings of the consumers' exploration) steps. From mid-April to early June 2017, the team managed to make sense of the massive amount of information. The one-week sprint took place in mid-June 2017 in Manila. The team selected five from nine personas to enter the sprint and decided to focus on three at the end of day one. Day two was dedicated to refining personas and point of views. Day three was dedicated to prototyping and testing in interactive loops meeting with fifty consumers. On day five, the team reviewed the learnings, decided what the following steps would be, and pitched them to their general manager. They were so convincing that they kept this team dynamic and working after the design sprint. The team went on more quick iterations around the product mix over July. They managed to find a shortcut in the product development process and put three products produced at a low scale on the shelves of a street market.

The story of this project was presented at the annual meeting to all the general managers and marketing directors of the Waters Division to showcase another way to innovate. Indeed, this project was initiated by the VP of Waters Division and became quite famous. People were curious about how it went. The highlights were that a design sprint called for a true collaboration among Danone functions and with externals (ethnography suppliers, designers) giving an equal share of voice to a diversity of cognitive styles. The key success factors were to start with a user challenge (i.e., how to design an attractive beverage for Filipino millennials?) and iterate with consumers until defining a product that provided the user with a holistic experience. This project proved several points:

- Design thinking can be applied successfully in a cheaper and faster way than via Fast&Furious projects.
- The Innovation and Organization team, together with central marketing, gained the credibility to catalyze this way of innovating.
- The local team learned by doing and adopted principles of collaboration, iteration, and fast prototyping and tested beyond the sprint week with the street market.

Yet the team also learned that if design thinking required a new attitude from team members inside the project team, it also benefited from close coaching of the decision-makers around the project (general manager, marketing director). They needed to learn to trust the approach and the team so that they could let it go. Moreover, the success relied on excellent preparation between a unified cross-functional global team (Jacinthe, Julie, and Sabine) and an engaged, dedicated local team. This preparation could hardly be done in less than nine weeks. Finally, the design sprints required a lot of energy, which directly impacted the capacity for the global team to handle several sprints simultaneously.

Applying Design Sprints to Renew a Brand

At the presentation at the annual general managers' meeting, the team hoped that this case would be enough to convince every CBU to try this approach, but it did not go that way. The Philippines was a small and new business for the Waters Division and therefore seen as different by the historical ones, convinced that their ways of doing things were good enough. However, the head of R&I Asia Waters kept talking to the Asian CBUs and identified another business issue that could benefit from design thinking. The Mizone brand[7] in Indonesia needed a renewal. The team had worked on the topic for several months, gathering extensive information on new consumers, profiling tribes, the evolution of the market, exploring technical new routes, and so on, but did not manage to make sense of all of these.

The collaboration with global marketing continued. Together with Jacinthe and Dieter, a newcomer from the central market study team, Julie and Sabine adapted a three-day sprint to redesign the Mizone brand. They did a similar job as in the Philippines, preparing the team for gathering content and data, shaping the team dynamic, and pushing for iterative consumer interactions. Yet the challenge was more extensive than the previous one since they were working with an existing business. Therefore, changing the local team dynamic was harder: they needed to leave their old paradigm and dare to test bold ideas. Moreover, renewing the marketing mix precisely was a must for the project. They leveraged the work on user experience to define new brand positioning.

The model worked: at the end of the three days, they had designed two new possible positionings for the brand illustrated with a prototype validated by early feedback from consumers. Those two positionings were ready to be further developed and tested for final selection. The local team built their confidence and aligned themselves with pursuing the chosen route.

From Telling to Showing

This project was very decisive because it was about using design thinking to renew an existing brand. This third successful project provided motivation and rationale for scaling design thinking within the firm. After February 2018, there were three success stories to tell: one about a new business model, one about new product, and one about brand renewal in a historic CBU.

The team started to advise innovative teams outside the Water Divisions, which included the Manifesto Innovation Accelerator (MIA)[8] and La Petite Fabrique,[9] the Medical Division, and the IT functions. They chose the same path as the Waters Division with light coaching: relying on external agencies first. The significant shift was that the team moved from pushing the messages internally to having people coming to them for advice, such as the R&I people who asked for help to secure and develop their external network, which led to a software project after using a design thinking approach. They also encouraged using design thinking outside classical product innovation, for example, redesigning training for the beverages-formulation expert or designing creativity rooms in the Paris and Barcelona research centers.

Inside the Tornado

The team had chosen a model where central expertise in design thinking coupled with market study and marketing could freely fly over a business unit to help solve a given challenge. This removed all barriers to try out the new approach. In 2018 and 2019, the Innovation and Organization team inspired six other projects in a sprint mode for innovation in France, Turkey (resulting in a new iced tea beverage, Hayat),[10] Poland, Argentina, Mexico, and China. The pace was intense; sprints were succeeding. They expanded the team to two newcomers (Mathurin and Mégane), reaching four full-time members to run sprints.

Yet all the teams that tried a project did not embrace design thinking in the same way. Some took the project as an exception to their work and went back to old habits afterward. The change was not consistent among all CBUs. The impact of each sprint had a very different depth according to whether the mindset in place was fixed on existing boundaries. The only CBUs that experienced long-lasting effects were the ones with a team already oriented toward growth and novelty. Those people, be they team members or leaders, could encourage new ways of working after the sprint.

However, a fast prototyping mindset and behaviors were adopted in every division, as this was very close to the Danone culture. R&I teams built capabilities inside and with externals to be able to speed up the production of prototypes. Teams started to use increasing numbers of fast prototypes, artifacts, or stimuli earlier in the project.

The Snowball Effect: Diffusing Design Thinking in the Organization

Approximately twenty people from other divisions, IT, and the Sensorial and Behavior Science team within R&I decided to be trained between 2018 and 2019. Sabine advised them to go to HPI. It was important to be trained in the same way as it ensured learning the same mindset and terminology, and it helped to unify a critical mass of internal design thinking experts within one community. That community was centered on one experience and philosophy.

While the Innovation and Organization team showed the path, project after project, some new employees experienced in design thinking joined Danone. In the United States, an ex-IDEO employee started to train the US R&I team.

A new head of the Sensorial and Behavioral Sciences team joined in 2018, coming from L'Oréal, where she had been exposed to design thinking. She amplified the pledge for change and adoption of human-centered innovation among the R&I executive team. She took the lead in organizing a new training event for 200 R&I leaders across divisions and across zones, which was known as the People Powered Innovation (PPI)[11] event and held in February 2019. Several past experiences from the Innovation and Organization team and other teams that had tried design thinking (MIA, La Petite Fabrique, the Flyte project) were presented. Starting from that moment, the label put forward became "People Powered Innovation" rather than design thinking. A new language was born.

Beyond the label, this milestone represented the mutation from design thinking as a process to design thinking as a mindset based on three principles: starting with a user challenge, adopting an iterative approach about the user experience, and emphasizing the multiplicity of perspectives linked to the diversity of people involved in projects.

Institutionalizing or Diluting Design Thinking?

The R&I executive team decided to rely on the Sensorial and Behavioral Science team to ensure a large spread of the PPI. This team had the advantage of gathering more than 100 experts on consumer science and being present in each division globally. It was necessary, though, to focus efforts in shifting the team from consumer science to user experience, integrating the design thinking mindset and expertise. This change was realized by a new name: the User

Experience team (UX). Because team members had been involved in projects in business units, they could infuse human-centered principles into everyday business life. Inside this new framework, new practices could be articulated with existing ones to bring together a massive buy-in from the entire company. This movement happened at the very exact moment as the initiative to renew training for marketing and R&I functions. This Innovation Academy could be fueled by the experimenting done so far, spreading the message widely. At a higher level, some leadership programs included the necessary shift in postures that innovation would require from leaders. All those training sessions were seeds disseminated across the company, and would prove their success in the coming months. Sabine's team worked hand in hand with the UX team and the human resources team to fuel the trainings. This was especially important as Julie, Mathurin, and Sabine left Danone in 2019 to pursue new opportunities. Mégane remained in the Waters R&I, ensuring the transmission of the acquired experience. Damien joined a new cross-division Open Innovation team, bringing the approach and expertise that had been developed in the Waters Division.

A Community of Addicts

Some would argue that design thinking became diluted within the corporate machine. But the first twenty design thinking addicts trained at HPI and the newly "contaminated people" gained through PPI continue to meet regularly, sharing the issues they encounter when working on this journey. They share the new projects submitted by business units, discuss how to approach them, share tips and failures. This community expresses their purpose as creating the best learning experience of PPI principles for them, their colleagues, and Danone. This is intended to set up an emotional and psychologically safe space in which to share worries and issues in order to grow collectively. They structured the community through rules to enter, behave, and leave the community. This group of people keeps expanding knowledge through experimentation of design thinking that can be integrated quickly into the organization, thanks to the UX team.

Lessons Learned

The story of design thinking at Danone is a story of a "change by design along the knowledge funnel."[12] It changed the way Danone manages product innovation. The change is significant among the R&I community as the user is now at the heart of the R&I mindset, and fast prototyping has become a habit. Beyond R&I, design thinking has touched other teams involved in innovation and other functions like IT. Overall, each of the three main phases of the initiative revealed important lessons and success factors.

- Top management sponsorship, a dedicated budget, and a person with the mandate to experiment and learn about design thinking were key.
- Experimenting with different types of innovation projects was essential to learn and show results. At the same time, it was important to try out different approaches to innovation so that the organization could learn quickly and develop its recipe for innovation.
- Collaboration with the organizational marketing function was crucial to understand and research the voice of the consumer and customer needs.
- To inspire other divisions and make the recipe for innovation relevant to the rest of the organization, a dedicated team with a mission to experiment was formed.

- Collaboration with the corporate and business unit level marketing function continued to be critical for early innovation projects.
- Training and development of the whole team in design thinking through the same education provider led to a homogenous and reliable knowledge base and the critical mass of internal design thinking experts.
- Building the opportunity for design thinking to be applied to major projects while carefully managing the energy of a small innovation team was critical.

Timeline

- 2014: Learning expedition with twenty-two high potential VP-level employees, including VP R&I. Visits to IDEO, P&G, and other leading organizations.
- 2015: Nomination of Sabine to explore design thinking; Fast&-Furious projects facilitated by different agencies including five projects across all divisions; learning from the projects and establishment of a Danone design thinking recipe.
- 2016: Creation of the Innovation and Organization team within the Waters Division; training of three key people via d.school at the Hasso Plattner Institute; development of an open innovation project using design thinking.
- 2017: New projects in the Philippines and further customization of the Danone design thinking recipe to suit the international and decentralized organization; training of twenty middle managers of the Danone Waters Division.
- 2018: Innovation of an existing product for the Indonesian market; increasing a variety of projects in France, Turkey, and other locations; training of an additional twenty people via d.school at the Hasso Plattner Institute; the design thinking team now

includes four people who facilitate design sprints at the global
level.

- 2019: New people familiar with design thinking join from IDEO,
L'Oréal, and other organizations; start of the People Powered
Innovation Program; further projects in China, Argentina, Poland, and other locations; start of the Danone design thinking
community; some members of the Innovation and Organization
team leave.
- 2020: Initiatives like the Innovation Academy are thriving; the
new Danone User Experience (UX) team with more than 100
experts across the globe is now in charge of design thinking that
has been renamed People Powered Innovation.

CHAPTER FOUR

Keeping the Momentum – The First Decade of Design Thinking at Intuit

WENDY CASTLEMAN

At **Intuit**, design thinking has been practiced successfully for over thirteen years. Seven years after its first adoption, and while design thinking had already been entrenched in the daily work of many employees, it began to fade from the skillset. It became necessary to gain a second momentum. Today, design thinking at Intuit is about integrating emotion with a crafted and iterative problem-solving approach (designated as Design for Delight) used in a wide range of situations. The scaling of this approach was based on two strategies: First, hands-on experiential workshops involving leaders to experience the potential of the approach and, second, a team of ten people who animate a community of engaged catalysts. Intuit demonstrated a remarkable openness toward learning from other firms and approaches.

As a business, Intuit, the financial software company that develops and sells financial, accounting, and tax preparation software and related services for small businesses, accountants, and individuals, had seen good growth in the 1980s and 1990s. However, growth became stagnant in the early 2000s. The core software products were still dominant in their areas, but the focus had been on incremental improvements in the ease of use of the software. There was a discussion at the Board of Directors level about whether Intuit should be considered a value company or a growth company. Given the lack of growth and flat stock price, the preference to lean into Intuit as a growth company may have seemed a bit audacious. Yet, the company founder, Scott Cook, believed in his company and decided to choose growth and thus change.

Intuit Inc. is an American business in the financial software industry. The company was founded in 1983 and is headquartered in Mountain View, California. Intuit's products include a TurboTax tax preparation application, a personal finance app Mint, and a small business accounting program, QuickBooks. In 2019, Intuit registered about US$6.748 billion in revenue, which it mainly generated from its activities within the United States. In 2021, over 10,000 people worked for Intuit.

The Challenge

From the start of the company, user experience design was a strong part of the product development process. The first product, Quicken, launched in the late 1980s, wasn't released until it reached its usability goals, and just a couple of years later, ethnographic research helped to highlight the importance of observing customers to understand the problems to solve. The company continued to invest in user research and design throughout its history. By the early 2000s, it was no longer unusual for a tech company to have user experience teams to research and design their experiences. Intuit continued to invest in user experience, and the focus was on making its products easier to use.

In 2004, Scott invited Fred Reichheld to Intuit to share the net promoter score (NPS) metric and story. Scott was very excited because, until then, there was no company-wide customer-based metric that was being measured to understand how the company was doing. Intuit used stock price, revenues, customer acquisition, and similar business metrics. The company also measured employee engagement scores, which it rigorously tracked over time. Each product was so unique that there wasn't a customer-focused metric. So, Intuit embraced NPS and began to track changes year over year. Almost immediately, it was clear that there was a big problem. While the products were becoming measurably easier to use (as measured by large-scale usability benchmarking studies), the NPS at Intuit was drifting downward. Although efforts decreased the detractors, they didn't see more promoters. This completely contradicted the internal belief that the value of Intuit's products was that they were easier to use than the alternatives. The CEO at the time, Steve Bennett, recognized that it was no longer sufficient for a product to be easy for someone to recommend or to buy.

In late 2006, a strategy team was assembled to figure out what was "beyond ease." Since easy-to-use products were now the standard, people wanted products that excited them and that exceeded their expectations. The team explored the question, "What should Intuit be designing for?" The strategy team was composed of members of the corporate strategy team and a member of the central Customer Centered Design[1] (CCD) team – Suzanne Pellican. Suzanne was a rising star in the Intuit design community, and Kaaren Hanson (head of CCD) saw that this was a perfect opportunity to make sure that design had a seat at the table for the future of the company. The brief project set out to define the next phase for the company – Design for Delight. The strategy team recognized that designing for ease wasn't enough and that designing for emotional engagement was key. To communicate that message, the team defined Design for Delight as "Evoking a positive emotion by exceeding customer's expectations in ease and benefit throughout the customer journey."

Intuit had a tradition of pulling teams of leaders together to define and lead changes at the company. Although consultants were part of the process, the aim was for teams to learn from the outside but make it their own. As such, instead of hiring a consulting firm to help with the roll-out and change needed for Design for Delight, the organization worked on creating the change from within.

Introduction to Design Thinking

In August 2007, Intuit held its annual leadership offsite workshop for directors and above. The theme of the conference was "Design for Delight," and internal and external speakers were brought in to talk about delight. One of the external speakers was Alex Kazaks from IDEO and the newly formed Stanford d.school. Alex guided the entire audience through an experiential workshop, the now-famous "The Wallet Exercise," that introduced everyone to design thinking.[2]

Scott also began learning about design thinking from Claudia Kotchka (VP Design Innovation and Strategy) at Procter & Gamble, where he served on the Board of Directors. Thinking that there was something to this design thinking thing, Scott connected Kaaren with Claudia, who brought their teams together for information sharing.

After the leadership offsite workshop, leaders were tasked with sharing what they had learned with their teams and applying a new Design for Delight lens to their work. As the design research strategist on the CCD team, I began to work with Kaaren and Suzanne as facilitators in the transmission of senior leadership learnings, running cascade and internalization sessions with teams to figure out what Design for Delight meant to them. During this effort, the CCD team recognized that many of the tools and skills were aligned to those we used in user experience design and we were able to crystalize some of the methods that were needed for various teams to understand designing for delight.

In early 2008, the CCD team pulled together Intuit's experience design (XD) community at Intuit's annual Tech Forum to craft a process for Design for Delight based on the best practices in the experience design field (see figure 4.1). The result was a phased process with a lot of back arrows pointing to iterations. The idea was that different activities would happen at four different phases in a project: discover, define, design, and deliver. Since Intuit had been very process focused in prior years, through its process excellence initiative, the process model made a lot of sense. It was rolled out as a best practice document for the XD community across the company. However, it was not immediately adopted for use.

Customer-Driven Innovation Workshops

To spur adoption of the new behaviors, I joined up with Nedda Cox (a design leader in CCD), Hisham Ibrahim (the product management community leader), and Roy Rosin (the former general manager of Quicken and a leader in the Personal Finance Group) to develop a series of workshops designed around the four-phase model (discover, define, design, and deliver), deeply rooted in the principles and tools of customer-driven innovation (CDI).[3] We chose four product teams from different business units whose members were tasked with addressing specific business challenges. As the teams were at different phases in relation to the process, each started at a different place. I led the discovery workshop and focused on customer discovery research and problem identification. Roy took the lead on the define workshop and focused on getting very narrow

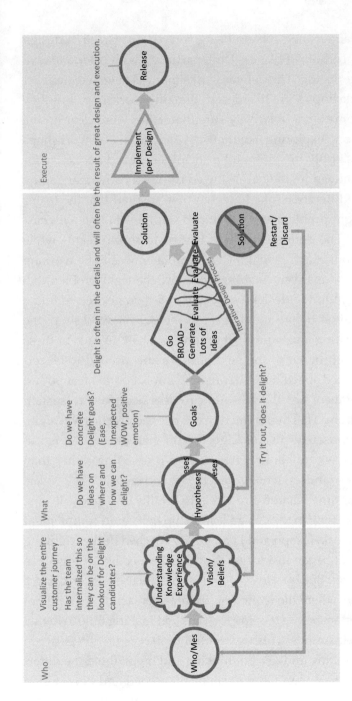

Figure 4.1. Design for Delight process diagram

and specific about the problem being solved. Ant Creed, a design leader in the Turbotax Business Unit, partnered with Nedda to lead the design workshop. The deliver workshop was never created.

These workshops were like design thinking workshops but they spent more time being relatively sure that teams were clear on the problem before exploring solutions. Although these workshops helped teams apply the tools and principles believed necessary for successful innovation, they also slowed the teams down. Engaging customers and iteration take time, but they ensured that the teams solved the right problem and developed solutions in line with customer needs. The define workshop tended to stump teams while they figured out exactly what the right problem was to be working on. Since the teams were required to know the right problem before moving on to the design workshop and then needed to know the right solution before moving on to the deliver workshop, the process of creating a new product ground to a halt. In each of these workshops, to proceed to the next phase, teams needed to be certain. The reduced speed had a depressing impact on the teams, and the team members lost the sense of progress necessary to sustain their momentum. This highlighted that while the practice was right, the teams' mindsets were still aligned with their old way of working, avoiding risk by being certain before proceeding rather than embracing the mindset of enlightened trial and error.

Around this time, Kaaren hired Joseph O'Sullivan, a design leader, to join CCD to bring in the design leadership that could complement my research work. Joseph and I had jointly coached design thinking workshops that began to address the mindsets needed to engage in design thinking. Specifically, the workshops focused on creating a learning cycle, where the team took an informed action that did not need to be perfect before moving forward and making time to iterate based on the learnings. This was central to the distinction between traditional thinking and design thinking and highlighted the difference between how the CDI workshops proceeded and how design thinking activities did. Implementing this bias-to-action approach, I observed that people moved faster and made faster changes. Hence, I shifted my entire focus toward teaching design thinking tools and facilitating design thinking.

Integration into Existing Leadership Training

Joseph and I were asked by the Human Resources Learning and Development team (L&D) to help update a leadership development program that had been around for a couple of years: Fast Path. Although the program effectively built emotional intelligence skills and assisted people in improving how they presented themselves as leaders, the actual work that the teams accomplished during the program – solving business challenges for the company – was below expectations. The L&D team thought that Joseph and I might be able to provide some lightweight Design for Delight (D4D) coaching to help teams move faster and more effectively. Pleased to have the opportunity to talk about D4D to high potential employees and get people to use these methods, Joseph and I jumped in.

After a few sessions with the program, Joseph and I interviewed L&D leaders to understand what value they saw in the coaching that they brought in. The leaders said that the sessions made for incredible teaching moments. For example, the teams would be arguing or spinning in place. Then Joseph or I would come in, listen for a couple of minutes, suggest a course of action (usually something as simple as asking, "Why don't we capture all of these ideas on Post-it Notes and stick them on this board?"). Suddenly the team would get unstuck and would start working together. This happened because it got the team from discussion to action, even in a small way, which immediately felt like traction. The L&D leaders described our work as being the catalyst that caused a change. We loved it because it exposed high-performing employees to some design thinking tools that they could take back and apply to their work. This was the origin of the "Design Catalysts" title that Intuit would use to describe its internal design thinking coaches.

Developing a Strategy for Getting D4D Adopted Widely across Intuit

In mid-2008, Kaaren invited a group of select designers from the XD community to join her, Joseph, and me in developing a strategy for getting D4D adopted more broadly. She knew that by inviting others from the XD community to help drive this, that design could increase its visibility and influence. Although Joseph and I were full-time employees working on this, the rest of these designers were employed full-time in design roles within the business units. Intuit had recently embraced the idea of "10 per cent time" (inspired by Google's 20 per cent time), and Kaaren thought that maybe these designers could spend 10 per cent of their time helping to drive the D4D strategy. Kaaren called these 10 designers the "Design Catalysts," inspired by the story from L&D.

CEO Offsite Workshop

Scott started getting impatient – he'd seen the scaling impact of P&G's design thinking workshops, and he wanted Kaaren's team to replicate that model. "Just do the workshop!" It was the fall of 2008, and the CCD team was still experimenting in small ways with discrete programs. Scott had the ear of Intuit's new CEO, Brad Smith, who was interested in encouraging commercial innovation within the business units. Influenced by Scott, Brad agreed to have the theme of his first CEO offsite workshop focus on commercial innovation. Scott turned to Kaaren and asked her team to lead a design thinking workshop. Kaaren engaged Suzanne, who was now working in another business unit, to join Joseph and me to develop the workshop.

In preparation for this high-profile event, Kaaren, Suzanne, Joseph, and I met with people on Procter & Gamble's design thinking team to get their best practices for a workshop with executives, including tips on facilitation and setting expectations and managing distractions. We decided to bring customers into the session, both for customer interviews and customer feedback. Since the offsite workshop was being held at a distant location, we assigned two extended members of the CCD team (an ethnographer and a logistics person) to manage the customers for the day.

Our team piloted the content and designed the workshop, but while doing so, we also looked back at the D4D process model and started thinking about how to simplify it for teaching the executives. Although the model had been rolled out to the user experience community, it hadn't been widely adopted because there was a certain amount of process fatigue in the organization and the belief that other process models (e.g., agile development) conflicted with it.

Our team took a step back to figure out what the main teaching objectives were. We realized that it wasn't the process itself that was important. It was the principles behind them. We decided to abandon the process and instead identified three principles that were easy to teach and understand: deep customer empathy, go from broad to narrow, and rapid experiments with customers. We realized that the principles were an effective way to teach design thinking. The principles were adopted and, as a result, are the central principles that guide Intuit's D4D program today.

The CEO offsite workshop was a resounding success, with general managers commenting on how different this way of working was from how people worked at Intuit at the time. Scott was thrilled, as was Brad, the new CEO. Several general managers asked for the CCD team to run an identical session with their leadership teams. As a result, Joseph and I planned and conducted workshops across multiple business units in various locations, collaborating with some of the original Design Catalysts over the next six months.

While we were running these workshops, two language issues began to arise. First, the Design Catalysts were seen as being experienced designers. Thus, they weren't seen as relevant to non-product development work. However, since D4D was about more than just products, the team needed the Design Catalysts to be taken more seriously. To signal this, they renamed the small crew of mostly volunteers: the Innovation Catalysts.[4]

As the goal was to get people at Intuit to behave differently, not just talk about D4D, Joseph and I took on any team that expressed interest in gaining knowledge and getting help. These included projects from product teams, support organizations, human resources, and sales. The design thinking methods and tools applied to any of the design environments they worked with, and the three principles became an anchor that could frame any of the work that they did.

When people began to understand the value of design thinking, they wanted help applying it to other things they were working on. At this point, things began to move very quickly, and there was a dramatic need for the scaling of coaching/teaching/facilitation capabilities to meet that new demand.

Increasing Innovation Catalysts (2009–2011)

Between the workshop requests and the L&D coaching, Joseph and I were stretched thin, but Suzanne decided to leave her role in the business unit and join the CCD team to help make D4D part of every employee's behavior. Soon afterward, though, Suzanne went out on maternity leave, and the resource issue arose again. Kaaren and her team realized that to scale these principles and behaviors across the company, they would need even more help. Of the initial ten Design Catalysts, only six were still at the company and available to help. They decided to train more catalysts that could conduct design thinking workshops, and upon returning from her leave, Suzanne was put in charge of pulling together the training for the Innovation Catalysts.

Suzanne worked with Joseph, Rachel Evans (an Innovation Catalyst and Design Researcher from the professional tax business unit), and me to develop the training. It was mainly based on the CEO off-site workshop, held nine months earlier, with some extra breakouts on facilitating and planning being added. The first "official class" of Intuit Innovation Catalysts took place in September 2009 and trained twenty-five employees. Many of these employees worked as designers or in XD-related roles because the focus was on employees who were instinctively using design thinking principles at work. Suzanne decided to build some community with the new recruits, creating community goals and a structure. Each Innovation Catalyst had to invest time in planning and facilitating at least four hours of workshops every month. She tracked this in a database. Employees could also make requests for Innovation Catalysts to help with workshops. Meetups and ongoing training events were created to educate the Innovation Catalysts further. An email alias was also created for a distribution list, and Innovation Catalysts started exchanging questions and experiences as the program gained momentum. Joseph, Rachel, and I flew to India, where we replicated the Innovation Catalyst training with twenty more employees, bringing the total number of Innovation Catalysts up to forty-five.

Over the next few months, it became clear that some of these Innovation Catalysts were more engaged than others. Suzanne was surprised that some of the designers in the group were not active. Digging into it, she discovered that some of the Innovation Catalysts didn't want to give their newly learned tools away. They considered them their "secret sauce" for how they were doing their work, so they didn't want to spend their time teaching it to others.

Other Innovation Catalysts, however, were highly engaged and felt energized from facilitating and teaching others. This informed the next round of recruiting Innovation Catalysts and we added an "attitude check" before admitting individuals for training. The Innovation Catalysts could have a broader impact by focusing on people who wanted to give D4D away to others. So we shifted focus from primarily training design professionals to be Innovation Catalysts to training employees who expressed interest in teaching others, regardless of the role.

Some of the Innovation Catalysts branched out on their training experience and created new types of workshops and new opportunities for applying design thinking. Rachel and some of the other Innovation Catalysts in San Diego started a "Painstorm" workshop. This format engaged customers in sharing their stories to identify and brainstorm on a customer pain point that would be good to solve.

I worked with the corporate Strategy Group to bring design thinking into a critical strategic project. The team moved significantly faster and generated much broader options for opportunities than the team traditionally explored.[5] Beyond these examples, many Innovation Catalysts were able to have a significant impact through participating and facilitating. Their involvement resulted in the filing of multiple patents. D4D gained momentum.

Soon, Rachel joined the CCD team to help rally the Innovation Catalysts, and the group hired two other full-time employees to increase the capacity to drive D4D. The CCD team renamed itself the "Design Innovation Group" and split its focus between teaching design thinking and nurturing the Innovation Catalysts community. A D4D intranet website was created for the company, including how-to materials and a series of short training videos around specific methods. This was the first time that the tools of design thinking were made openly available at the company. However, most people continued to rely on the Innovation Catalysts to help them plan and implement workshops and activities.

From Special Events to the Everyday

From the start of the Innovation Catalyst program, design thinking activity was going on at the company, primarily in "engagements," mostly one-to-three-day workshops. While in 2008 there was only one workshop, by 2011 there were hundreds. By 2011, it was clear from the activity data and stories across the company that D4D was starting to gain a foothold, but that employees were looking at it as something that you did outside of your everyday work. That is, D4D was something you did in a workshop or a session of some sort. Innovation Catalysts helped run workshops and "jams," and this reinforced the idea. Since the move to the three principles, Kaaren and her team recognized that these could (and should) be applied all the time in everything that employees were doing.

I worked with Suzanne to create an offsite workshop for the Innovation Catalysts where the focus was on the vision for "D4D in the DNA" and, what they identified as, the most critical and misused tools in the D4D toolkit: empathy mapping, problem statements, brainstorming, and 2x2 narrowing. Each of these was familiar to the Innovation Catalysts. Still, they were not being used effectively because of weak facilitation skills, misunderstanding the tools, and misunderstanding the value of the tools. For example, the empathy map was frequently used in debriefing customer empathy research, but teams just stuck Post-it Notes into the various quadrants and then moved on. I created an activity for the offsite workshop that walked people through the quadrants, challenging them to find patterns and to think more deeply, and based on the analysis, to identify the underlying motivation for the person. Changing how this tool was used made the tool more valuable and less of a checkbox. It was clear that focusing on providing specific feedback and tips on facilitating these few tools would help the Innovation Catalysts have a greater impact and think about applying the tools outside a workshop context. The offsite workshop was held in October 2011,

D4D in the DNA MEANS...

PROFOUNDLY DELIGHTING OUR CUSTOMERS IS WHY WE EXIST AND D4D IS INSTINCTIVELY THE WAY WE DO IT.

LOOKS LIKE...

It's like riding a bike towards growth. Everyone is doing it naturally and with mastery and ICs are the expert coaches. **WE'RE DROWNING IN HUGE CUSTOMER INSIGHTS.** Everyone is challenging and pushing each other to delight our customers. And we have amazing business outcomes. We're #1 on the Forbes Most Innovative Companies list.

Specific Behaviors

FEELS LIKE...

To our customers, it feels like they are understood by us so much that it's almost telepathic. Because of that, they feel in control and they're fanatical about working with Intuit.

To our employees, it feels like we're in love with the problems, not our solutions. It feels natural – almost indescribable when D4Ding. We feel united in caring for our customers and each other. It's effortless, everyone, everyday.

To Innovation Catalysts, it feels like we're no longer needed – and that's a good thing.

To our Customers. Employees, Us

SOUNDS LIKE...

"Intuit has changed my life so profoundly that I can't imagine going back. **Intuit REALLY gets me.**"
— *Customer*

"D4D is just what we do. **What's a session?**"
— *Employee*

"I want my company to be as innovative as Intuit!"
— *Tim Cook, Apple CEO*

Figure 4.2. Innovation Catalyst community workshop vision

and its results (see figure 4.2) reinvigorated the Innovation Catalysts community.

First Organizational Restructuring

By the end of 2011, the importance of D4D was becoming more visible, so the Design Innovation Group created a new group to focus on scaling D4D. Suzanne led the newly formed D4D Strategy Group, and a variety of changes occurred in the core team, including hiring Lionel Mohri (a new hire formerly at IDEO) and Suzy Wise (previously of the Stanford d.school), and later, Larry Cheng (also from IDEO). By bringing in outside expertise to facilitate design thinking, the team was able to turn its focus onto the culture shift that it was trying to create.

By 2011, Suzanne and I started accepting more Innovation Catalysts into the program from other fields and other parts of the company. There were, by 2018, 300 employees who expressed interest in being trained as Innovation Catalysts in addition to those who were already trained. They had recognized that when there was a group of catalysts co-located or on the same team, they tended to be more active and have a greater impact. So, the idea of a "posse" was created – and the Innovation Catalysts were trained in groups to go back and invigorate the local culture.

One such posse was based in Tucson, Arizona, and was composed of people in finance, support and sales. None of these Innovation Catalysts had design-related experience. Instead, the skills of this group focused on operations. So, they operationalized everything they learned and systematically went through the Tucson office, identifying areas where they could drive change. This led to an impressive transformation in the Tucson office, which saw improvements to its revenue through innovation, operational enhancements, and cultural change.

Integrating Lean Startup into D4D

In 2012, after his book launch, Eric Ries was invited to present it at a company-wide Delight Forum.[6] Delight Forums were quarterly, all-employee meetings that Scott Cook arranged to inspire the company with outside perspectives and stories. Scott was such a fan of Eric's work that he enlisted Lionel to help bring lean experimentation to the World Economic Forum. To design an experience for them, Lionel created a poster that he called the NEXT poster. NEXT introduced a synchronized path for developing ideas – from the idea to the key assumption to a hypothesis to an experiment and finally to a decision: pivot or persevere. In testing these materials, Lionel and I took the poster and a simple set of challenges to some of the Innovation Catalysts.

Inspired by Eric's presentation of the lean startup mindsets and empowered by Lionel's NEXT poster, the Innovation Catalysts began to look for ways to run experiments to test assumptions and encourage people to pivot when their assumptions were rejected. Two of these Innovation Catalysts, Aaron Eden and Bennett Blank, attended one of Steve Blank's startup weekend events after Eric's talk. They loved it so much that they decided to pilot it inside of Intuit. The first pilot was transformative for the employees who participated. Aaron and Bennett conceived of a challenge and brought it to the entire company: the Lean StartIn, which would bring 100 Intuit teams from around the world through the two-day workshop over 100 days. They convinced Hugh Molotsi (Intuit's first Innovation Award winner and a VP in the Innovation and Advanced Technology Group running the Intuit Labs) to fund their travels. They adopted Lionel's NEXT poster and adapted other materials as they went, offering a two-day immersive, guided, intense experience in rapid experimentation, which massively accelerated the internal teams that attended, and led to some significant return on investment (ROI). Over time, Bennett and Aaron determined that having Innovation Catalysts embedded on the teams attending the Lean StartIn sessions helped teams be more successful. This also gave many Innovation Catalysts firsthand experiences that they could use when they returned to their day jobs and when engaging with others.

The Innovation Catalyst Community was taught the NEXT tool at an offsite workshop in San Diego, and I encouraged the Innovation Catalysts to make it a year of experimentation. Over the course of the following year, formal and informal sessions were run, and teams began adopting them into their everyday work processes.

Institutionalizing D4D

The Learning and Development Group had continued with D4D and taught courses at varying levels of the company that focused on teaching employees the tools and mindsets. Although the format of these programs differed, depending on the audience, the core of D4D was based on the three principles of deep customer empathy, go from broad to narrow, and rapid experimentation with customers. The former Fast Path program was changed into a new program called "HIPO," which was an immersive, multi-day D4D boot camp that included leadership training and invited notable speakers. An additional program called "Intuit Youniversity" was developed to train new employees on the value of the three principles alongside the values and operating mechanisms that they would need to succeed and grow inside Intuit. The class was taught about a month after onboarding, so new employees could focus on the content rather than common onboarding issues like choosing insurance and getting computers up and running. In addition to teaching hundreds of new employees, these two programs gave Innovation Catalysts and others additional opportunities to facilitate and coach.

Throughout 2013, D4D was being used in groups across the company, and was cited as the primary behaviors that led to new products, increased employee engagement, increased revenues, and higher NPS. It seemed as if D4D was getting into the DNA of the company.

Seven years into the journey, the original aim of the program – to get D4D into the DNA of the company – was gaining sufficient traction that other challenges became more urgent and new priorities emerged throughout the company. Leaders and executives believed they could dial back on the resources and still carry forward the cultural growth.

Dissolution of Programs

In 2014, a couple of key things changed. First, the bulk of the D4D Strategy Group broke up and moved into different roles within the company. Suzanne, who had been leading the group, moved into a design leadership role in the QuickBooks organization, taking Lionel with her. Bennett moved into the Intuit Labs space to be the product manager of Intuit's Brainstorm product, an internally developed tool for tracking ideas. Larry moved into a strategist role and ultimately into a design leadership role in the QuickBooks organization. I stayed within the Strategy Group and continued leading the Innovation Catalysts community and working with teams across the company to apply D4D to their work.

The Intuit Youniversity program was starting to uncover a challenge. Although the class taught new employees about using design thinking in their work, some of the excited employees returned to their teams and found that their managers were not supportive of using these methods. This was because many longer-term employees had only experienced minimal exposure to D4D. Even though almost 50 per cent of company employees had some D4D training, the rest of the employees had none. Therefore, it was not apparent how these behaviors would apply in some teams, and employees were discouraged from developing them further. The challenge was that when middle managers were unconvinced of the short-term gains of using D4D, they put up barriers to adopting it. This was because they were still being rewarded based on short-term execution. The Learning and Development Group attempted several training approaches to teach mid-level managers, but they felt that none of these approaches had the impact they needed to.

Around this time, Intuit also rolled out a refreshed set of values to the company to bolster behaviors around being bold, decisive, learning fast, and winning together.[7] These were related to the mindsets encouraged by using D4D (not surprising, since one of the team members who created them was Suzanne, who was on the original D4D team). The Learning and Development team had limited resources and decided to stop the Intuit Youniversity program since they couldn't solve the mid-level manager challenge. They moved those resources to training the company on the new values. After another year, they also eliminated the HIPO program.

At the end of the summer in 2014, Kaaren left Intuit, and I remained the sole leader of the D4D initiative and the Innovation Catalysts program. To maintain momentum of the program, the Innovation Catalysts were encouraged to create local communities to support D4D in their locations. They were also encouraged to train more Innovation Catalysts as needed. The community of Innovation Catalysts grew from 250 to about 400, but much of the nurturing and growth for the Innovation Catalysts came from within the community itself during this time.

Between the loss of training and high-level leadership, D4D began to falter. As is typical of technology companies in the Bay Area of San Francisco, Intuit turns over nearly a third of its employees each year, so new employees and managers were joining the company and not being trained in D4D methods. The efforts to make D4D part of the company's DNA weren't successfully keeping up with the need to onboard new employees with the basic principles.

Turning the Tide

In the spring of 2015, I moved the D4D program and the Innovation Catalysts community leadership from the Central Design Group to the newly formed "Innovation Systems" team (later renamed the "Innovation Capabilities" team) within the Transformational Change team in the Technology Innovation Group. This brought a team back to the challenge of building D4D capabilities and a new focus on the cultural barriers that became visible. The team started teaching introductory D4D workshops and boot camps to any employee who wanted to learn.

By the fall of 2015, some of the long-term behaviors related to customer-driven innovation and D4D had begun to fade from the skills of leaders. This "aha moment" struck leaders when they were asked to identify the customer benefits for their respective offerings. Although senior leaders believed that this should have been a trivial effort, it ended up being very difficult because leaders focused on tracking NPS, customer acquisition, and revenues. When asked to reflect upon what they knew from customer visits, it came out that many senior leaders had not visited their customers to understand what value their offerings had. As a result of this "aha moment," Brad, Scott, Eileen Fagan (the leader of the Transformational Change team), and the Innovation Capabilities team worked together to reintroduce Customer Site Visits (known as Follow-Me Homes) at a series of leadership meetings over the next year. Buoyed by the reconnection to customers, the team created a "Customer Obsession Tour" during the annual State of the Company tour that Brad made at every site during the 2018 fiscal year.

Around the same time, a consultant named Tom Chi came and worked with teams and reintroduced the concept of rapid prototyping, which had faded over the time that the company focused on lean startup and then away from D4D. Although it was not new to the core Innovation Capabilities team and the Innovation Catalysts, the outside influence was able to reignite energy around conducting rapid prototyping sessions with customers. This was so important to the company that Tom and the Innovation Catalysts led the top 400 leaders at the company through a half-day rapid prototyping workshop. Fueled by these events, the Innovation Catalysts then were able to restart sessions and workshops with teams who had never learned (or forgotten) D4D behaviors. The tide had turned again, and D4D became an important focus for Intuit.

In February 2017, I decided to leave Intuit. The Innovation Capabilities team maintained the 300-person Innovation Catalysts community leadership along with their efforts to grow and sustain experience with D4D, including skills around customer research and supporting the customer obsession efforts. In September 2017, Sylvia Greenley, a long-term, active Innovation Catalyst, took over leadership of the Innovation Catalysts Program and began rebuilding the program as it had started to lose ground over the churn of the prior three years.

In 2019, Intuit was riding a new high with new leadership and a renewed vigor around D4D. The new CEO, Sasan Goodarzi, was one of the executives who participated in that first CEO offsite workshop in 2008. He is passionate about customers and encourages all employees to use D4D to improve the experiences they create constantly.

Intuit continues to consider D4D to be the primary way the company innovates and to be the set of core capabilities that all employees, no matter what level or role in the organization, should be able to use. However, the company has learned an important lesson about the need to continue nurturing and funding programs that differentiate it from standard practices – that is, it cannot assume that the work of teaching people new behaviors and mindsets is ever over.

Having learned the lesson that the company could not assume that things would continue to grow without delegating resources, Intuit has now bolstered its investment in building D4D capabilities and supporting the culture of human-centered innovation that gives results. In 2019, a program was introduced to train all new employees in D4D, including middle managers. Today, there are hundreds of case studies and examples from all parts of the company, and there are 375 active Innovation Catalysts globally at Intuit. However, all 9,000 employees are encouraged to use D4D in their everyday work. Essentially, Intuit has finally embraced D4D into its DNA.

Not coincidentally, Intuit's growth has skyrocketed. In 2007, when this journey began, Intuit's stock price had been stagnating around US$30 for seven years. On 30 August 2019, exactly twelve years later – the same twelve years during which Intuit embraced design thinking – the stock price closed at US$288.36.

Lessons Learned

- Always continue adapting design thinking to the best practices and tools that come onto the company's radar and the observations you make along the way. You are never done adapting.
- Don't get complacent. Scaling efforts are bound to fail if you think momentum alone can carry you forward.
- The initial team should have the freedom to experiment with how to adapt design thinking to work with the company's current culture and allow growth to seem like a natural extension of what you already do.

- Top management visibility is constantly needed. Most senior managers want to have an innovative culture and believe that design thinking helps contribute to innovation. They need to hear about the wins and failures and be actively involved in challenging and coaching the team. When they aren't in the loop, they may think it is thriving when it needs attention.

Timeline

- 2006: A low net promoter score (NPS) prompts an initiative to use customer-centered design (CCD) methods and explore opportunities for innovation; start of Design for Delight (D4D) projects to exceed customers' expectations; two people are dedicated to CCD projects.
- 2007: Several workshops are held with directors and staff to explore D4D based on IDEO methods and P&G benchmarks; new design thinking tools are aligned with what is already being used.
- 2008: Start of the experience design (XD) community; establishment of the D4D process (discover, define, design, and deliver); workshops with product teams highlight the differences between a design mindset and current processes; successful application of new methods with executives; introduction of a simplified process; ten employees become Design Catalysts and explore how to adopt D4D more broadly.
- 2009: Increasing demand for workshops to apply D4D beyond product development; training of forty-five additional Innovation Catalysts; creation of a community of practice; further exposure and momentum; CCD is renamed the Design Innovation Group.
- 2010–12: Growth of the Innovation Catalysts community to more than sixty people; the Design Innovation Group has eight

members who are shaping the vision of D4D and developing a scaling strategy; further increase in the number of workshops; development of NEXT initiative mixing D4D with lean startup methods.

- 2013–14: Development of a multi-day immersive boot camp and "Intuit Youniversity" teaching employees D4D alongside the values of the company; over 200 Innovation Catalysts are active; some core team members move into leadership positions or leave the company; some D4D trained employees are not supported by management; D4D Youniversity canceled; Innovation Catalysts leadership joins the Technology Innovation Group.
- 2015–16: Leadership realizing how vital skill sets are being lost and resumes D4D workshops with Innovation Catalysts.
- 2019: The new CEO, who was part of the initial CEO offsite workshop, confirms D4D as the way Intuit will innovate; training set up for all employees, including middle managers; over 375 active Innovation Catalysts assigned to drive innovation.

CHAPTER FIVE

Design for Joy – How Kaiser Permanente Created a Human-Centered Design Movement

CHRISTI ZUBER AND LISA CARLGREN

At **Kaiser Permanente**, design thinking found its way into a relatively risk-averse, data- and evidence-driven healthcare nonprofit. Nevertheless, this is the story of a very pragmatic approach driven by a small enthusiastic team. The initiative's objective was to prove the value of a human-centered approach and build capability using storytelling and training. Accordingly, the projects and the people involved were critical and deliberate. Kaiser Permanente chose projects that featured diversity in locations and business units, a direct impact on customers or front-line staff, and a possibility to share results within and outside the organization. The small team in charge of design thinking considered the scale-up of the initiative as a design challenge. It was open to adopting other methodologies, including behavior design and behavioral economics, Agile and Lean Six Sigma. The importance of using external communication to fuel an internal fire and gain legitimacy helped to grow the "movement" and the central role of leadership for design-thinking implementations helped to build it into a legitimate trail-blazing practice.

The nonprofit, Oakland-based healthcare giant Kaiser Permanente is a unique healthcare organization with an amazing story in American healthcare. Starting in the Second World War, industrialist Henry J. Kaiser paired up with physician Sidney Garfield to address a critical need of the Allied forces: the availability of warships and a healthy enough group of workers to build them. In the early 1930s, the ability to quickly build and send battleships into the war waging on the seas was becoming more and more critical. Most of the healthy men had already been deployed to war. Those men still left in the United States were often referred to in jest as the "petri dish of the American workers," people who were too old or too sick to fight in the war. This is where the creativity and fighting spirit of Henry J. Kaiser and Dr. Sidney Garfield came into play. They created an approach to health and healthcare that was predicated on addressing the fundamental need to keep people as healthy and productive as possible, sometimes even managing such simple things as picking up rusty nails on the job site and making sure everyone was immunized. It addressed the need for preventative medicine, not sick-care, and it filled the gap for affordable care.

At the time, the plan was scoffed at for behaving like "socialized medicine" and shunned by the American Medical Association. Still, the popularity and success of this model grew thanks to the Shipworkers Union, which was the primary beneficiary of the health plan and of the builders who built the ships. While adversaries tried to shut down Kaiser Permanente, its care recipients rallied and fought for its continuation as the industrial health care program for construction, shipyard, and steel mill workers. This partnership and innovative approach to healthcare was opened to the public in 1945. It created the foundation for the non-profit now known as Kaiser Permanente, an organization celebrated for paving the path for preventative medicine in the United States and responsible for the lives of more people than the entire population of Sweden.

Kaiser Permanente, or KP for short, had been known as an innovative company for nearly a century. This story shows how the spirit of innovation and an approach to creativity was rekindled again through the emergence of human-centered design (HCD) almost fifty years later after a small, scrappy group of people and supportive advocates were willing to try.

Kaiser Permanente is an American integrated managed care consortium based in Oakland, California. Founded in 1945, it comprises the Kaiser Foundation Health Plan, Inc. (KFHP) and its regional operating subsidiaries; Kaiser Foundation Hospitals; and the regional Permanente Medical Groups. Kaiser Permanente runs one of the most extensive nonprofit healthcare plans in the United States, with over 12.6 million members, operating 39 hospitals and more than 700 medical offices, with over 300,000 personnel, including more than 80,000 physicians and nurses.

A Shopping Cart with Major Consequences – Teaming Up with IDEO

A future-looking group of KP executives discovered what was later called human-centered design (HCD) by a chance encounter. The spark was lit after seeing the now-classic *Nightline* television segment in which Ted Koppel spent time at IDEO, the design and innovation consulting practice then headquartered in Palo Alto, California. In the TV program, IDEO practitioners took on the challenge of redesigning a shopping cart. Most importantly, in the process of doing so, they shared their perspectives on innovation, a methodology used to create innovations, and their leadership philosophy. With the strong legacy of their founders – a constant curiosity and care for humans – the KP executives deemed it worthwhile to test out for a fit with the organization's values and the ability to internalize the approach within its workforce.

This was back in 2003 when the terms design thinking and human-centered design had not yet been used pervasively in business, especially not in healthcare. For IDEO, trying to teach its approaches to non-designers was new, and the company was only at the initial stages in attempting to teach its method to a few other organizations overall. Additionally, IDEO had clients in healthcare, but they were mostly technology companies, and healthcare services were a relatively new focus area. A group of KP executives asked Christi Zuber, a former practicing nurse and hospital administrator, to lead the first effort and put together a team to try out the IDEO methods in hopes of a cultural fit for the organization. She reached out to a handful of fellow employees, Chris McCarthy, a business analyst and clinical information systems implementer, and Adrienne Smith, a change management practitioner, to join her in the quest in the field. This KP team and IDEO partnered together to see how HCD would work for healthcare services in addition to diving into how to make the methods teachable and useful for people who were not self-proclaimed design professionals. The KP team would bolster the consulting company's ability to navigate healthcare service delivery and more importantly, would sharpen their understanding and ability to teach their "secret sauce" for innovation and design to others. A unique and win-win partnership was created between IDEO and KP.

A Small Innovation Team and Their Under-the-Radar Love Affair

At the outset, a strategic choice was made to focus and develop deep skills with a small group to become specialists in the methodology, rather than to "go abroad" and expose a maximum number of people to a minimum set of skills. The IDEO and KP teams were hoping to get a snowball effect – starting small and building momentum. Without worrying about getting everyone on the same page at the same time, they planned to learn deeply through a small, committed team, and prove value through genuine work efforts in the field, with the belief that the others in the organization would become interested and follow.

Zuber decided that to truly test out the cultural fit and alignment with organizational values, the labor unions needed to be a part of the work and the evaluation process. It harkened back to the days when the labor unions were involved in the foundation of KP during the Second World War. Therefore, the handpicked, non-designer KP core group was enhanced with one union representative co-lead named Maureen Sheahan, who had a background as a labor representative of the auto workers unions. There were few sanctified projects jointly co-led by management (like Zuber) and labor (like Sheahan) within the organization as they were complex and rather high stakes. However, it was decided that the possible partnership and the insights gained from the front-line staff were worth it and the right thing to do to try out the methodology and determine a cultural fit within KP.

The team was quite diverse in all aspects. However, while the team members all had different cultural and professional backgrounds, they shared some important aspects of their personalities. They were energetic, creative, and scrappy, and had a strong ability to empathize and engage with others across KP to gain their support and trust along the way. It was an exciting time to see if their transfer of skill sets and mindsets was possible to non-designers within an organization, and particularly within a risk-averse industry such as healthcare.

Their initial engagement was in a three-month apprenticeship-style project approach with IDEO. A substantial advisory group was put together to help learn about and assess the project and methods, but the work of the team was still kept fairly "under the radar" at the time. After three months, it became apparent that it was an instant love affair. The initiative turned into an eighteen-month engagement (2003–5) where the team worked full time with the consulting group. It was done in a 1:1 pairing between IDEO and the KP team to learn deeply how to use their methods and transfer the skills to Kaiser through a series of medium and large-scale projects. KP began the engagement without an existing innovation process, so the new team had to both find their place in the organization as well as model how this innovation project might look within the organization. The idea was to see if KP could create its own "internal IDEO," with innovative approaches and solutions equal to KP's. A full-out transfer of expertise was the goal.

Initially, the team was enthusiastic about using the methods, but how to crosswalk future-looking innovation efforts with run charts and statistical significance initially eluded them. This was a glaring reality they faced when undertaking their third large-scale engagement during this time. The group was asked to focus on the flow of patients across the various hospital departments and functions in what is called "bed management." After six months and thousands of hours working on it in the field with clinicians and hospital managers, the team had very few implementable solutions ready to be put into action. The complexities of process ownership and change management had overcome their efforts. They learned a hard lesson in the measurement (or lack of it) of a system's complexities and of first seeking existing best practices before going into full design and innovation mode.

The team needed to learn to apply their experience and creativity to meet the needs for measurement and existing best practices if they were to succeed in the prevailing data-driven and evidence-based culture. To build a thorough understanding of performance improvement and of how to test and measure ideas, in 2004 and 2005, members of the team attended the one-year Improvement Advisor Training program at the Institute for HealthCare Improvement (IHI) in order to become certified improvement advisors. This eventually led to an adapted version of IDEO's approach. On the surface, the innovation process resembled the typical five-step HCD processes we are used to seeing today. However, phases with thorough planning, measurement, and, when appropriate, statistical testing was built-in, as opposed to IDEO's more relaxed approach to testing and measurement at the time. With the team growing its skills and having proven its value, the formal partnership with IDEO was phased out as planned, and the goal of an "internal IDEO team" was realized. The group was named the Innovation Consultancy (IC) team.

A Nascent Innovation Microclimate

The IC team and the projects with labor and IDEO were the sparks. In comparison with other well-funded large-scale corporate programs, KP's scrappy and vulnerable approach to implementation was essential for starting the movement in a large organization with distributed decision-making and operating structures. Zuber, who led the first project, served as the group's first director and worked with a talented group of new innovators. Even though at the time the organization at large was more focused on best practices than innovation, the work of the IC team and their internal partners began to create a microclimate of their own. If you think of a microclimate as an area that fosters the growth of things that are slightly different from the surrounding areas, this describes what was occurring at KP. Innovation microclimates[1] provide a way for a small, committed group of people within an organization to visibly show to others what can be possible. It was the first microclimate model created (see figure 5.1), and the energy and excitement of those who participated in it were palpable. Developing HCD within an organization is sometimes a bit like a fish swimming upstream in that it's counter to the broader culture and organizational flow. The KP executives provided a bit of protection to the team to function differently than the rest of the organization, and they continued to grow in skill sets and structures to do the work at hand.

Microclimate Model

Overarching combination of **advocate support and protection** along with **enabling conditions** and **change agent behaviors**. Together they create the ability for HCD to flourish in a group of people, despite it not being a predominant culture of the broader organization.

Conditions

ADVOCATE
Leverage support for time, resources, and protection to work differently than predominant organizational culture.

PARTNER
Have a partner for emotional support and to work with.

PLAY
Create a playful and trusting workplace for contributors.

CAPACITY BUILDING
Begin with small low-risk projects and build up as desired skills, mindsets, and behaviors increase.

Behaviors

CONNECTING
Display deep curiosity and commitment to people.

IMPROVISING
Mix together methods of design with methods for change, lean, and others when needed.

STORYTELLING
Share experiences and work verbally and visually.

SCAFFOLDING
Offer up ideas and examples to start and to refine the work.

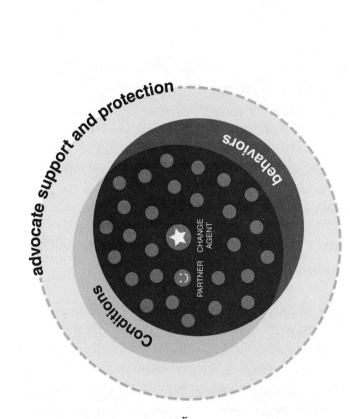

Figure 5.1. Microclimate model

Marilyn Chow, the VP of National Patient Care Service, was one of the early leaders who initiated the effort and sponsored the team. She stated that one of the keys to success was to be found in finding the right people from the start: "I don't know where we had been if it hadn't been for the fantastic personalities of the initial members of the Innovation Consultancy [team]. It is very possible that we would not have had any of this."[2] She was referring to the core team of people who were both skilled and supportive ambassadors of the methods, especially at the beginning of the program when others needed to see how it could work within their own organization. The modeling became a way of spreading the desire to be a part of this broader change and way of working and collaborating.

Building Skills and Spreading the Passion through Careful Project Design

Early on, the IC team realized that if the solutions they crafted in innovation projects did not gain spread, their projects would not be viewed as successful, no matter how good the solutions seemed in a few departments or hospitals. Additionally, the concepts with the potential to make substantial improvements for staff and patients would not get implemented if larger spread could not be achieved.

It is sometimes forgotten and underestimated that most organizational employees have some choice, even if it is a small choice, about how they spend their time and energy at work. When people are part of a movement, they think it is purposeful and exciting, and the excitement has the power to influence others to make a choice to put what extra time and effort they have toward the cause. In the same way, the IC team started leveraging the approach of an organizational change movement into the work. They also began building in strategies to help with buy-in and potential implementation from the start of a project. Some of this included making a conscious choice of which hospitals and units to collaborate with on project efforts. By selecting diverse parts of the organization, they helped to avoid feelings of "not-invented-here." Projects were led by members of the IC team, but in different phases also involved many front-line staff (nurses, doctors, and other stakeholders who were educated in and using the methods) who took on various leadership roles. Depending on the challenges, the projects would often span a couple of areas, such as IT, quality, administration, and patient care services. In various stages, as many as fifty to seventy participants could be involved in a single encounter, and as hundreds could be involved over a single project. This was not because it was always necessary for the research or testing, but it helped create ownership, facilitate spread, and keep building the movement within KP.

The efforts were time-intensive and sometimes quite intimidating to the teams. Clinicians, leadership, and support staff were wary of trying out half-baked ideas in front of their patients. It went against their desire for a more polished experience and professional image. Still, taking part in innovation projects often evoked positive feelings of excitement and collaboration and the IC team and its partners were quick to provide support and encouragement. One member of the IC remembers an experience at the beginning of one project journey when the importance of trust in belief in each other showed up:

> We had nurses crying at our debriefs; they said, "Nobody in seventeen years had ever asked me what I thought, or what my dreams were." And this is the first time that they could even reference that this was happening. And so, I think between our passion and the passion of our front-line staff, that convinced our folks that we don't know the evidence of this, there's no evidence of what you guys are talking about, but everybody is so passionate, we have just to keep going and see what we can get out of this.[3]

In the early years, the innovation teams struggled with overextended and under-resourced situations. The IC team felt the weight of being a small organizational team whose ratios were one team member to 50,000 employees. This ratio demonstrated the struggle of scale. The organizational requests and needs far outweighed the group's ability to meet the demand within a few years of the team's conception. Two actions were put into play to aid with this, one was to amplify the wow factor of the path they were taking, and the other was to focus on the right work. Their work was mentioned in the *New York Times*, *Fast Company*, and numerous books, including a few by IDEO leaders. They took full advantage of the external press[4] to fuel the internal fire and grow the legitimacy and social proof of the organization's value. This led to others who wanted to develop comparable HCD skills and build them into the organizational culture more deeply.

As for focusing on the right projects, given the size of the team in relation to the size of the organization, it was also important to focus their efforts on the right problems. Zuber created a filter to guide their work, and so they took on problems that fell within the following guidelines:

- The problem and the potential solution would need to have a direct impact on customers or front-line staff,
- More than one geographical region would need to be involved in demonstrating the scale and consistency of the problem at hand and the cross-regional willingness to address it,
- The effort would need to be more of an innovation project than an improvement project, meaning that it had not yet been solved elsewhere in healthcare,
- The topic area and/or skill-set used was exciting to the IC team and created energy and passion to work through the tough times,
- The sites involved had people who were also excited to partner directly with the IC team to do the work and further develop HCD skills,

- The project was a strategic priority for the organization and/or a key stakeholder,
- HCD methods and skillsets were likely best suited for the project based on the need to focus on the desirability of the solution and the collaborative nature involved in addressing it,
- The project outcomes could be shared with others inside, and ideally outside the organization as well, through both data and meaningful stories.

Through several well-chosen projects strategically aligned and showing tangible impacts across the organization, an awareness of the innovation team started to grow within Kaiser. Through this, the support for both the team and the human-centered approach to innovation grew as well. Two years after their first project, the Innovation Consultancy team had demonstrated that they could lead impactful and exciting projects on their own. New opportunities to grow the innovation infrastructure more broadly were right around the corner.

Reaching New Audiences and Developing Tangible Flagships

The momentum for HCD was beginning to build. Through the support of a grant from the Robert Wood Johnson Foundation, Chris McCarthy on the IC team took on the role as the first executive director of the effort to build a network of healthcare organizations, aptly named the Innovation Learning Network,[5] in 2006. The goal was to share innovations, learn how to be better innovators, and create friendships between all the entities to help foster them both. This network served as an excellent way to propel the thinking and development of infrastructures to support the HCD and innovation efforts.

Adding to this, in 2006, the Sidney Garfield Innovation Center[6] was opened within Kaiser. This cutting-edge center was created in response to the need to design the workflow, technology solutions, and physical spaces for eight new hospitals planned to be built. The "Garfield Center," as it's more commonly known, was led by Jennifer Lieberman and created a Hollywood studio-type building (the building was a former warehouse in which many mocked-up rooms were set up – e.g., a patient's room, an operating room – where the team could test new ideas) that could show stakeholders how the future hospital facilities could function and look. It also created a shared space that the people in the organization could point to as a tangible symbol of innovation. The stories of organizational innovations the IC team and others had been a part of were captured and shared for those who visited it.

Also, during this time, a team of technology innovators was created, the IAT (Innovation and Advanced Technology) group under the leadership of Naomi Fried and, shortly after, Faye Sahai. This expanded on the HCD approach brought in by the IC team and developed it through technology testing support in the field and within the Garfield Center. The reach of HCD was growing. HCD was now actively applied to process changes, space designs, role and workforce changes, and new technology solutions and applications. Most importantly, the groups began working together to use HCD to design their collaborations better.

The IAT engaged the IT side of the house and the physician partners in testing new technologies. KP's internal facilities department, the National Facilities Services (NFS) group, also ramped up its work and made the physical design of hospitals and clinics collaborative and exciting. Zuber and the team had the opportunity to work across and partner with these groups. Leaders from each team had been a part of the team's original Advisory Group when they started the work with IDEO in 2003, so they had exposure and an understanding of the possibilities.

The groups were technically separate departments funded through different budget lines. This created tensions in what strategic priorities to focus on from the beginning. The groups spent a lot of time and energy doing independent work early on in their creation, sometimes in a way that was at cross-purposes or redundant. They collaborated loosely and had slightly different ways they would talk about HCD. They naively thought the differences allowed the audiences to customize an approach that worked for them. However, they learned that the seemingly innocuous differences were more distracting than they were helpful. They found that the people inside of KP were spending unnecessary time and energy trying to reconcile the differences. They learned that even slight variations in wording and visuals of their frameworks took away energy and time to do the real value-added work of trying to understand the problem and trying to test and find a good solution.

In reaction to this, the five groups decided to work together to form an entity called the Design and Innovation Groups (DIG). They created common frameworks and assets and supported each other in project efforts. The work, and just as importantly, the camaraderie, helped them to continue to grow professionally and to feel a tighter connection to peers across KP. This exposure turned into action and impact. The small microclimate begun by the IC team was now a group of separate but interconnected microclimates that reached across diverse functions in new and exciting ways (see figure 5.2).

Adding New Methodologies and Team Members to the Core Group

Yet, while the small but mighty teams were gaining recognition and street credibility for the solutions they created and implemented, they were still struggling with scale. They needed to find ways to reach more people and grow the reach across the massive organization. Adding headcount to support innovation wasn't easy in a non-profit healthcare organization where most resources, understandably,

Infrastructure of Design

Diverse and complementary group, aiming to extend impact through collaboration.

Methods

Innovation Consultancy (IC)
Human-centered design experts co-design solutions with members and clinicians

Spaces

Garfield Center (GC)
Simulated care delivery environment for testing new ideas and designs

National Facilities Services Planning (NFS)
Facilities design and deployment of innovative care delivery environments

Tools/Technology

Innovation and Advanced Technology
Research, assess, and prototype new, emerging technologies

Networks

Garfield Innovation Network/Ideabook
Connect innovators and innovations together

Roles

Organizational Change, Performance Improvement, and Human Resources
Support behavior change and performance assessment across the organization

Figure 5.2. Interconnected microclimates

would go to direct patient care. Now that an HCD approach to innovation had the attention of leaders and peers and a solid track record, the KP innovators needed to find creative opportunities to show what a larger team of internal experts could really do.

Two efforts began to accomplish the scale challenge. One was a dedicated focus of 20 per cent of the team's time on capability-building to develop skill sets in the organization through various programs and mentoring during on-site projects. The other was a real gift of an opportunity to grow the department itself. In 2007, in a true innovative spirit, the team, still under the guidance of Marilyn Chow (sponsor of the team), applied for and received a sizable grant from the Gordon & Betty Moore Foundation. This allowed the team to add ten new members during the duration of the grant, including a subset of classically trained designers. Thus, they began to take on larger and more complex projects.

As the innovation teams developed into experts in HCD and innovation, they began to push the boundaries of its potential. They started to layer in other methodologies and scientific practices like behavior design and behavioral economics, design charrettes, change management, and Agile and Lean Six Sigma. The growth in practices was mirrored by the growth in the IC team. When the grant ended two years later, the team was able to triple its size officially.

Going beyond Projects – Capability Building and Using HCD for Implementation

The project work of those years also grew the team's understanding of large-scale change. This came out of necessity: even when the outcome of an innovation project proved to improve patient safety, efficiency, and staff well-being radically, it was still hard to gain traction in the larger organization for implementation beyond the initial pilot sites.

There was no formal receiving role or process in place to transition an innovation project into a large-scale diffusion effort. The team realized that the approach to spreading and scaling initiatives was a design challenge on its own. They saw that if they desired broader impact, they needed strong partners in implementation. One of the tests of how to drive large-scale implementation came with two improvement advisors from Southern California. They started exploring the collaborative, visual, empathy-based approaches to innovation to facilitate change across an organization. Using HCD, they could bring people to understand what the change was all about and to help make it theirs through visualizing and testing out the ideas in rapid easy ways. They called this a human-centered approach to change.

Through the projects, the team's broader awareness and approach grew, leading to a growing number of training requests. After learning and applying the methods within the core team, the challenge became how to create capabilities in others so they could improve on and best implement innovative ideas. The IC and DIG colleagues still had limited bandwidth and needed to find ways to work on projects – their main priority – and support others to learn independently. The KP Improvement Institute and the HR learning function also stepped forward to collaborate. They created training for video ethnography and storytelling to reach wider audiences. This also created a more robust approach to involve legal and compliance in order to develop clear and actionable processes for teams to follow during the work. Training approaches were also enhanced with virtual training courses to expand the reach, as well as an advanced course and standardized training through existing training structures, such as a development program for middle managers. To support more real-time project needs, every second Friday afternoon, employees who had learned HCD methods on their own or through participating in projects could call the IC for a "curbside consultation." During this time, team members would take turns giving support to their KP colleagues who called in for advice. IAT and the Garfield Center were offering training and project support as well. While still modest in relation to the organizational size overall, the infrastructure for HCD and innovation was building.

Shifts in Management and the End of the Core Team

In 2013, the original DIG community went through ups and downs as executive leadership changes occurred, causing shifts in strategic direction and management styles. Despite the team having a solid track record and deep skills, the prerequisites for doing this work also changed when the microclimate changed. With more exposure, leadership conflicts over ownership of innovation and design and the strategic direction emerged across corporate leadership. The leadership of the facilities group and the technology team changed, and the IC was split into two groups, a Design Consultancy and an Innovation Consultancy team. Between 2014 and 2016, a significant portion of the deep senior design talent pool at the corporate level moved onto other organizations and opportunities.

With a new reorganization of functions, the groups began to re-establish and stabilize within a few years. The Design Consultancy team was now housed in the Center for Care Innovations and focused on large-scale quality and safety efforts. The Innovation Consultancy team was brought into a newly created entity, the Office of Transformation. The teams have found their paths again and have been in the process of understanding how to leverage the newly developed entities across organization-wide efforts. The Health Hubs was one of the efforts the IC and other DIG partners collaborated on with Southern California. The main sponsor of the work moved into the newly created role of chief transformation officer and oversees the IC and Garfield Center, among other things.

The changes were not all easy, but the reach and impact of the founding work and the new teams can be seen across KP. Change and evolution are never a straight path. HCD has spread far and wide, and the regional and local microclimates developed over the years have been firmly rooted and have spread the word to others. While building up a strong, cohesive team like the IC and other DIG partners is paramount initially, it is also of equal importance that groups like this take on the responsibility to spread to others in the organization. The more roots that are created, the stronger the tree. Start small, be scrappy, but eventually spread through involvement and collaboration. This approach worked for project efforts, and it also worked for extending the capability of HCD itself.

Use Today and Impact

While most of the original innovation and HCD effort founders have moved on from KP, their legacy continues. Even years later, the effort has become much bigger than them and continues to thrive and push the boundaries of US healthcare. Today, design occupies a central position in innovation work at KP: first and foremost, through a human-centered perspective where the needs of patients and front-line care providers are woven into a diverse range of organizational efforts.

The innovation process where HCD has been adapted and combined with other methods is still present in innovation projects and facilitation. With HCD tools incorporated broadly into improvement training across hospitals, clinics, and support functions, the use of HCD is also supporting a range of diverse initiatives. KP has developed a broader innovation and design ecosystem and uses its multiple innovation centers for this purpose, training approaches, and leading active efforts across a diversity of departments and geographical areas. The use and skillsets around HCD as well as the role of more professionally trained designers has grown in the organization. While still working toward being a fully "design-driven organization," KP uses HCD in marketing, IT, clinical care delivery, quality improvement, and facility design. It isn't pervasive across all 220,000 people within KP and maybe never will be, but it continues to grow. A more nuanced view on innovation and innovation leadership abilities is also growing. Overall, there is now a shared language to discuss it and a common set of skills to apply to it.

Implementing HCD at KP has resulted in several successful innovations related to the delivery of care, and examples can be found in numerous publications and across healthcare organizations globally. KP continues to be featured for its innovative ideas and its approach to innovation. It seems true that the innovation DNA of the organization has been reactivated.

Conclusion

How did all this happen? One of the main lessons learned is the importance of focusing on individuals as human beings. It is important to thoughtfully consider who might be involved, how to craft efforts to be as inclusive as possible, and how to create a sense of being part of a movement. Through the early-stage projects carried out by the IC team and their DIG counterparts, people got engaged and felt that they were part of something important. It was then that people took the extra effort of doing rigorous testing, or walked the extra mile when implementation was tough.

Another important lesson is to be mindful of the necessary microclimates needed to allow people in various parts of the organization to put their new skills into practice. Today, HCD is more well-known than at the start of its application in 2003. More buzz, general awareness among managers, and strategic resources are put into large-scale training programs. Yet organizations change slowly. The individuals who are now trained and who are working to change their practice can still face similar challenges as the IC team did in the beginning. Those who bring the HCD methods into new areas of this massive organization still must understand how HCD will fit into their context and when to apply it, who should be involved, how to convince others, and how to face resistance. For this, they need to develop a microclimate in which they can thrive and spread the approaches.

How HCD was implemented at KP is characterized by some of the fundamental aspects of the concept: starting small, dreaming big, trying it out, and making mistakes. During a research study of KP in 2012, Carlgren asked Zuber about her thoughts regarding implementation. Zuber reflected upon the difference between then and when the IC started about ten years earlier: "At the time, there weren't other organizations to look at, to say 'oh this is how they did it.' Human-centered design wasn't out there in the world; they didn't have the coined terms and things in *Fast Company* about designers being the new rock stars." Today, with all the attention that design and HCD have received, there are often high expectations to deliver already from the start, something that might kill fledgling initiatives. As Zuber pointed out: "If it's an executive mandate, there's a very high bar for expectations because of all the things that they have read or seen or heard about at conferences. Then you throw people into that and say deliver on this – they are just like a deer in headlights. So, I am very grateful that that's not how we started."[7]

Lessons Learned

- Starting small gave KP a chance to learn how the methods really work within its organization. Most movements begin with a small group of excited people, so the small, scrappy approach proved to have a scaling effect that may have been far superior to a well-funded, overpublicized big program. Patience was key: not worrying about getting everyone on the same page simultaneously; they learned on their own, proved value, and people came.
- Creating opportunities for capability development through real project efforts, storytelling, and training. HCD and innovation are best learned with the help of a more skilled practitioner working with the new learner.
- Keep a mindful and realistic focus on learning: dream big but begin by working on project efforts that are not overly complicated. You are still learning how to do the work and how the organization responds.
- Design with the end and with implementation in mind. If you can get a reasonable percentage of your innovation project to translate into real implementations, the innovation and HCD work will sell itself.

- Don't underestimate the importance of the press. It helps to legitimize the work and to make it sexier. Use outside accolades to gain internal support.
- Developing HCD within an organization is sometimes a bit like a fish swimming upstream. It's counter to the broader culture. Change agents can develop microclimates to help create and support the teams' success (and retention).
- Leadership changes leave innovation teams (even seasoned ones) vulnerable. It makes it more critical to share with and support others in the organization to build HCD skills and success stories across geographies and divisions.
- Learners can eventually become advocates for others in the organization. And so, the cycle continues.

Timeline

- 2003: The executive team become aware of design thinking and IDEO; start of a three-month apprenticeship project with IDEO on how human-centered design (HCD) can enhance healthcare services; one executive sponsor, an advisory group, and a team of four commence activities.
- 2004: The team explores the issue of hospital bed management, but only creates few implementable solutions; involvement of the Institute for Health Care Improvement and creation of an Innovation Consultancy (IC) team that is backed by executives.
- 2005: A range of projects are underway in different business units and across various business functions involving a diverse set of people; projects are led by the IC team and engage frontline staff; training of everyone who is involved and demonstration of HCD at work.
- 2006: Start of the Innovation Learning Network; Garfield Center features the innovations developed by the IC team; a first team

of technology innovators adopt HCD; new methods are also adopted to improve processes, spaces, role and workforce design, and applications to new technology; creation of Infrastructure of Design (ID) to all groups

- 2007: Scaling of HCD initiative; 20 per cent of time is dedicated to build design capability through training; recruitment of ten people grows the core national consulting team to twelve and regional teams begin developing; commencement of larger and more complex innovation projects.
- 2009: Experimentation with other methods, including behavioral economics, design charrettes, change management, and Agile and Lean Six Sigma; leveraging HCD to scale organizational adaptation of HCD; involvement of the KP Improvement Institute and HR learning.
- 2010: KP named on Fast Company's Most Innovative Health Care Company list.
- 2015: Capacity-building efforts continue and formalize; Center for Care Innovation, Gravity Tank, and KP are awarded the Design Management Institute's Design Value Award for a capacity-building program "Innovation Catalyst."
- 2016: Changes in leadership; many of the senior design talent pool at the corporate level moved to other organizations and pursued other opportunities; IC team is split into the Design Consultancy and Innovation Consultancy teams.
- 2019: Talent continues to grow and is distributed across regional operational entities and national project focus areas such as Metal Wellness and Care at Home.
- 2022: KP awarded Design Company of the Year by Fast Company for its groundbreaking member app and website, making it the first healthcare organization to receive that honor.

CHAPTER SIX

Throwing a Hand Grenade at the Bureaucracy – MindLab and Wicked Problems in Government

DAVID DUNNE

This is the story of a lab created by the Danish Ministry of Business Affairs to diffuse and apply methods of user-centered design to public services, and beyond, to influence and establish these different ways of thinking in government. Founded in 2002, **MindLab** progressively scaled up to become an instigator of system change and a global thought leader in user-driven public sector innovation. With the objective of disrupting the Danish bureaucracy, MindLab transformed over the sixteen years of its existence from small beginnings to an international reputation. While MindLab facilitated over 280 workshops in its first four years, showing a real value as a process catalyst and a project initiator, the impact of the lab more generally was limited. Thus, the scope and strategy of the lab were extended and in the following years resulted in moving from an idea lab to a lab that brings about lasting change and thought leadership in public sector innovation. In 2018, it was shut down and replaced by the Ministry of Business' Disruption Task Force.

The Need for MindLab

While MindLab morphed over the years, it was always about wicked problems in society – hopelessly complex problems in which cause and effect are intertwined. Wicked problems demand different ways of thinking; yet establishing these different ways of thinking in government is a wicked problem in itself.

MindLab was established in 2002 by the (then) Danish Ministry of Business Affairs, both as an internal incubator for creativity and innovation, and to make the policy development cycle more effective. However, it soon confronted the limitations of this approach and, with the full support of senior levels of government, expanded its activities, first to apply the methods of user-centered design to public services, and later to influence the system at a deeper level. Throughout its history, it sought to influence the bureaucracy's culture and ways of thinking.

In its heyday, MindLab was an international thought leader in public service innovation. However, in 2018, in the wake of a policy shift in the Danish government, MindLab was shut down and replaced by the Ministry of Business' Disruption Task Force. MindLab's development, growth and ultimate demise offer important lessons for design labs everywhere.

MindLab's Development: A Story in Three Eras

Era 1: The Innovation Catalyst, 2002–2006

In the early 2000s, the Permanent Secretary of the Danish Ministry of Business Affairs was provoked by leading business school academics who would ask him, "Where does innovation live within your ministry?" His inability to answer this question led to the founding of MindLab.

At the time, the Permanent Secretary had a vision of "open engagement" in the public sector that involved making government more transparent and accessible to citizens. At the same time, private-sector organizations were experimenting with innovation labs. This looked like it might be an interesting – indeed, revolutionary – approach to innovation in the public sector.

MindLab was initially about disrupting the bureaucracy – "throwing a hand grenade" at it, in the words of its founding director, Mikkel B. Rasmussen. Its radical interior design, by Bosch & Fjord, internationally renowned architects with a reputation for bright, functional learning and creative spaces, was one signal that the activities that would take place there would be distinct from the day-to-day routine of government. In this adventurous spirit, a poster exhorted visitors to be fearless, reading "Replace fear of the unknown with curiosity."

MindLab's goal was to create the optimal conditions in the ministry for creativity and new ideas. With five full-time employees, it was in no position to disrupt the government on its own. However, with skills in creative facilitation, team building, hosting, and policy development, the team could exert an influence, by:

1. Reducing reaction time to new challenges,
2. Reducing the time span between idea and result,
3. Developing creative competencies in the ministry, and
4. Acting as a catalyst in policy and organizational development.

The group hoped to increase the efficiency of the policy development cycle by becoming a catalyst of change at the level of processes, policy development, and organizational development. The outcomes would include faster reaction times and shorter time to implement ideas and improved creative competencies within the Ministry itself.

In all, MindLab facilitated over 280 workshops in its first four years. Mostly, these were meetings to kick off projects by helping teams within the ministry articulate a vision and goals and define a process. The workshops also demonstrated a different way of working from the accepted routine of reading, debating, and report writing. In addition, MindLab offered help with developing project processes, underpinning the development of a professional project organization, supporting a mindset change among employees and helping bring about an organizational culture shift.

An external evaluation was commissioned in 2006.[1] The report concluded that, as a process catalyst and as a project initiator, MindLab had proven its value. While many units in the ministry remained interested in using MindLab for their projects, there were uncertainties about how its work changed the results; moreover, there were limits to how much change a small unit could bring about. According to Christian Bason, its director from 2007 to 2016, MindLab's "activities were a little bit too superficial, too short to have a deeper impact. [There was] not enough follow-up, lack of user focus; there was some experience over time, but it wasn't systematic. There were areas within the Ministry of Business that had been impacted deeply, and then there were areas that had hardly been impacted at all."[2]

After four years as an innovation catalyst, MindLab needed to change. The external evaluation indicated four alternatives:

1. Status quo: remain a "general store" with several services.
2. Narrow the focus: specialize in process assistance in the development of policy and organization.
3. Scale up: become a Danish center of excellence in user-driven innovation.
4. Close down: recognize that MindLab has run its course and transfer some of its activities to other units.

Around the same time, the Ministry of Taxation was thinking of establishing a unit like MindLab. Both ministries wanted to create an opportunity for mutual learning and create a space for collaborative innovation, rather than have separate units. It was decided to scale up and adjust MindLab's mission, services, competencies, and staffing to meet the needs of the whole ministry, in line with the third option.

Era 2: The User-Centered Policy Designer, 2007–2011

MindLab would now strive to become a national and international thought leader in public sector innovation. Bason, a former innovation consultant, was recruited to lead the organization in this new direction. A third partner, the Ministry of Employment, joined the (then) Ministry of Economics and Business Affairs (later the Ministry of Business Affairs) and the Ministry of Taxation and co-invested in the MindLab initiative.

For the most part, MindLab's work consisted of workshop facilitation within the ministry itself. The new MindLab would be governed differently, would work differently on different problems, and would use different approaches. At the core was the principle of user- (or human-) centered design: policy development that focused on the needs and aspirations of those affected by services and policies. Specifically, this comprised a shift from the emphasis on creative methods, team building, and collaboration to a much more human-centered approach. MindLab would also aim to develop academic research to become a centre of excellence in user-driven innovation.

With this overall direction clear, Bason and his colleagues developed a program of action. The new MindLab would enact this major shift in five ways:

1. By impacting policymaking across the three ministries.
2. By impacting the design of services.
3. By impacting the culture.
4. By building capacity, tools, and methods.
5. By sharing, expanding, and disseminating MindLab's work.

MindLab would extend its involvement in projects beyond the kick-off stage and be a long-term partner if the project lasted by identifying projects based on user needs, analyzing and testing ideas, deploying them, and evaluating their impact.

The nature and scope of MindLab's project work would also change. In the past, much of its work had been internal to the public service – specifically, within the Ministry of Business Affairs – primarily concerned with organizational development and productivity. Now, MindLab would shift its focus externally, to wicked problems in society.

One project from this era was the "Burden Hunt'": on behalf of the three ministries, MindLab conducted observations and interviews at 284 companies to identify obstacles and irritants that were created by red tape. The project led to the "Away with the Red Tape" project to simplify processes. It also provided concrete evidence of the success of MindLab's methodology within a politically supported agenda and attracted international attention.

In the first of several projects for the National Board of Industrial Injuries, MindLab facilitated working labs and cross-ministerial project manager networks as part of a project management education initiative in the three ministries. The program was MindLab's first foray into upgrading the skills and approaches of civil servants.

In some cases, MindLab's methods pushed the boundaries of acceptability, as in one specific example in which art installations were proposed to popularize citizens' rights in taxation. The approach did not resonate well within the bureaucracy; from this, the team learned that radical experiments could come at the cost of opportunities to collaborate with colleagues. It was important to empathize not just with end-users, but with government actors responsible for implementing change.[3]

To build its credibility, MindLab also hired PhD students to conduct research in innovation methods. The results of this research were disseminated through publications and speaking engagements.

Together, these initiatives sent a strong signal that MindLab was a major initiative. With an annual budget of about €1.2 million (about US$1.6 million at that time), it was anchored at the top of the organization and advised by a senior, high-profile board of the Permanent Secretaries and the three sponsor ministries, as well as external experts in innovation. It conducted an active research program in innovation methodologies and set out to become a national and international thought leader in public sector innovation.

Era 3: The System Architect, 2011 Onwards

By 2011, MindLab had become a widely recognized, globally respected institution, both through landmark projects such as the Burden Hunt and through its program of conducting and disseminating innovation research. It had a staff of fifteen and was regularly engaged in a diverse set of projects; three examples follow.

MindLab and the design firm 1508 collaborated with a regional enterprise incubator, Vaeksthus Syddanmark, to provide a service suite that would attract entrepreneurs. Using personas (rich descriptions of archetypal user types) and user journeys (maps depicting the user experience), MindLab and 1508 involved the Vaeksthus client in a series of workshops. The outcome was a greater focus on client needs and ultimately improved service, growth, and productivity at Vaeksthus.

Another project, for the National Board of Industrial Injuries, explored the reality of industrial injury victims' experiences with the system. By making videos of interviews with industrial injury victims, MindLab developed user journeys of each victim's experience of the handling of their entire case. The videos and journeys provided the National Board with a convincing picture of how the system appeared from the perspective of the user. The result was a series of changes in the National Board's protocols for dealing with injury victims.

Denmark has a shortage of skilled labor and needs to pay attention to the retention of highly qualified foreign workers. In a further project, on behalf of Branding Danmark, MindLab looked at the challenge of how to encourage these workers to stay in the country. MindLab helped design a major workshop attended by officials, companies, and representatives of foreign workers and their accompanying spouses. One of the outcomes was a social network with an associated website that functioned as a bulletin board for a range of different activities.

Successful as its track record was, Bason and the staff felt that MindLab could play a larger role – not only to challenge the system but also to help bring about real change. Looking back, they could see that MindLab was at its most effective when it could help bring about an *outside-in* perspective – that of users of services, as opposed to the *inside-out* perspective of providers.

It was not just about ideation, though this was still important. It was about fundamentally flipping the way change managers looked at things; to do that, MindLab staff would have to become ever more intimately engaged with projects and ministries. In a 2012 article, Bason and co-author Helle Vibeke Carstensen wrote:

> Sustainable innovation – if that was truly to be MindLab's objective – would not happen via isolated projects. Innovation should lead to lasting public value across multiple bottom lines. In MindLab's experience, this required … even deeper, longer-term, top-level engagement.[4]

There was an opportunity for MindLab to move from idea lab to broad influence across the Danish government. To accomplish this, MindLab would have to adjust its strategy to focus more tightly on bringing about lasting change and thought leadership to the future of government.

The expanded role took shape in two major initiatives: organizational change and exploring new policy directions. In the first, its *change strand*, it consulted with senior management to support organizational change. In the second, its *think strand*, it used its research capability to identify and develop new findings on policy trends. In undertaking these two directions, it hoped to broaden its role as a thought leader in public sector innovation, while continuing to promote a deep awareness of users' perspectives in policy and service development.

Core Principles and Governance

Core Principles

Central to MindLab's approach was the idea of bringing a citizen's perspective to government, as the basis for better ideas about policies and programs. MindLab worked in partnership with colleagues in government, providing facilitation, a physical space for ideation, and research.

Questioned by the author in 2014 about which aspects of Mind-Lab's many facets were truly essential to its identity, Bason emphasized two aspects: human-centered design and MindLab's role as a colleague and facilitator rather than a consultancy. The mantra was "facilitate, don't consult."

Governance and Organization

MindLab's organization and modus operandi were all about fostering collaboration across its three sponsoring ministries.

A significant aspect of the mandate was to break down silos between government departments. As MindLab expanded to become a collaborative venture between three ministries, it was important that each had an equal role in running it. MindLab's aspiration to be a "centre of excellence" on public sector innovation also needed to be considered.

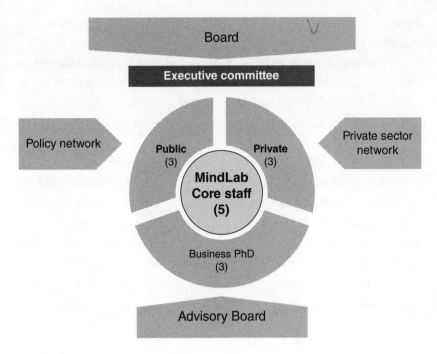

Figure 6.1. MindLab organizational model.
Carstensen and Bason (2012) "Power Collaborative Policy Innovation," 12.

The result was a carefully balanced organizational model that included the three ministries along with representatives of the public and private sectors. It was set up not only to conduct project work, but also to use its experience to build a deeper understanding of how innovation works in a public sector context. The organizational model from 2007 onwards is shown in figure 6.1.

MindLab's Board of Directors consisted of three Permanent Secretaries from the three departments, three private-sector representatives, and one representative from a university. The Board was responsible for overall strategy, for overseeing the project portfolio, and for acting as an ambassador within and outside the Danish government. A secretariat facilitated this process by advising the Board about MindLab's work and identifying projects within the ministries. An Advisory Board included external experts in design and public sector innovation.

Each of the three ministries contributed two core staff members and one PhD student. In addition, each ministry seconded an additional staff member tied to a specific project. Private-sector companies seconded a total of three staff members to a project that was of interest to them.

Core staff had a mix of skills in design, social research, and policy development. Initially recruited on the promise of an opportunity to change the public service from within, the process of bringing them on board was not easy. In effect, they were being hired by one ministry and working in another that was located in a different location, and that had different IT permissions and different rules: for new hires, this was an early encounter with the wickedness of working in the public sector.

Implementing the Strategy

As MindLab scaled up in 2007, it adopted the five major strategies mentioned earlier: policy impact, service design, cultural change, capacity, and publicizing its work. These strategies were put into operation in the following ways.

Policy Impact

To run a workshop is one thing; to develop great solutions from user research is another; and to make them work in practice is still another. Innovation in government takes place within a context of overlapping policies, systems, and regulations. Costs are tightly constrained, and the risk of unintended consequences can be high.

Contributing to the wickedness of public sector problems are the legacies of previous attempts to solve these and related problems over time. As Bason put it in an interview:

When you talk about wicked problems, we have two types of complexity trying to connect. You have the complexity and the wickedness of the problems out in society, and you have the complexity and
the wickedness of the systems we have designed – and those systems
have legacies that go back to the eighteenth century; and they have
sediments and layer upon layer upon layer of regulation, of procedure, of ways of doing things.[5]

Scaling an innovation could be the biggest challenge. According to
Bason: "It's one thing to design a user experience, but if you want
to make the user experience happen for 500,000 school kids, for
150,000 unemployed persons in Denmark, then you have to redesign the system."[6] In a large, complex system, those responsible for
implementing an innovation may be different people, subject to different constraints, and with different interests from those who came
up with it.

This was where MindLab's "facilitate, don't consult" approach
came into play. As a cosponsored unit within the Danish government, collaboration was in MindLab's DNA. Working as a peer with
governmental colleagues meant that it could extend its reach into
the implementation of projects and thus have a greater effect. It was
a two-way learning process in which MindLab staff, as well as helping develop solutions, learned how the system worked and how the
hierarchy functioned.

Influence through Collaboration

A large part of MindLab's raison d'être was to break down silos,
streamline overlapping regulations, and create a seamless experience for those affected by government policies. MindLab staff-led
cross-departmental workshops on problems such as the day-to-day
experience of regulations for those faced with them or simplifying
the process of claiming compensation for industrial injuries.

MindLab worked collaboratively with ministry personnel, guiding, and teaching them as they went through the steps in the process. Colleagues were trained in interviewing techniques and brought into the field to participate in the ethnography; they were heavily involved in workshops and encouraged to take ownership of the ideas and ultimate recommendations.

Service Design

Almost every project involved exposing a team to the "lived experience" of those affected by the policy. MindLab embraced *user-centered design*, a movement to bring users to the center of the design process by deeply understanding their experience.[7]

Taking such an outside-in perspective could be challenging, as it confronted teams with the often-hidden assumptions they were making about users. MindLab strove to shape how public service managers *think*, by exposing them to an external perspective through both research and workshop facilitation. Beyond participating in ethnography, managers were trained to think more broadly and deeply, to recognize their own assumptions, biases and mindsets, and to imagine what it would mean to be someone else.

MindLab did not usually do exploratory ethnographies – loosely directed "fishing trips" – to look for hidden patterns or insights. Usually, these insights were discovered through a discussion of a physical object in some form. As a MindLab designer, Jakob Schjørring, put it:

> It's really important for us to stage these engagements with citizens, to enable them to give some good feedback to us ... we do that partly through prototyping, where we simply sketch up, for example, the future scenario ... I put forward a suggestion, they can ping-pong with me on that.[8]

The involvement of users, however, could take many forms. In one project, MindLab was asked to find a means of ensuring that Common Objectives (COs) were incorporated into planning, implementation, and evaluation in schools. MindLab's research revealed that COs were implanted in schools through the annual planning system, so a prototype was developed in the form of a game that would facilitate this process. Teachers and educators tried out the game in a workshop.

However, it was not always obvious who constituted the "user." The experience of the recipient of a service, such as unemployment insurance, can depend on the experience of front-line staff, which in turn can depend on the experience of managers, and so on. Even then, it was not clear whether one should be concerned with the experience of actual recipients, or of those who may be recipients at some time in the future, or of advocates of the unemployed. Wicked public service problems demanded an approach that was flexible and open as well as empathetic.

Cultural Change

Evocative as the idea was, perhaps throwing a hand grenade at the bureaucracy was unrealistic from the beginning. Yet MindLab remained faithful to its goal of changing the nature of the bureaucracy and intensified its efforts after 2007.

Nevertheless, wholesale cultural change was extremely difficult. Recognizing the limitations of efforts to change culture, Bason argued that the way forward was to *model* the change:

> [Changing the culture of the bureaucracy] is something we used to have in our strategy explicitly, but it's just a huge task to take on ... what we are trying to do is to model the new culture and the new behavior through our work, again in collaboration with our colleagues.[9]

The culture modeled by MindLab embraced design attitude, an attitude that arises from designers' focus on inventing new alternatives to choose from, rather than selecting a course of action from existing alternatives.[10] To invent new alternatives, one needs to learn about what currently exists, the context for an innovation, what has worked and what has not, and find fresh perspectives. The task involves deep research and the ability to suspend preconceptions to be open to new possibilities; it requires a culture that encourages curiosity and learning, and in which it is okay to be wrong.

Learning was central to MindLab's culture. This was in part a result of the changes made in 2007: by becoming a center of excellence, designers like Schjørring had the opportunity to exchange ideas with other experts in the field of innovation:

> We are in the pipeline of new thinking, so we can use time on learning about new trends, talking to the right people, finding out what's going on in the world. I can take that, I can apply that in my projects and get some personal experience with it, then I'm also able to share my experiences with others.[11]

Bason stressed the importance of learning from mistakes. In his 2018 publication, *Leading Public Sector Innovation*,[12] he argued that "smart errors" can yield important learning, but that this learning needs to happen in a safe and supportive environment.

Capacity

If culture was the "soft" side of public sector management, it was supported by some more tangible elements, such as space and staffing.

Space

MindLab's office, featured in design and lifestyle magazines such as *Monocle*,[13] was a source of pride. The space was bright and airy

Figure 6.2. MindLab space

Figure 6.3. "The Mind" pod space

(see figure 6.2). Furniture was on wheels so it could be moved around as the task demanded. Three workspaces provided differing emphases on project focus, conversation and resources for reference. The main workspace had room for about fifteen staff who worked in pods of three desks on wheels, some filing cabinets – also on wheels – plus a desk for visitors. Curtains separated this from a space containing couches, chairs, and plants, which was devoted to lounging and informal dialogue. The third space had a worktable, a library, and a TV screen. This area was next to the kitchen and was used as a breakfast area where the team met and socialized informally at the start of each day.

MindLab's unique pod space, "The Mind," provided a safe area and isolation from "busy work" when necessary, so a team could work closely with a client.

Staffing

In its initial phase, MindLab consisted of five core staff, with expertise in creative facilitation, team-building, hosting, and policy development. Activities that were undertaken in the ensuing years reflected this skill set: MindLab's staff used their workshop facilitation skills to develop change from within the bureaucracy.

By the time MindLab underwent its 2007 expansion, just one member of the original core staff remained. Under the new strategy, the permanent staff complement doubled to ten, but the new approach demanded new skills. Design thinking required a skill set closer to that found in design firms like IDEO and Gravity Tank than in government: in addition to policy development skills, there would be a need for expertise in design and social research.

However, the new MindLab was not built around specific deep skills; instead, it looked to create an environment where diverse perspectives were welcomed. As it turned out, only two of the new hires had extensive experience as civil servants. The new team came from varied backgrounds; all were change agents, hired with the promise, and the challenge, of changing the public sector from within. Secondees from external organizations and PhD students provided additional diversity, fresh thinking, and research.

By 2012, well into MindLab's third life, its fifteen or so staff (a mix of permanent staff, secondees, students, and visitors) boasted backgrounds in anthropology, sociology, history, policy, and other disciplines. In addition, while MindLab employees were expected to model different behavior, they needed to be likable. According to Carstensen and Bason:

> The employees have to be different but not too exotic, have to understand the work of a civil servant without thinking like one. And first of all, the staff has to be so likable that their colleagues will want to work with them, even when there are challenges. Recruiting cannot be too thorough or too careful.[14]

Embedded as it was within the bureaucracy, MindLab adhered to the same salary scales as other parts of the Danish government. To attract and retain the right people, it needed to offer something more: team members were encouraged to travel to speak at conferences and be seen as experts, providing them with recognition and inspiration.

Methods and Process

Fundamentally, MindLab did three things: collect ethnographic data, conduct workshops to understand the data, and prototype innovations. These activities could be undertaken in any order.

Almost all projects were centered on developing a deep understanding of users, mostly through ethnographic research. The results formed the basis of a workshop, or series of workshops, with the sponsor. Where there were multiple sponsors, all were included in a collaborative workshop.

These workshops sometimes resulted in a complete redefinition of the project, as in one case where MindLab was asked to develop a mobile service for the Danish Tax and Customs Administration

(SKAT). MindLab translated SKAT's proposals for five different types of mobile service into drawings and showed them to taxpayers; however, when the taxpayers saw them, it became clear that mobile services were not being eagerly embraced – among other reasons, confidentiality and security were an issue. As a result of this insight, an inappropriate and costly initiative was taken off the table.

Visualization is an important part of making abstract ideas real, and MindLab was constantly looking for new ways of doing so. One approach was to develop games: as noted earlier in the educational Common Objectives project, a game could represent complex issues and engage users.

Some projects stopped at user understanding and problem definition, as in the case of a project for the Consumer Agency exploring why bank customers appeared to behave "irrationally" (from the perspective of an economist). Customer stories revealed that a different logic was at work, one which challenged the agency's assumptions. Another example was the Burden Hunt project noted above, which identified areas in which red tape was an irritant, as an input to policy.

While there were common steps, this was not a cookie-cutter process and there were many variations. Some projects used art to represent wicked problems; one of the more counterintuitive examples of this was the development of ideas around "legal certainty" for SKAT. Three young artists each presented their suggestions about the experience in the form of works of art. These were shown to members of the public in a workshop and users were encouraged to discuss what the pieces evoked in their own experience.

Several projects focused on the stories of individual users: the individual experience of a young business owner, an industrial injury victim, and a young taxpayer were all explored through storytelling.

As shown in table 6.1, MindLab's approach was about building ideas in collaborative teams, based on user insights and compelling

Table 6.1. MindLab's problem-solving approach

Core Elements of the Process	Core Elements of the Process	Extensions Used in Some Projects
User experience focus	Ethnographic interviewing and observation	User stories, video interviews
Development of insight	Personas, journey maps	Citizens' stories
Ideation	Brainstorming, prototyping	Brainwriting, artistic representation, mood boards
Problem representation	Storyboards, concept development	Games, works of art
Collaboration	Workshops	Site visits, training

representations of the problem. These core elements were usually applied through a limited set of methods, though the application of these methods would vary from project to project. Depending on the requirements of a specific project, new methods were introduced.

The process could play out in any order – a good deal of preliminary research might go into defining the problem, or, if the problem was well-defined, concepts might be developed and tested early on.

In summary, while there were core principles, the exact process and methods used in each situation were specific to each project, might be adapted to different needs, and might change during the project in response to emerging information. A great deal of flexibility was required of both MindLab staff and each project's sponsors.

Publicizing MindLab's Work

MindLab's openness to learning extended beyond the confines of its Copenhagen office and its interactions with various sections of the Danish government. Seeing learning as a two-way street, it actively sought to be a part of a global conversation about innovation in the public sector. Members of its staff were invited to speak around the world and published many articles and books; it hosted several visitors who wrote reports; it was featured in several papers on innovation labs, in magazine articles, and in books. It invested heavily in its website, where it posted comprehensive case studies of its work.

MindLab's Journey

In 2016, MindLab published "The Journey of MindLab,"[15] mapping the unit's growth from its origin as a "Creative Platform" in 2002 to it becoming a "catalyst of an international movement" by 2011, and ultimately becoming an "enabler of a new public sector culture" by 2016. (See Timeline below.)

In February 2015, Bason left MindLab to take up a position as CEO of the Danish Design Center. He was replaced by Thomas Prehn, a former independent consultant and entrepreneur.

To the surprise of many around the world who had been following MindLab's progress over the years, it was shut down in May 2018. The move reflected a policy shift in the Danish government toward digital transformation. MindLab was replaced by the Ministry of Business' Disruption Taskforce, which was established to contribute to "one focused on inciting a digital transformation across the Danish government."[16]

Conclusion: Innovating in the Public Sector

There are many disincentives against innovation in government. Budgeting of public funds favors established and readily measurable initiatives. Outcomes are not merely financial but can involve trade-offs between the well-being of one group and another group; they may be difficult to define and measure; they may be realized only in the long term, or they may be hidden within a larger project or combination of initiatives.

Government innovation, unlike that of the private sector, needs to be open to public scrutiny. While governments are elected by majorities, programs are often targeted at subgroups whose interests differ from the majority. It can also be difficult to conduct experiments that provide temporary advantages to one group over another.[17] More challenging still are cross-functional or cross-ministerial collaboration; trade-offs between groups; initiatives that show results only over the long term; and scaling of promising programs to larger groups.

Simplistic notions about innovation abound. One report by the National Audit Office[18] in the UK found that public agencies tended to approach innovation as "one-off" change, seeking a single "big bang" rather than a systematic series of new initiatives that add up to substantive change. Innovation was equated to idea-generation methods such as brainstorming.

The result is that the public sector is best at predictable, quantifiable, routine activities that have short- to medium-term impact. In such an environment, workflows are smooth and continuous, changes are incremental, the organization is hierarchical, and risk is minimized.

At first, MindLab responded to this environment with the tentative step of facilitating workshops and later, as its learning developed, by scaling up. As its influence grew, it expanded from its original role as a creative platform, to an innovation lab based on user-centered design, and finally to an agent for change (see table 6.2).

Table 6.2. Three generations of MindLab[19]

	First generation (2002–2006) / Creative platform	Second generation (2006–2011) / Innovation unit	Third generation (2011 onwards) / Change partner
Process focus	Ideation	Value-creation	Insights to drive innovation
People focus	Employee-oriented	User-centered	User- *and* organization-centered
Capacity focus	Training and facilitation	Innovation projects	Core business transformation
Primary methods	Creativity tools; emphasis on individual coaching, etc.	Research, project, facilitation tools; involvement of users and teams	Co-creation with users, professional empathy, rehearsing futures
Management involvement	Management not involved	Management passively supportive	Management actively involved
Main role of design	Graphic design	Plus interaction design, service design	Plus systems design, organization design, managing as designing
Key challenge	Buy-in to new ways of working	Integration of innovation processes in the wider organization	Adopting a new narrative in the organization

Based on MindLab's evolution, Carstensen and Bason found eight major points of learning, which may be grouped under three headings: organization, education, and people:[20]

- Organization: Take charge of ongoing renewal; maintain top management backing; don't be too big. MindLab reinvented itself several times, and to accomplish this it had been the epitome of a "learning organization" in which experimentation was encouraged. At the same time, it derived legitimacy and authority by insisting on solid support from top management and maintaining a positive culture by staying small.

- Education: Do – don't only think; communicate. In keeping with the design focus in its second iteration, demonstrating by doing was important to MindLab. For public servants to learn its methods, it was important that abstract concepts like "empathy" be made tangible and real; in addition, a toolkit was provided so public servants could undertake their own projects. MindLab also broadly disseminated its message through its internal and external communication work; this, in turn, helped build a powerful brand.
- People: Create professional empathy; insist on collaboration; recruit and develop likable people. A fundamental part of MindLab's role was to help public servants develop an "outside-in" perspective that looked at services from the point of view of the user. In keeping with this perspective, the need to collaborate across agencies arose from the fact that users do not see the distinction between different silos and expect an integrated experience. MindLab also needed to reach out to the ministries by recruiting people with whom they would want to collaborate; this was not just a matter of an appropriate skill set – balancing an understanding of the public sector with a fresh perspective – but of being pleasant to deal with.

Lessons Learned

- A separate space reflects a different culture. Innovation, while greatly desired by MindLab's sponsoring ministries, was a difficult fit within departments preoccupied with the task of policy choice. MindLab occupied a separate office that looked and felt different from a government office and was designed to support an open and collaborative culture.
- Collaborate closely with the mainstream. Despite the early rhetoric of throwing a hand grenade at the bureaucracy, MindLab

worked closely with it. It moved from facilitating kickoff workshops to increased involvement of ministry staff in fieldwork,
analysis and evaluation of results, and ultimately to engage with
ministries in project implementation.

- Evolve, to build engagement. MindLab's evolution through
  three strategic phases progressively increased its engagement
  with the bureaucracy. As it evolved, it came ever closer to changing the bureaucracy itself.
- Actively engage with the external community. MindLab staff
  was regularly engaged as speakers on public sector innovation
  and design: this was considered an important part of their role.
  External speakers were invited to Copenhagen to offer their perspectives. The research program engaged PhD students in the
  study of innovation. By these means, MindLab remained open
  to perspectives from outside the confines of Denmark and its
  government.
- No innovation lab has a "right" to exist. MindLab made its mark
  as a thought leader in design-based innovation and an exem-
  plar of what an innovation lab could be. Nevertheless, it was
  replaced in 2018 by a completely different initiative. Innovation
  labs are cost centers whose benefits are usually difficult to measure. They are an arm of the organization's broader innovation
  strategy and can be highly vulnerable to shifts in prevailing
  power structures.

Timeline

- 2002–6: MindLab as a creative platform;[21] after having run
  nearly 280 workshops, the demand for MindLab's support decreased; MindLab was turned into a cross-ministerial innovation
  unit focusing on user-centered methods to enhance innovation
  across government.

- 2007: MindLab as user-orientated innovation unit; a new team of five is hired with a focus on design, social research, and public administration; the Danish Ministry of Employment becomes part of the ownership of MindLab; debureaucratization and digitalization become the focus; the Burden Hunt project is about identifying administrative burdens for businesses.
- 2008: MindLab project leading to a new organizational strategy in a large public organization; facilitation of "working-labs" and cross-ministerial project manager networks as part of the project management education in the ministries; first successful attempt to build new capacity for civil servants; partner ministries invest in three PhD projects.
- 2009: Financial crisis leads to reflection on core operations and new ways of developing the public sector; MindLab owners are recognized as innovative top managers because of MindLab; "experienced legal rights" using art as a central component in illustrating a public challenge; experimenting with the limits of knowledge input to decision-making processes.
- 2010: MindLab as a catalyst of an international movement; "Away with the Red Tape" is the first larger cross-ministerial project; Christian Bason published *Leading Public Sector Innovation* based on experiences from MindLab, and the book becomes an international reference point in the literature on public innovation; MindLab launches the public sector innovation toolkit.
- 2011: MindLab's existence is questioned; a new left-wing government is elected with the significant eagerness of making big reforms in several policy areas; the two first industrial PhD projects affiliated with MindLab are completed; scientific research process and insights are exposing delicate bureaucratic practices challenging the relationship to the Ministry of Employment and MindLab's loyalty; Ministry of Taxation withdraws from MindLab; the How Public Design Global conference hosted by MindLab is catalyzing an emerging community of public innovation practice.[22]

- 2012: MindLab as a strategic change partner; the Ministry of Education becomes a new partner; board structure is replaced by a more strategic, decision-oriented model; a new advisory board is formed with international experts; the seminar series "Denmark Is a Great Country!" is a proactive use of the government platform to explore innovative potential; first longer-term research collaboration between Nesta and MindLab on the publication of innovation in public policy.
- 2013: Strategic advisor to the Danish Minister of Education; MindLab is leading the work for the EU publication *Powering European Public Sector Innovation: Towards a New Architecture;*[23] launch of a new research program; public design policy workshops to let design methods work everyday challenges of bureaucracy; a new approach to reform implementation; a first project focused on applying human-centered design in core reform agendas; partnership with UNDP around developing their innovation skills and capacity.
- 2014: MindLab as a developer of capacity; changes from being cross-ministerial to "cross-public," adding the municipality of Odense to the circle of owners; Christian Bason leaves MindLab; MindLab helps the UK government set up a policy lab in the Cabinet Office; strategic cross-ministerial project defining the future of Denmark's production policy; governance labs as a temporary partnership with the Ministry of Interior focusing on exploring new governance models for more trust-based public service systems.
- 2015: MindLab assists various governments set up innovation labs in their government administrations, including Uruguay and Canada; development of new generic implementation model/mindset for the Ministry of Employment; Thomas Prehn is appointed new director of MindLab; MindLab recognized as an enabler of a new public sector culture.
- 2016: MindLab publishes "The Journey of MindLab."

CHAPTER SEVEN

The Making of a Design-Led Innovation Strategy – How Mirvac Launched the Hatch Program

NATALIA NIKOLOVA, JOCHEN SCHWEITZER, AND CHRISTINE GILROY

Mirvac is an example of how a company, which was lacking a formal structure and process for innovation, successfully built its internal innovation capability, within a short period of four years. The journey started with a change in the top leadership of the firm. A new CEO set the innovation agenda, brought along the top leadership team, and resourced an initiative, initially supported by external consultants. To achieve both incremental innovation and disruptive innovation outcomes, the small corporate innovation team started to engage with key business units and central departments. However, balancing the need for tangible outcomes and successes that would satisfy the business unit managers and secure further buy-in with achieving long-term strategic and possibly disruptive innovation outcomes proved difficult – if not impossible. The team leveraged design thinking, tried out different and clever ways of engaging with various stakeholder groups, and introduced new methods that included open innovation, agile management, and design sprints, to ultimately succeed. Overall, a design-led innovation strategy played a key role in making innovation a priority. Whether Mirvac will succeed in managing the tension between incremental and radical innovations in the long term remains to be seen. However, the implementation of design thinking in many aspects of what Mirvac does already represents a significant shift in the culture of the company. Further, design thinking has had positive effects on various aspects of the company's life.

A Company at a Crossroads

Due to its diversified portfolio, funded largely through bank loans, Mirvac faced significant challenges during the financial crisis in 2008. Indeed, at one point, the company's share price dropped 80 per cent in only six months. Slowly recovering, the company got into a more stable position by 2012. This year also marked a time of change in Mirvac's leadership and strategic direction; Susan Lloyd-Hurwitz was appointed as the new chief executive officer (CEO) and given the mandate of setting a new direction for the company. As one of her first steps, Susan transformed her vision of three core business areas (residential, office and industrial, and retail development) into a focused strategy for Mirvac.

Mirvac Group is a leading Australian property group that owns and manages over AUD$18 billion worth of assets in Australia. Established in 1972, Mirvac has been listed on the Australian Stock Exchange since 1982. It has its headquarters in Sydney, a workforce of approximately 1,400 employees, and had a revenue of AUD$2.275 billion in 2017. Mirvac's focus is on property ownership and development. Its three core business units are residential, office and industrial, and retail.

Members of the executive leadership team turned their attention toward strengthening key organizational drivers and introducing the cultural changes required to support the new strategy. Several key priorities were identified, including increasing the company's capacity to innovate, developing more sustainable work practices, and increasing employee engagement. Mirvac had never articulated a dedicated innovation strategy. The company had previously produced several notable product innovations; however, in general, these innovations had been ad hoc rather than strategic. Mirvac had no processes or methodologies in place for innovation, no funding allocated to innovation initiatives, and no dedicated innovation roles. Nor was there an overarching strategy about Mirvac's role in addressing large industry-related or societal issues. As one member of the leadership team, who later led the firm's innovation efforts, recalled, "We were really, really bad at actually stepping back and saying, this whole universe of problems that exist out there – what is the biggest problem to solve? What should our biggest priority be?"[1]

Until this point, Mirvac's innovation efforts and outcomes had been mostly incremental. Susan and the leadership team were particularly aware that Mirvac lacked the capacity to create disruptive or ground-breaking innovations. Further, the company had failed to create a space, time, or culture in which the status quo could be radically questioned and new opportunities explored. Christine Gilroy, who was later appointed Group General Manager of Innovation, reflected, "No one knew what innovation was, so everyone had a completely different definition of it if you asked different people. No one connected it back to the customer. It was all, it's an idea, it's a tech, it's an app, it's something that IT does but nothing that was customer-related … So, there were no resources, no funding, no strategy, no process, no nothing."

Taking the First Steps to Set Up an Innovation Program

Realizing that innovation represented a key gap in Mirvac's capabilities, and with the objective of developing a more strategic approach toward innovation, two senior leaders had taken the initiative to plan the next steps for developing innovation at Mirvac. Consequently, a position paper was drafted that recommended the appointment of a Group General Manager of Innovation and an annual operating budget. The paper also recommended that the executive leadership team put aside a "ring-fenced amount of money" to securely fund the innovation initiative. In 2014, Christine Gilroy, a long-term employee of Mirvac and a manager in the Mergers and Acquisitions and Strategy Department, who had been involved in the development of the Mirvac Group strategy, was appointed Mirvac's Group General Manager (GGM) of Innovation.

Christine was well regarded in the company, having worked across a few portfolios over the years. She was also well connected, and her colleagues appreciated her analytical prowess and ability to drive change. However, Christine had no experience in managing innovation. As she herself stated, "While I had the strategy background, I knew the business, the people and the culture ... I really needed to bring in the expertise on the innovation front." Being aware that innovation "can be a murky and elusive concept; a buzzword," and that the company's culture was largely influenced by its construction and engineering background, Christine quickly realized that "a science-based approach" toward innovation needed to be adopted, and that the approach would have to be "evidence-based" to successfully embed innovation throughout the organization. Christine began to look outside Mirvac for ideas on how to set up an innovation program that would "fit" the Mirvac context.

In 2013 Christine had attended a conference at which she saw a consulting firm give a presentation on the topic of design thinking and how a design thinking approach had enabled strategic innovations among their clients. The consultants presented a design-led structured approach to innovation that pricked Christine's interest, as she knew the structured approach would be well suited to Mirvac's culture.

The design-led approach used by the consultants was based on nine key drivers of innovation, which they claimed had been proven to work through scientific research. Innovation performance was driven by three underlying pillars: structure, leadership, and people. Horizontally, their framework comprised three levels of innovation maturity that applied across each of the three innovation pillars. The design thinking innovation process was the key to the nine building blocks and was the prism through which the other eight blocks had to be understood and designed.

The consultancy firm's approach of combining design thinking with other scientifically proven approaches to innovation was precisely what Christine had been seeking. As she later explained, "This is what's been missing – the rigor, the structure, the thinking around customer problems – we had all the passion and the motivation and the intention but there was no process, and this gave us the structure." Christine arranged a meeting with the presenting firm's consulting partner and Mirvac's CEO, Susan, who was similarly impressed with the well-defined structures and processes of the approach. Susan and Christine wanted to create an innovation program for the long term; one that would truly be embedded in the company. They believed that as a methodology, design thinking would enable innovation to become embedded within the company. It was thought that a combination of top-down strategic guidance and bottom-up idea generation with a focus on internal and external customer needs would enable the development of organizational innovation capability; a capability that would produce innovation outcomes for Mirvac.

In 2014, Mirvac engaged the consulting company to work with them to help implement the innovation framework, which included the development of an innovation strategy and training staff in design thinking. Hatch, Mirvac's innovation program, was also launched and Christine was appointed as its first director. Hatch's overarching aims were to provide a platform for, and a strategic approach to innovation that was supported by a strategy, process, and resources.

The program budget for Hatch was set at AUD$1 million, a sum that covered the GGM of Innovation's salary, consultant fees for training and support, and any experimentation costs that arose during the prototyping and testing phases of innovation projects. The budget for the experimentation costs was set at AUD$300,000 and was to be used as a seed fund for numerous ideas in amounts of up to AUD$10,000. To address the potential concerns of external and internal stakeholders about financial risks, the lean startup methodology became another building block of the innovation program. This small budget also allowed Susan to openly commit to never reducing or removing the Hatch budget and thus signaled her long-term support of innovation.

Organizationally, Hatch was established within the Culture and Reputation Portfolio, a broad portfolio that comprised several areas, including human resources (HR), sustainability, innovation, health and safety, media, and communications. As the GGM of Innovation, Christine reported to the Head of the Culture and Reputation portfolio, who was also a member of the Executive Leadership team.

One part of setting up the Hatch program included running a competition within the Mirvac Design team to design a logo for Hatch. Many interested employees participated in the competition. Following the announcement of the winning logo, it began to appear on all of Hatch's communications.

Implementing the Key Building Blocks of the Innovation Program

In the months that followed, Christine was assisted and advised by a consulting partner as to how to set up and embed the key building blocks of the innovation program.

Table 7.1. Missions driving Mirvac's innovation initiatives

Missions
Focus on objectives that aligned with organizational strategy

Key question:

- Which of the biggest opportunities should we focus on if the business is to create value?

Mission characteristics:

- Deliberately broad, yet specifically targeted at a customer group
- Defined scope regarding what was "on" and "off the table"
- Annually reviewed to ensure continued relevance

Exploit Missions Focus on *Current State*	*Explore* Missions Focus on *Future State*
Key questions: • What do we do now? • Where do we currently create value? • Where do we currently capture value? • What opportunities are there to capture more value?	Key question: • Where are the biggest opportunities for creating value in the future?

Defining Missions to Set a Strategic Direction

The first task was to clarify which strategic direction would drive Hatch's innovation efforts. This was particularly important given that Hatch had to operate within a culture focused on minimizing risks. In a series of workshops, Christine and the Executive Leadership team developed Hatch's strategic direction by defining its *missions*. Derived directly from Mirvac's corporate strategy and company vision statement, these missions sought to provide direction to employees and ensure that energy would not be focused on areas outside the core strategic business objectives. Missions were seen as the front end of the design-led innovation process. The Executive Leadership team differentiated between *exploit* missions and *explore* missions (see table 7.1).

To foster ideas for explore missions, the team used a range of stimuli, including trends and thought leaders' presentations and reflections on Mirvac's culture, and focused on value net customers, suppliers, complementors, and competitors.

After several workshops, the leadership team agreed to eight missions, ensuring a good balance between missions focused on fostering incremental innovations (exploit missions) and missions focused on fostering disruptive innovations (explore missions). The first incremental innovation mission (related to retail business) was to "ensure continued relevance to retail customers so they will dwell in our shopping centers and spend more." Conversely, a second disruptive innovation mission was to find "radical ways to revolutionize the way we build."

In addition to top-down, mission-driven innovation, Christine also proposed a bottom-up approach to innovation whereby innovations that originated in the business units could also be supported by the Hatch team. The aim was to involve more employees in the innovation process and to create an innovation culture at Mirvac that supported both top-down and bottom-up innovation. A third route was proposed for within-project innovations (see figure 7.1).

A Design Thinking Innovation Process That Follows Three Different Routes

As developed and practiced by the Hatch team, the innovation process comprised a journey of innovation via three different starting points:

1 Top-Down Innovation: This type of innovation occurs when a broad business strategy drives the direction of innovation so that employees understand where to focus their efforts. It begins with a mission that is directly linked to a broader business strategy from which the subsequent steps (i.e., scan, challenge, ideate, decide, experiment, implement and promote) all flow (visualized by the white diamond in figure 7.1).

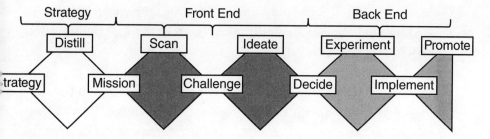

Figure 7.1. Mirvac innovation process

2 Bottom-Up Innovation: This type of innovation occurs when employees identify an opportunity or an idea over the natural course of their work. In this case, innovation is driven by employees' personal experiences, as they are exposed to opportunities that might increase the value of the business. It begins at the ideate phase when an employee conceives an idea that could increase the company's value. After an idea has been conceived, it must be subject to the core innovation process (i.e., a specific mission must be retrospectively identified) to ensure that the idea can be linked back to the company's broader business strategy (start at the second dark diamond, then go back to connect to a mission in figure 7.1).

3 Within-Project Innovation: This type of innovation occurs, for example, when an employee identifies an opportunity for innovation after they encounter a problem while working on a project. For innovations that originate late in a process (i.e., at the experimentation stage), the solving of the identified problem should be linked to achieving the project objectives. Naturally, after a problem has been identified, ideas to solve the problem will be generated. As this type of innovation requires quick solutions to solve well-defined problems, the experimentation phase can be bypassed to allow any solutions to be implemented quickly. However, if an idea requires a

major "leap of faith" that requires testing, experiments to validate the idea may be undertaken (start at the first light-gray
diamond in figure 7.1).

To the GGM of Innovation, supporting bottom-up and within-project innovation, rather than only top-down innovation,
mission-driven ideas, was an important way to embed the innovation
program and design thinking throughout the organization. Unlike
many other organizations, Christine did not wish to separate the
innovation unit from the other business units. Indeed, Hatch has
"a group-wide customer-centric ideology" that "involves building a
business-wide innovation capability." As one innovation champion
explained, "Hatch is a culture piece – it needs to be permanent and
long-lasting and something that is needed to infiltrate culture and
influence the way we do things on a permanent level."

Implementing a Governance Structure for the Innovation Program

With Hatch's missions defined, a dedicated Innovation Council was
formed in 2014 to oversee Hatch's progress and make funding decisions. The Innovation Council included the CEO, CFO, Head of
Culture and Reputation, GGM of Innovation, and the relevant divi-
sional head. The Innovation Council aimed to:

- Ensure that both exploit ideas (focused on the current customer
  and incremental improvement) and explore ideas (focused on
  the future customer and disruptive ideas) from missions would
  be implemented.
- Provide greater oversight and visibility of the spectrum of the
  work being undertaken by Hatch.
- Approve experiment funding over AUD$10,000.

• Instill a greater sense of ownership in respect of the work being carried out by Hatch in the individual business units.

Building an Innovation Workforce

At the same time that the above efforts were being implemented, a cross-organizational team had to be trained in design-led innovation to drive any innovation efforts. Christine called for applications from employees across the company who wished to apply for the role of innovation champion. She was not looking for "creative geniuses or top-idea generators," but "connectors, inspirers, and facilitators," who would become "positive influencers." Her objective was to build a team of people from all areas of the company who were passionate about innovation and would be able to gain support for innovative ideas in their areas of operation.

She received ninety self-nominations. Excited to see so many applications, she handpicked a group of twenty-five individuals who were then trained by the consultants in the Hatch methodology based on design thinking principles (mission, scan, challenge, ideate, decide, experiment, implement, promote). These twenty-five individuals – the Innovation Champions – were assigned to the previously defined missions, and they started by conducting customer scans to define a set of challenges for each mission, moving through each phase of the process.

For Mirvac, starting a project for new services or products by focusing on customers' needs represented an entirely new way of thinking about innovation. Previously, innovation initiatives had been solely driven by employees' ideas or the application of emerging technologies. Customer research was conducted only after a business case for a project had been developed and was typically executed following large-scale surveys, often conducted by external research companies. Seeking out and talking to their own customers about their needs was a new and often uncomfortable experience for the Innovation Champions. To ensure they understood the processes and the rationale behind a design-led innovation approach, the entire Executive Leadership team also completed the training in late 2015.

In 2015, the company largely focused on building the capability of Innovation Champions in the Hatch methodology and working through the Hatch innovation process for the eight missions. Christine was committed to a thorough setup phase, determined to follow a design thinking process, and would not be rushed to show quick outcomes. She was of the view that the structure, process, and roles had to be properly implemented to ensure the success of the innovation program in the long term.

The Innovation Champions attended three days of training and were then asked to work in small teams of four to six people and to dedicate two to three days per month to their mission-related challenges. For an innovation champion to apply, their manager needed to approve two-to-three-day time requirements, a process that was supported and encouraged by the Executive Leadership team. The business units were not compensated for the time that the Innovation Champions spent on the innovation projects.

One of the first ideas to be delivered was a "Shopping Nanny." This project was part of the incremental retail mission that was to "ensure continued relevance to retail customers so they will dwell in our shopping centers and spend more" and was led by an enthusiastic innovation champion with a marketing background, Teresa Giuffrida (Teresa would become the new GGM of Innovation in late 2016 when Christine went on maternity leave). Champions on this mission went out into Mirvac and competitor shopping centers and spoke directly to over twenty-five customers. Many customers told the team that they were at the shopping centers for reasons other than shopping, and one specific reason or "job to be done" that was mentioned often was that customers were at the shopping center to "get the children out of the house." They also talked about needing to leave the shopping center once their children became tired or bored. The mission team set a challenge to "find new ways to make Mirvac's shopping centers the ultimate destination for entertaining children." At their ideation session, which included both internal and external participants, one of the ideas was "a shopping nanny who would follow you around and look after your kids while you shopped." After considering more than 100 ideas, the team decided to focus on this one as it would have a high impact on solving the customer challenge of entertaining customers' kids and increasing dwelling time at shopping centers. The team of Innovation Champions started testing the concept using lean startup methodology.

Another early phase project which emerged from the second mission was dedicated to "finding new ways to work as one Mirvac team" focused on the colocation of temporary project teams to address an internal organizational challenge. Colocation is typical among project-based organizations, such as consulting companies; however, it is not common in construction companies. Traditionally, employees are located and work from their respective business units and departments (i.e., design and architecture, construction, residential, retail, office and industrial, HR, and information technology). The champions uncovered a challenge around "improving consultation and transparency during the decision-making process" and one of the ideas from the ideation session was to apply the work practices of other industries to physically colocate team members (e.g., construction managers, designers, sales and marketing people) for the duration of a project.

By 2016, more Innovation Champions were needed across the organization. This was partly due to the increased number of projects driven by Hatch. Word had begun to spread about how certain projects, such as the two mentioned above, were beginning to show positive outcomes. Christine began to receive more requests from employees across Mirvac asking how the Hatch team could support innovation in the business units. However, more champions were also needed because some existing Innovation Champions stepped down from the role due to pressures they were facing in combining their normal workload with a commitment to Hatch projects. Another cohort of Innovation Champions was recruited and trained by early 2016, bringing the total number of champions to fifty. To accelerate the embedding of the innovation program, continuing to build capability by giving everyone at Mirvac a chance to get involved in innovation without the formal commitment of a champion role, and addressing the time pressures Innovation Champions were facing, the Hatch team created a new role to allow employees to join ongoing and new projects on an ad hoc basis. The "Hatch Helper" role was created for employees who were interested in learning about the innovation process and who wished to contribute to a specific project but could not commit to the full training and the expectations associated with the innovation champion role. Innovation helpers underwent training in the Hatch methodology when they committed to a project and the training was specific to the part of the process they were undertaking.

Christine also added Hatch design thinking training to Mirvac's Learning Academy to train new recruits as well as summer interns. The Hatch team invited all employees to contribute ideas to the eight missions and organized special challenge sessions at which employees could contribute ideas. These initiatives were part of a planned "ripple effect." The number of employees involved in Hatch initiatives grew exponentially.

Spreading the Word through Communication and Artifacts

Updates about Hatch and its progress were included in all official communications. Information was shared via email, electronic poster campaigns, and presentations at meetings and Mirvac events. Hatch also had an internal online presence whereby news and updates were published on the "Hatch Hub." A "Hatch & Chook"[2] animation video was released in 2016 to introduce the Hatch innovation process to all employees. Externally, the GGM of Innovation gave several presentations at conferences and events and was interviewed by a range of media outlets.

In 2015, Hatch crowd-sourced the creation of creative spaces in each of the company's capital city offices in Sydney, Melbourne, Brisbane, and Perth. As part of the "Hatching Space Challenge," teams of four to five volunteers from across Mirvac were given AUD$12,000 and four weeks to create a space for people to think creatively and be inspired – whether that be in groups or alone. They were required to adhere to a small number of design guidelines to ensure that the spaces were in keeping with the science behind stimulating creative thinking. After four weeks, the spaces were presented to the CEO and the Executive Leadership team.

When a larger space for training or ideation sessions was needed, a space in Mirvac's headquarters or a space outside Mirvac was booked (this often occurred when external participants attended the ideation sessions). Hatch also often used shared virtual spaces, most notably, Slack and Skype.

In 2015, Mirvac won the award for the Best Innovation Program at the BRW Most Innovative Companies awards and was ranked as the third most innovative company in Australia in the same survey that ranked it in the bottom 20 per cent in 2014. The firm that conducted the research and released the rankings noted, "Mirvac showed the greatest improvement between 2014 and 2015 on the innovation drivers of Strategy, Resources and Process."[3]

Fostering an Inclusive, Diverse, and Supportive Culture

At the same time that she was establishing and supporting Hatch, Mirvac's CEO had also committed to building an inclusive, diverse, and supportive organizational culture. Susan strongly believed that in addition to being critical to the financial success of a company, employee well-being was an important enabler of innovation. Several key initiatives were adopted and implemented to create an inclusive and supportive culture, including initiatives under which employees were offered the following incentives:

- Time to invest in upskilling at Mirvac's internal Learning Academy.
- Twenty-weeks of paid parental leave, which was offered in addition to the legislated paid parental leave in Australia.
- Flexible working hours (in 2019, 75 per cent of Mirvac employees had some sort of flexible arrangement in place, compared to 44 per cent in 2015).

Mirvac also increased gender diversity in key committees. In 2017, Mirvac achieved a 50:50 gender representation on its Board of Directors. It continues to be one of only a few companies in Australia to have a gender-equal board.

In 2019, Mirvac achieved an overall employee engagement score of 90 per cent in the Willis Towers Watson's Engagement Survey, placing it above the "Global High Performing Norm," the survey's highest external benchmark.[4] These initiatives were also seen as enablers for the development of Mirvac's innovation culture. As one Mirvac employee explained, "There is this healthy respect; it's appreciating people's ideas; it's not, 'we go to a board meeting and we are frightened to say anything'; it's very open. So that's why it's important building a culture – building an environment where people want to come and work and really believe that they can contribute – not fear of being 'smacked over the head.'"

Going Solo: Building an Internal Innovation Capability

After working with the consulting partner for two years, the Hatch team felt that they had developed a sufficient understanding of the process and of the tools to run projects and could conduct the training of Innovation Champions independently. At the start of 2017, four new full-time roles for the most engaged and successful Innovation Champions were created: Innovation Leads. To be funded by consulting cost savings, these roles were designed to:

- Drive innovation without the support of external consultants.
- Dramatically increase innovation resources by providing both mission support and internal business guidance and support for bottom-up and business unit-initiated innovation.

In 2017, the Executive Leadership team supported the proposal, approved the appointment of four full-time Innovation Leads and increased the Hatch budget to AUD$2–3 million. Each of the four appointed innovation leads would be responsible for working with their "home" business unit (construction, residential, office and industrial, or retail) and would also be aligned with two to three of the missions and champion teams.

In 2017, after almost three years, Mirvac maintained a core team of four Innovation Leads and the Hatch GGM of Innovation (the role was now shared between Teresa and Christine, who had recently returned from maternity leave). The aim of the core team was to establish Hatch as a center for "best-practice innovation" that would drive innovation across the organization by:

- Delivering outcomes on Mirvac's stated innovation missions and supporting the Innovation Champions working on the missions.

- Developing methodologies and frameworks to drive innovations across the business.
- Providing access to knowledge and resources to assist diverse areas of the business in developing value-creating innovation.
- Acting as a driving force of innovations across the business and challenging the business to innovate and evolve by providing support when needed.
- Facilitating Hatch innovation training for Mirvac.

In addition to creating the role for Innovation Leads, Teresa and Christine also asked each business unit to nominate a business partner (a senior leader in the business unit, who was well connected and would assume a conduit role) to work with the Innovation Lead associated with the unit. These business partners were to assist the Innovation Leads to ascertain how Hatch could help each respective business unit and assist the mission teams to connect to different people in the business units. It was thought that the business partners would also accelerate innovation engagement across the company.

Resourcing Challenges Slowed Progression

Despite the success of Hatch projects, not everyone at Mirvac was sharing enthusiasm for the program. Even though managers had to sign off on the time commitment when the Innovation Champions applied for the role, some managers of Innovation Champions were skeptical about Hatch and did not make it easy for Innovation Champions to spend the required time per month to drive innovation projects. As one Innovation Champion explained, "Even from day one, you have skepticism from a lot of senior managers … I am very hesitant to even go up to my manager and say, 'I need less time doing this and more time doing Hatch' because they'll go, 'Well that's generating money for the business, [but] is that [your involvement in Hatch] generating money for the business?'"

Innovation Champions often worked on Hatch projects on top of their day-to-day work as de facto overtime. Every year, several Innovation Champions stepped out of the role because of their inability to combine their commitment to the innovation program with their jobs. The inability of champions to spend the required two to three days was a challenge for mission progression.

Another challenge that slowed progression was that Innovation Champions were often reluctant to "get out of the building" and speak with customers, as required by the design thinking methodology. This created additional delays in the progress of missions and projects, and sometimes decreased the motivation of the champions.

Teresa and Christine believed that the introduction of the Innovation Leads would speed up the progress of Hatch projects and that this would address the concerns of some in the organization that Hatch was too slow. Consequently, following the introduction of the Innovation Leads, an increased number of innovation projects initiated by the business units were supported by Hatch. In 2017, thirty-two business projects were completed. The Hatch design-led approach was in high demand for these business projects and showed the results of Hatch's investment in the business units. However, Hatch's focus on business projects in 2017 meant that work on missions again took second priority. Teresa and Christine knew that it was the mission work for which Hatch would be known and it was important that the required time was also dedicated to progressing missions and driving outcomes.

In early 2018, to gain faster progression on missions, Teresa decided to focus the efforts of the Hatch Innovation Leads and Innovation Champions back on the Hatch innovation missions and particularly on some of the more promising radical innovative ideas that had emerged. Consequently, she introduced the concept of "mission sprints": intensive six-week sessions contributed to by Innovation Champions and led by an Innovation Lead. These mission sprints enabled teams to more quickly reach a stage at which a decision could be made as to whether to fund the more innovative concepts proposed. Some of the ideas that progressed as part of these missions were radical whereas others were incremental in nature. The mission sprints were successful in obtaining rapid progression on missions.

An Evolution to Governance

Additionally, Teresa and Christine were of the view that the structure of the Innovation Council needed to be addressed. Over time all members of the Executive Leadership team had been added to the Council and this meant it was very difficult to have all members available to meet on short notice. Further, the Innovation Council tended to be more supportive of incremental ideas that could support Mirvac's current business, rather than the more radical, disruptive ideas presented. As one Hatch participant explained, "If you take an exploratory idea into our Innovation Council and it's viewed through the lens of how does it help our current customer? Then we will never get an exploratory idea off the ground, we're talking about the future customer and our future value proposition. So that is probably a big challenge."

Teresa and Christine knew that a focus on the current situation and customers would not support the breakthrough, exploratory innovation that Hatch had promised to deliver. In mid-2017, in a meeting with the Executive Leadership team, Teresa and Christine outlined the challenges Hatch was facing and asked for renewed commitment from each Executive Leadership team member to pursue exploratory innovation alongside exploit innovation. A new, more agile, structure for the Innovation Council was proposed: a delegation from the Executive Leadership team, a smaller team, comprising Mirvac's CEO, the Director of Strategy, the Head of Culture and Reputation, and the Hatch GGMs of Innovation. Other Executive Leadership team members would be invited to participate when the projects they were sponsoring were being discussed. The new structure was approved and implemented shortly thereafter.

Taking Stock: Ongoing Challenges and the Ripple Effect

In 2018, there were some parts of the business that lacked understanding of the design-led innovation strategy, however, there was also strong evidence of a ripple effect. The Hatch program had become increasingly visible and employees from across the organization continued to contact the core innovation team and the Innovation Champions seeking support for their projects. Additionally, more people began to use design thinking principles when attempting to promote new ideas and develop strategies. For example, instead of developing a business case and relying on surveys when working on new products or services (as once occurred), employees began to conduct customer scans and run experiments before applying for funding. The Executive Leadership team would often ask employees to apply the Hatch methodology before granting funding for projects.

More generally, there was a significant shift in the culture of the organization such that it became much more customer orientated. Employees began to only apply the design thinking methodology and tools to their work on innovative ideas but also to their day-to-day work. As one Innovation Champion explained: "I've found the design thinking training to be an amazing tool not just for the missions, but for everything I do. I look at things from a totally different perspective." Many employees began to think about how they could improve and change what they do based on using the design thinking tools. They felt that their ideas would be appreciated. There was also a sense that this type of thinking, which had previously been perceived as risky, was now accepted and supported. As another Innovation Champion explained, "Now you can have conversations with people and explore things without people fearing that their idea is a bad one or that they're too junior and so it won't be heard." The Executive Leadership team's endorsement of Hatch was a clear sign that Mirvac supported innovation and wanted to encourage employees to think about ways in which every aspect of Mirvac could be renewed.

Hatch's key innovation initiatives include the following examples:

- Build AI, a business using artificial intelligence and visual data analytics to automate construction processes on site.
- Cultivate, an urban farming initiative in basements and car parks (the initial launch in the car park of Mirvac's headquarters attracted 200 urban farmers, which was followed by a second location under another corporation's headquarters).
- The Third Space, an innovative new co-working space, was launched at one of Mirvac's shopping centers.
- Shopping Nanny provided nanny services for children in shopping centers.
- Pet Concierge was an Australian first service for pet owners.
- Solar energy was upgraded for residents in high-density apartment buildings.

Going Forward: Partnering Externally

By mid-2017, Hatch was also seeking to further incorporate the notion of open innovation processes in internal innovation efforts. Until now, open innovation (i.e., working with a larger group of internal and external contributors on innovative ideas, products, and services) had been ad hoc. However, a formal open innovation strategy called an "External Partnering Strategy" was developed at the end of 2017. This provided a clear decision-making framework for Hatch's interactions with the outside world and brought consistency and structure to decisions around buying, building, or partnering. Partnering became a big focal point, as a way of efficiently and flexibly, engaging with the outside world and tapping into new capabilities.

To create another funding avenue for innovation, a new initiative, Mirvac Ventures, was announced at the end of March 2018. Mirvac Ventures has a funding budget of AUD$10 million and focuses on making minority investments in early-stage non-core companies that bring strategic benefit to the Mirvac core business. In addition to sourcing internal opportunities coming out of Hatch, Mirvac Ventures directly targets opportunities outside the Mirvac boundary by investing in promising new technologies and new businesses relevant to Mirvac. Thus, Mirvac Venture is an internal venture capital unit that can invest in both internal Hatch initiatives and external opportunities. This also provides opportunities for larger investments in ideas coming out of Hatch which can be spun out, resourced, and funded as stand-alone entities. With this initiative, Mirvac's Executive Leadership team has further signaled its commitment to innovation. As of April 2019, Mirvac Ventures had made four investments, three of which were sourced through the Hatch innovation pipeline.

Lessons Learned

Mirvac is an example of how a company, which was lacking a formal structure and process for innovation, successfully built its internal innovation capability, within a short period of four years. In Mirvac's case, a design-led approach to innovation played a key role in making innovation a priority. Whether Mirvac will succeed in managing the tension between incremental and radical innovations in the long term remains to be seen. However, the implementation of design thinking in many aspects of what Mirvac does already represents a significant shift in the culture of the company. Further, design thinking has had positive effects on various aspects of the company's life.

- Mirvac as an organization has benefited from developing their internal design thinking and innovation capability. External partners/consulting companies can introduce best practices and help to implement innovation programs and processes; however, to succeed in the long term, organizations like Mirvan need to develop and assume ownership of their innovation processes (this is what Mirvac referred to as "the ripple effect").
- Senior leaders play a critical role in supporting innovation. They need to balance their focus on meeting financial targets and managing risks and reputation with the need to foster radical innovation. To do so, senior leaders need to learn about innovation tools and methodologies, such as design thinking, to ensure that they understand the nature of, and the challenges facing, radical innovations.
- Design thinking is a very effective way to acquaint employees with new tools and practices that enable the development of innovative outcomes.
- Over time, it is the behavioral and attitudinal change, which comes from practicing new design thinking tools

and techniques, that is critical. It allows the organization to develop an innovation culture. This is also referred to as the design thinking mindset. Developing an innovation mindset goes together with developing a supportive work environment in which employees feel safe to share ideas and take risks.

- Incentives (e.g., key performance indicators and rewards) need to be implemented and time needs to be allocated to ensure that innovation initiatives are recognized and rewarded appropriately. This enables employees to participate in and contribute to innovation initiatives.
- Winning the support of middle and senior business unit managers is a key step in achieving innovate outcomes, since they are the ones who must manage the tensions between short-term goals and long-term innovations.

Timeline

- 2008–11: Mirvac recovers from the global financial crisis.
- 2012: A new CEO is appointed who makes changes to Mirvac's strategic direction by creating three core business areas and focusing on strategic innovation.
- 2013: Key staff learn about design thinking and explores its potential for the organization.
- 2014: Engagement of a consulting company to help implement an innovation framework; Hatch initiative is launched and its budget set at AUD\$1 million per year; explore versus exploit missions set.
- 2015: Building capability begins; training of Innovation Champions and leadership team; Mirvac wins award for Best Innovation Program at the BRW Most Innovative Companies awards.

- 2016: Fifty Innovation Champions trained; Hatch budget is now AUD$2–3 million; "Hatch Helper" role is created.
- 2017: CEO commits to building an inclusive, diverse, and supportive culture; new Agile structure introduced for the Innovation Council.
- 2018: Introduction of mission sprints; a significant shift in the company's culture starts to emerge.
- 2019: Mirvac achieves an employee engagement score of 90 per cent.

CHAPTER EIGHT

From Department to Consultancy – Building Human-Centered Design Capabilities at Swisscom

KATJA BÜRKI

Swisscom is Switzerland's leading telecom company. The development of a human-centered design capability at Swisscom did not start at the top. To get buy-in, build awareness, and attract the attention of top management, a group of managers started by creating an open and visible creative workspace in a central location. The space acted as an embodiment of human-centered design methods, featuring interdisciplinary teamwork, prototyping, co-design with customers, and so on. Additionally, the team started teaching people human-centered design methods, which resulted in the development of a community of facilitators who were determined to develop a design-driven innovation culture and to diffuse its methods. Over time, other roles were created, so that human-centered design could play a more active role in business projects and its value could be demonstrated. The success at Swisscom was being able to measure the value of design thinking: new KPIs with a focus on customer centricity were implemented. Swisscom's HCD team merged with an external innovation company called Creaholic, which enabled Swisscom's team to learn from external clients and projects and gain internal legitimacy. The partnership allowed mixing employees and gaining access to complementary resources and competencies, which enabled Swisscom to address larger innovation projects faster.

Digitization has introduced new dynamics of speed, creativity, and the continuous invention of a business. It evolved and developed customer needs and behaviors, which must be addressed to ensure a company's long-term success in the market. Like many technology-based companies, Swisscom,[1] Switzerland's leading telecom company, has been affected by this development. Swisscom's key performance indicator, the Net Promoter Score (NPS),[2] became volatile, demonstrating to the management the criticality of reaching a new benchmark to sustain the business into the next decade.

Swisscom is Switzerland's leading telecom company. The Swiss government holds a 51 per cent majority of shares in the business, which offers mobile telecommunications, fixed networks, and Internet and digital TV solutions for business and residential customers. Swisscom is also one of the largest providers of IT services in Switzerland. The company develops and maintains the wireless and wireline network infrastructure, distributes broadcasting signals, and is active in banking, energy, entertainment, advertising, and healthcare. About 19,000 people work at Swisscom. The company generates around 80 per cent of its net revenue of approximately CHF 11 billion and operating income from business operations in Switzerland. In 2017, Swisscom

had a share of about 60 per cent of the Swiss mobile market, 67 per cent of the broadband, and 33 per cent of TV
telecommunications. Swisscom also maintains a presence in
the Italian market.

Discovering the Next Big Thing

In 2003, two of Swisscom's top-level managers announced that they
would visit Silicon Valley in the hope of finding groundbreaking
and forward-thinking technology. They reached the Swisscom's innovation outpost in Silicon Valley where two innovation experts –
Christina Taylor and her colleague – were established. Their role
was to attend talks, startup presentations, and business networking
events. Thanks to visits to the d.school, the Stanford Research Institute, and design firms such as IDEO, Philips, and HP, they also
developed an understanding of a human-centered perspective that
facilitates and nurtures successful innovations.[3] This perspective is
known as human-centered design (HCD).

The schedules of the Swisscom's top-level managers at Silicon
Valley only permitted short meetings with various technology startups. However, Christina and her colleague planned a visit to IDEO
without specifying it in their official program as it was not a technology company and therefore might have been rejected. During
their visit at IDEO, the managers were immediately attracted to
the company's specific work method and its cultural aspects (e.g.,
the team's mindset and interdisciplinary collaboration). They were
convinced that such a unique design approach would introduce
groundbreaking innovation at Swisscom.

However, they had one main question to answer: How could
they implement this agile human-centered work method in their

established company, which had over 150 years of tradition? They realized that there were thousands of books, methodologies, and approaches that companies can use. There was no right or wrong way to implement such a change; it was important to simply start experimenting with it.

Creating Visibility to Increase Awareness through a Dedicated Space

The first HCD team was established at Swisscom in 2008. Christina led a small team of three and worked on putting ideas into practice within Swisscom's residential customer department. Faced with limited resources to implement this approach, the HCD team prioritized gaining the attention of Swisscom's top-level management. They aimed to achieve this by increasing the visibility of HCD working methods. Since physical spaces and rooms shape corporate culture and are visible to everyone in the company, the team decided to create a designated space for HCD to place it on the top-level management's agenda.

To do this, they initiated the renovation of a 1,500-square-meter space at Swisscom's Bern location and created an open space creativity room based on HCD methodologies that encouraged cross-functional discussions between Swisscom employees and people from other ecosystems. Dedicated project rooms were built around the open space to support interdisciplinary teamwork at specific times and each room involved flexible infrastructure to support different HCD work methods for each phase of the project. The rooms featured white surfaces for visualization during discussions and concept work, tables to activate teamwork, and materials to create ideas and prototypes in the early stages.

The space was situated in the center of the most populated campus building. The room – named BrainGym – played a pivotal role

Figure 8.1. Swisscom BrainGym

in unfolding HCD at Swisscom (see figure 8.1). It acted as a hub that frequently enabled people, both internal and external, to collaborate. The team soon realized that the space emphasized the purpose of HCD: it inspired people to spread ideas beyond BrainGym into other parts of the company. Further, BrainGym provided a platform for HCD to reach the Swisscom CEO's agenda. Christina used the space to host regular exchanges with representatives of the top 100 executives and Swisscom's CEO. These meetings were instrumental in garnering the attention of the Swisscom top-level management team, which convinced them to support HCD efforts.

Developing Internal Capabilities with Facilitators and Co-Creators

Top management's attention increased the expectations from and the demand for HCD. Consequently, there was a growing need to train Swisscom employees in HCD, which was difficult to manage because Christina's team was very small. Hence, the team developed a facilitator program. And facilitators who trained in HCD methodology extended the team. Swisscom reached an important milestone in winning allies and scaling HCD to an organization-level with those facilitators coming from different units. In 2008, there were twenty trained facilitators; that increased to over 100 in 2010. Facilitators spent 20 per cent of their time moderating workshops and projects using HCD methodologies with the permission and support of their direct managers.

To sustain momentum, the team got top-management exposure. They decided it was time to demonstrate HCD's influence on projects and its success. However, facilitators reported challenges in implementing project-based HCD work within the company. Indeed, technology and business development teams were accustomed to working within separate line functions, which prevented them from completing cross-disciplinary work. Further, project-based HCD working methods were unfamiliar to most untrained employees. Therefore, facilitators only minimally influenced projects. It was sometimes challenging for them to convince their teams and management to work differently with these new methodologies. Facilitators were mostly trained on a tool and process base, which meant that they had not gained practical project experience during their training. They were missing knowledge to strengthen their HCD skills in their everyday work.

On top of these critical issues, the HCD team noticed that facilitators were isolated and dispersed throughout the company. They, therefore, decided to create a facilitator community. This community brought HCD knowledge to an organization-level to exchange methodology experiences and discuss difficult HCD business challenges, so that empowerment was guaranteed on different levels. It also relieved some of the HCD team's duties, which increased their efficacy.

On top of that, a dedicated team of HCD experts called "Co-Creators" was established in 2010 to support project teams in various business units. A Co-Creator worked on business projects and took responsibility for empowering project leaders and teams to embody HCD working methods. A Co-Creator's main tasks were (1) creating an interdisciplinary project team, (2) being at the start

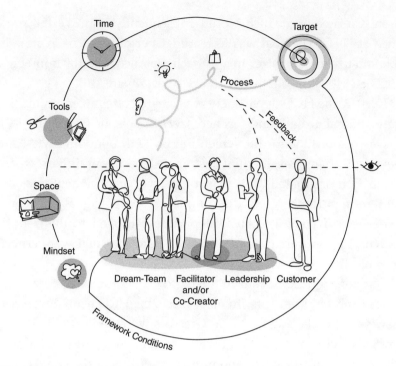

Time

Target

Process

Tools

Feedback

Space

Mindset

Dream-Team   Facilitator   Leadership   Customer
and/or
Co-Creator

Framework Conditions

Figure 8.2. Co-Creator guiding an interdisciplinary project team

of a concrete design challenge, (3) bringing customer insights into projects based on market reports, interviews, and observations, (4) ideation, (5) building prototypes, and (6) asking for feedback in the early stages (validation). Therefore, the project teams experienced a new work method and developed their understanding of HCD. Moreover, their projects led to tangible outcomes, which were used by the HCD team in showcasing best practices and examples of how HCD processes, tools, and methodologies were central to Swisscom's innovation (see figure 8.2).

Christina and the HCD team soon became aware of the positive influence that Co-Creators had within business units. They initiated a close exchange with the top-level manager of each unit with the aim of convincing them to provide the financial resources to employ more Co-Creators, which would subsequently improve the presence of HCD. The goal was to recruit 1 per cent of Co-Creators in relation to each unit size, an approach that increased the number of HCD employees from three in 2008 to seventy in 2013.

In 2013, the HCD department was created after an enormous organizational growth and reached seventy persons (see figure 8.3). It was responsible for implementing HCD throughout Swisscom, beyond the single residential customer department in Bern where BrainGym originated. This was a top-level management decision and an important sign of the company's strategic goal to become experience-driven. The HCD department reacted to this repositioning by centralizing important competencies that were crucial in projects.

Christina quickly realized that growth introduced new challenges and requirements. To meet these, the HCD team developed new skills, tools, and roles. Co-Creators were dedicated to developing novel projects for all Swisscom units (e.g., residential and enterprise, infrastructure, and human resources). Additional teams were initialized to address other functions and offered specialty services for Co-Creators and business units to run projects with a strong business influence. An Innovation Culture team developed a culture compass (see figure 8.4), processes and skills (e.g., methodologies), led training to strengthen interdisciplinary teamwork and capabilities (e.g., facilitation, prototyping, and visualization), built a creative working environment, supported learning communities, and further developed key performance indicators. An eight-person Research team published and introduced market and customer insights into Swisscom projects. A Prototyping and Testing team developed digital tools and apps to scale HCD in a larger digital dimension. However, Swisscom's business units did not completely understand the new structure. Recognizing this confusion, the HCD team quickly developed a story to address that issue.

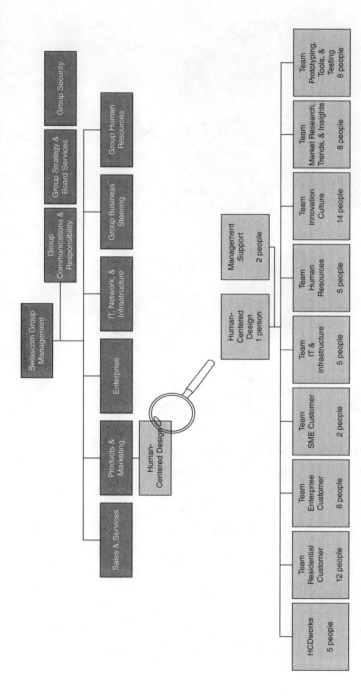

Figure 8.3. Organization of the HCD department

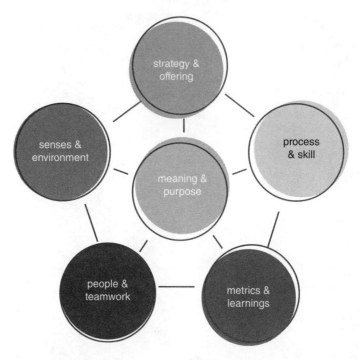

Figure 8.4. HCD department's culture compass

From Storytelling to Measuring Outcomes with the Customer Centricity Score

Customer needs were evolving, and Swisscom had to update the products and services it offered on the market – not only by addressing the technology but also by giving customers the best experience. The story was clear: Happy customers would continue buying products and services, which, in turn, would ensure that Swisscom was economically viable.

The HCD department had the capacity to provide the core foundation for Swisscom employees to create products and services that would satisfy customers. The NPS was the main tool used to transform customer satisfaction into a KPI. However, the department still needed an instrument that showcased the necessity of a customer-centered work style from an organizational perspective. This would ultimately demonstrate the HCD department's achievements and how it influenced the NPS. In the search for this instrument, Innovation Culture team employees scouted the market for suitable tools but quickly realized that no tool suited their needs. Instead, the team consulted a team of researchers at the University of Lucerne. The two teams collaborated for eighteen months, focusing on developing a KPI that was scientifically valid, practically oriented, and proven to be effective. In 2015, they introduced the Customer Centricity Score, an instrument that depicted customer-centered activities at Swisscom on three levels: management, collaboration, and implementation. Generally, management focused on how top-level management enabled customer centricity within the company. Collaboration measured the presence of a customer-oriented working method. The level of implementation confirmed that employees had all the tools, systems, and processes they needed. The results were examined by several management boards and reflected upon during workshops, which fostered a common understanding of a customer-oriented company's purpose and the HCD department's contribution. From these conversations, the management boards changed their mindset and asked how they could support Swisscom's transition to becoming a customer-oriented company (see figure 8.5).

Addressing the Middle Management Barrier

By 2015, there was the HCD department, a community of facilitators, a team of Co-Creators, and a new KPI, that is, the Customer Centricity Score. However, despite knowing that facilitators and Co-Creators contributed to Swisscom's overall success, middle

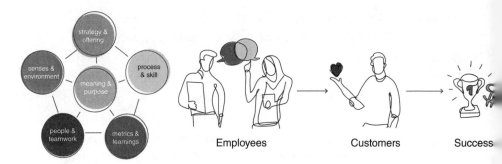

Figure 8.5. Swisscom internal operations and how HCD influenced the market

management focused on concrete and measurable outputs linked to incentives. Middle managers were the biggest barrier to the implementation of HCD and had the highest potential to foster it. To address this, the HCD department collaborated with the Swisscom Leadership Academy to align the HCD mindset with management's understanding and leadership. Together, the two created a training program that educated middle managers in how to develop the HCD mindset and achieve HCD working methods. HCD was fundamental to the Swisscom Leadership Academy. By leveraging capabilities and collaborating with transformation-related departments, the management had now adopted HCD. The focus was now on connecting themes and discovering the right collaborations to strongly transform Swisscom.

Initially, the HCD department struggled to reach various important and internal target groups because of insufficient political power or credibility. Working with different departments led to creating additional entry points for the most elusive stakeholders so that they could delve into the HCD mindset and methodology – consciously or unconsciously. This approach allowed them to reach those from various units with different backgrounds and roles from different angles. Additionally, the facilitator program created more than 500 trained facilitators who assisted the HCD department in reaching almost all units within Swisscom, which increased acceptance and influence.

Extending from Internal to External Consulting to Learn and Develop

In 2015, a new HCD department team – HCD Works – was created with five (out of seventy) HCD experts. This team acted as an external consultant firm that worked for large German-speaking companies and attempted to implement HCD or co-create new products and services for them. HCD Works shared the knowledge and experience gained from projects completed for Swisscom with these other companies. A close relationship between HCD Works and the HCD department was strategically important because it allowed HCD Works to engage with internal projects if necessary and the HCD department to understand external developments. Progressively, companies throughout Switzerland were more and more willing to pay HCD Works to learn from them. The team's external recognition and financial success assisted the HCD department to gain internal credibility.

The learnings and insights from HCD Works projects in other industries were shared internally at Swisscom to improve business through this outside-in perspective; for example, other companies used the Customer Centricity Score. This additional data enabled the HCD department to establish an interbranch comparison, which also allowed Swisscom to identify issues and opportunities for improvement.

The performance and achievements of HCD Works projects were recognized as hugely influential in Swisscom's overall learning journey. However, the projects raised new issues. Because several project teams focused on product life-cycle development, there was often no time to take on the innovative, disruptive ideas generated from HCD Works' outside-in learnings. Further, the length of time before the business acted on these new ideas, including forming the right teams, was not supported by the existing organizational structure. It was soon realized that the organization's ability to foster disruptive innovation was compromised. The HCD department's position and the HCD employees' roles in business projects did not allow ideas to be taken beyond development to implementation. A new question emerged from the HCD department's team leader conversation: "What type of setup would be needed to bring disruptive innovation to Swisscom?"

Developing a Strategy to Foster Disruptive Innovation in Partnership with Creaholic

Christina and her team worked for several months to consider different strategic options, noting that the best way to foster disruptive innovation was through a strategic partnership external to Swisscom. It was necessary to complete a market analysis of potential partners who would complement the HCD's internal capacities portfolio. Since the HCD department and HCD Works were knowledgeable in HCD methods and service design, it was important to identify a partner that possessed deep technological knowledge and was experienced in other industries. In the search for this partnership, several discussions were held with important stakeholders.

The team identified Creaholic, a well-known innovation company in Biel/Bienne, Switzerland, that was founded in 1986 by inventor Elmar Mock – who had played a role in developing the revolutionary Swatch watch. Creaholic had technical innovations from many industries in Switzerland and abroad (e.g., the medical technology, automotive, and cosmetic industries). In 2016, Marcel Aeschlimann, the managing director of Creaholic, and his team discussed the potential of a new partnership to take Creaholic to the next level.

Christina and Marcel met to discuss merging the HCD department and Creaholic. Swisscom's partnership with Creaholic was viewed as beneficial for multiple reasons.

The technological knowledge that the HCD department was looking for was present in various spin-offs, in the number of registered patents, and in the skills and competencies of the Creaholic team. The objective was to merge HCD knowledge and tangible technical knowledge. Further, the similar mindset, principles, and values of the people were key for cross-industry expertise to reinvent elements of Swisscom's offering and push an innovative culture.

Convinced of her plan, Christina's team presented the idea to Swisscom's top-level management in 2016. After reviewing and discussing the partnership opportunity for six months, management agreed. In 2017, Swisscom and Creaholic established a strategic partnership and Christina and twenty-seven HCD experts merged with Creaholic. A new team of inventors, customer experience experts, engineers, designers, software developers, IP experts, and change agents was created to explore new possibilities for Swisscom and other multinational companies.

Swisscom became a member of Creaholic's Board of Directors and had a shareholding of 5 per cent, whereas the other shareholders were Creaholic's employees. This contribution demonstrated that Swisscom and Creaholic's strategic partnership was a shared long-term interest. Through this partnership, it was not only HCD processes and methodologies that empowered Swisscom's innovative culture but also additional practical engineering expertise and the development of new tangible prototypes (e.g., 3D printing, laser printing, injection molding, and CAD designs) made it possible for Swisscom to have a full invention package. Creaholic's portfolio grew in both its competencies and customer base.

Sixty Creaholic employees – seventeen of whom were former Swisscom colleagues – collaborated with Swisscom's business units to create new product offerings and train employees in advanced skills, such as Agile and Visual Facilitation to foster the innovation mindset. Creaholic developed Swisscom's innovative culture and led strategic product and service innovation with project teams. Simultaneously, the remaining thirty-two employees in the HCD department at Swisscom focused on creating process innovation and customer interaction experiences. Because processes depend strongly on a company's organization and structure, these had to be approached internally; creating customer journeys and coordinating interfaces was significant to produce continuous experiences for customers. This strategic partnership demonstrated the ideal interdisciplinary team setup, with the term "dream team" becoming integral to Creaholic's working principles. For each project, those with the skills and experience relevant to the topic contributed to a specific business challenge. Unlike other external companies, Creaholic's relationship with Swisscom meant that each company was able to directly enter each other's projects with little to no notice. This "plug and play" collaboration procedure supported agile working methods where Swisscom could drive and experiment with new topics and challenges within a short period of time with less internal politics – elements that usually postpone a project's commencement. Additionally, it added a broader perspective that served as a benefit as Swisscom was often too close and too operationally involved in its own projects.

Reaping the Benefits of the New Strategy

After the announcement of Creaholic and Swisscom's new partnership, several business units and middle managers approached Creaholic with projects. It appeared that the strategy to move externally from the organization increased the credibility and demand for HCD. Creaholic was asked to develop new business fields with the strategic department because they brought technical expertise, cross-industry know-how, and a broader ecosystem perspective to projects. Before 2017, when the HCD department was fully integrated into Swisscom, many business units asked Christina and her team to run projects. However, Christina's team was unable to prioritize projects, and this became a difficult balancing act as these units paid for a certain percentage of HCD employees. The new setting enabled this shift to prioritize projects with a strong influence on disruptive innovations. Creaholic viewed Swisscom's potential holistically, without it being integrated into the system and its politics. Swisscom gave Creaholic several project requests to accept, and Creaholic was required to filter and argue for or against an initiative externally as the strategic partnership clearly framed the goal of the partnership.

In 2019, two and a half years after the start of this strategic partnership, Swisscom and Creaholic have run several projects. Creaholic has developed two feedback questions to be asked of anyone involved in a Swisscom-Creaholic project in order to continuously measure and report the quality and value of the collaboration: How likely is it that you will recommend Creaholic to your colleagues and friends? Has Creaholic created value in our collaboration?

A Closed Loop

When reviewing this journey, it is important to consider the role of HCD within Swisscom and how HCD was organized. The small team focused on creating awareness and reaching as many people as possible to build a facilitator community. This followed the desire to demonstrate HCD's influence in projects. Consequently, the team grew with Co-Creation experts, and HCD reached new heights as teams received project support, which made the process and results tangible and experiential. The influence of project results was leveraged and supported by developing a focused KPI, which heightened HCD's visibility and impressed project teams and decision-makers.

The project teams created a company-wide appreciation of HCD, which also resulted in new demands. Consequently, the HCD department grew to seventy people across different subteams. Close collaboration with other transformation teams created further influence as specific themes were addressed from various angles and strengthened each other in a corporate transformation context. To fulfill the call for Swisscom's disruptive innovation, an additional step had to be taken: in 2017, twenty-eight HCD department members joined Creaholic in a strategic partnership. This partnership enabled Swisscom to leverage Creaholic's development and implementation experience, which provided Swisscom with knowledge beyond innovative concepts. Additionally, relying on an external structure allowed Swisscom to drive innovation against the structural and political limits that naturally exist within any organization.

The partnership between Swisscom and Creaholic was an experiment. Evaluating organizational changes can only occur retrospectively – there is no single correct approach. As HCD promoted its prototyping and experimentation, its implementation spread and found the right path through trial and error, benefited by its constant ability to reach new heights. After a few years, the influence of the Swisscom and Creaholic partnership was evident and the goals were reached. The five-year experiment has transformed into a long-term collaboration and continues to evolve today – proving that even partnerships can serve as successful prototypes.

Lessons Learned

- Management buy-in is instrumental in the struggle against limited resources in implementing HCD. The team invested in creating awareness through visibility (a dedicated open space to creativity and HCD methods), which resulted in gaining management's attention.

- Grouping the facilitators in a community to assist in developing a human-centered culture and working methods is advantageous. It also enabled awareness of the time before reaching a quantitative number of trained facilitators and the understanding of when to invest to achieve the desired result.
- Co-Creators play an essential role because of their direct influence within business projects and their ability to adopt HCD methods within projects and to demonstrate the value built.
- Create a department with Co-Creators dedicated to projects and shared services to capitalize and gain time (prototyping, etc.).
- Create new KPIs; for example, the Customer Centricity Score.
- Design a program within the leadership academy of the company.
- Create an external consultancy that has external clients to learn from external projects and gain internal legitimacy.
- The strategic partnership between Swisscom and Creaholic resulted in mixing employees, enhancing complementary resources and competencies, and gaining legitimacy internally.

Timeline

- 2003–8: Some top Swisscom executives visit the Swisscom outpost in Silicon Valley and IDEO. They see the potential of HCD for innovation at Swisscom.
- 2008–9: A team of three people take the lead in spreading HCD within the organization; launch of the BrainGym as a visible and open creativity room embodying HCD methods to attract attention of the top executives; creation of a training program and teaching of twenty facilitators.
- 2010: One hundred facilitators trained; identification of Co-Creators highly involved in projects.

- 2013: Seventy Co-Creators involved; creation of the HCD department.
- 2015: The Customer Centricity Score is introduced; start of the Leadership Academy; 300 facilitators trained; creation of HCD Works as an external consultancy with five people from the HCD department.
- 2017: Start of the partnership with Creaholic, an external innovation consultancy; thirty-two people remain in the HCD department.
- 2019: Evaluation of the projects undertaken by the partnership to determine if they have worked.
- 2022: The five-year experiment between Swisscom and Creaholic transforms into a close collaboration that continues to this day.

CHAPTER NINE

From Underdog to Design-Led Innovation – Scaling Design Thinking at Thales

SIHEM BENMAHMOUD-JOUINI AND DIDIER BOULET

The implementation of design thinking at **Thales**, a high-tech company in the global aeronautics and defense industry, started by partnering with the Stanford d.school, which convinced the top managers of the great potential that design thinking would have for innovation. What is unusual in this case is that the first internal sponsor was the manager of the Thales Corporate University. In fact, the university was where the first Thales Design Center – a space for learning about and applying design thinking – was hosted. This way, the Design Center escaped the attention of the Research and Technology unit, which in high-tech firms like Thales would typically oversee delivering innovation. The implementation of design thinking started with training and facilitating workshops, which gradually turned into innovation projects involving various business units. The Design Center adopted an internal consultancy operations model that allowed accommodating different mandates from customers across the large organization. The consulting model enabled the delivery of results and outcomes rather than evangelizing and advocating for a method. Innovation projects were co-designed and involved business unit staff throughout all phases, which ultimately resulted in business unit staff taking responsibility for the destiny and outcomes of their projects. The first Design Center developed a "franchise" model that enabled the diffusion of design thinking via more than thirteen Design Centers worldwide and allowed other innovation teams to leverage the approach and benefit from network effects.

"My dream job would be to establish the first Design Center of Thales." This is how, in 2012, Didier Boulet, founder and director of the Thales Design Center, pitched his vision of a corporate design thinking center at Thales, an 80,000-employee-strong firm in aeronautics, defense and security, space, and transportation that operates globally and is headquartered in Paris.

Nine years later, in 2021, the firm counts thirteen Design Centers around the world located in the main business units of the company. In these Design Centers, a large variety of innovation projects are explored by employees from different business units within the company that engage with users and customers. Since 2014, design thinking has been an integral part of every top management leadership program and has become instrumental to the digital transformation of the company. In February 2020, Didier was appointed chief design officer at the corporate level.

What was the journey of a growing ambition from a low-profile design thinking facility to a global network of Design Centers? How did Thales manage the integration of a design mindset in a technologically driven firm?

Thales is a high-tech multinational company in the global aeronautics and defense industry with 80,000 employees in

sixty-eight countries, including 30,000 engineers. It is composed of five business groups: aerospace, ground transportation, space, defense, and identity and security. Thales is
a EUR 17 billion revenue business that spends about EUR 1
billion on research and development in addition to the research and development funded by its global, mostly government customers.

The Genesis

When Didier Boulet pitched his "dream," Thales was certainly not
unfamiliar with design thinking. Three years earlier, in 2009, Thales
Corporate University (which operates as an independent entity
within Thales) had organized a learning expedition to Silicon Valley
for thirty high-potential managers (VP level). The group included
Hervé Multon, ESVP Strategy; Jean-François Pernotte, VP of Strategic Partnership and Development; Patricia Viviani, VP of Professional Development; and Alain Oumeddour, General Manager of
Thales University. This executive program had been created to expose the group to disruptive approaches to innovation, and so the
group visited IDEO, the Stanford d.school, Jump Associates, among
other organizations. This first encounter with design thinking resulted in a three-year collaboration with Stanford University's famous ME310 program, which includes international student teams
working on innovation projects of the participating firms.

Three projects explored different technologies or domains that
were strategically important to Thales: (1) new applications for un-
derwater drones, (2) redesigning the helicopter cockpit, and (3) the
reinvention of filmmaking. The students from the d.school worked
on these briefs and delivered very promising innovation concepts,
but afterward, none of the identified opportunities got any traction

at Thales. Although the ME310 project results were presented to the business unit managers and their strategy director, it proved very difficult for the internal development teams of the company to transform these concepts into new offers. A primary reason was that the opportunities that the students had identified were not embedded in the environment of the business units and the firm did not have the technological capabilities to develop them. Others would have required developing completely new business models for the firm.

However, participating in the ME310 program was an insightful experiment that showed Thales managers how design thinking could make a difference. According to Didier, these projects showed that "design thinking really works, and this was good news," and it created the conditions to push the idea of internalizing design thinking inside the company in order to "create something."

During the same period (2009–11), Didier was managing software technology innovation within the office of the chief technology officer. He had the opportunity to discover design thinking on his own and experienced what the approach could offer. He had tried several times to inject more design thinking into the techno-dominated research and development context, however without much success. He was also closely following the d.school projects, thanks to Antonin Caors, the program coordinator at Thales.

By 2012, Thales had conducted insightful design thinking experiments with the Stanford d.school, even though they proved rather unsatisfactory in terms of business impact. Despite this, Didier, who was dreaming of a corporate design thinking facility, and a group of senior managers from the learning expedition persisted in their pursuit of design thinking. They all were convinced of the potential that design thinking could have for Thales. One of them, Alain Oumeddour, the general manager at Thales Corporate University, took the leap and agreed to experiment and test the Design Center concept within the university: a very unusual place for Thales to host such an innovation initiative. It was then that the convergence of two journeys – a corporate and a personal one – took place.

Didier secured an open office space covering more than 180 square meters on the university campus. He received initial funding of Euros 60,000, which was used for the refurbishments and was given twelve months to demonstrate the internal traction of the initiative to the university's leadership. The first Design Center (DC) was born.

For six months, the "team" was composed of only two people, Didier and a designer intern. Together, they undertook an intense phase of benchmarking and understanding best-in-class design thinking practices and their applications within other firms, and a lot of self-guided training. They created the Design Center space and its brand. They also put together a one-day design thinking training and a range of support materials for workshops. They used the d.school framework as a reference to the five main phases of a design thinking project (empathy, define, ideation, prototype, and experimentation). At the same time, they conducted many meetings with potential early adopters within the firm, including the members of the 2009 learning expedition, who would ultimately become their first internal customers. This was how the first DC was bootstrapped: a low-cost, time-limited, low-risk prototype to experiment with the firm's acceptance and to determine if design thinking could gain traction.

The Year of the Underdog

In January 2013, after three months of space refurbishments, some Ikea raids, a few DIY projects including the assembly of twenty Ikea storage boxes the night before the opening, the Design Center space was officially opened. Based on early positive feedback and first training contracts, Didier was joined by another undercover design thinker, Charles-Antoine Poirier, bringing the team to two full-time staff and two designer interns. The team's growth was supported by Alain and the Thales Corporate University.

From day one, the Design Center adopted a key structuring element – an agency business model: all activities were contracted with internal stakeholders and were fully invoiced. The objectives at this early stage were simple: (1) demonstrate the viability of the agency model, (2) touch a maximum of people through workshops and training, and (3) secure a first full-fledged design-led innovation project. Several years of experience at the firm informed Didier to stay under the radar and to avoid exposure. His objective was to show what design thinking could bring to the table: that is, don't tell (i.e., evangelize) but rather demonstrate as quickly as possible what the business impact of a full-fledged design thinking project could be. His obsession with delivering projects proved to be essential for the long-term success of the DC.

Another important factor was to remain independent and not get absorbed by other departments or teams. Didier knew that becoming institutionalized would endanger the integrity of the approach as well as the DC's existence. Over the years, there had been some instances of poor implementation of design thinking, resulting in negative perceptions and bad press for the approach. This was primarily due to an interpretation and implementation of design thinking that reduced it to a list of facilitation tricks to be used and abused in workshops. The belief was that under the wrong leadership, the DC would succumb to the same short-sighted interpretations. So, to protect the strong drive toward a design-led and project-led DC, the team took a strong "let's stay independent" stance.

During the first year, the DC had started to make some waves and generate outcomes such as training and projects (as discussed in the sections below), prompting different groups within Thales to lay claim to the ownership of the initiative and overall use of design thinking as an approach to innovation. These groups consisted of various innovation methodologists and human factor practitioners. However, these groups were anchored in their own discipline and failed to recognize and embrace the interdisciplinary and creative elements of design thinking. The (relative) independence of the DC and its self-sustaining business model helped to protect the initiative from these friendly takeovers. The early growth in terms of activity, footprint, and credibility played a key role in closing these initial takeover attempts.

What were the results after the first twelve months? The DC's results exceeded everyone's expectations. The one-day training courses, delivered to more than 200 people from different units, were a great success. This led to design thinking becoming an integral part of the Thales management leadership programs. Alain's strong sponsorship was not only a powerful enabler of success but also turned out to be a very effective indirect channel for developing the activities of the DC. As a result, many post-training opportunities to pitch design thinking and the DC's value proposition were created.

The DC completed more than fifteen creativity workshops and two projects within the first twelve months. One of these first projects, the 6-Watch, to date remains an emblematic project for Thales due to its pivotal impact on the reputation of design thinking across the organization. It is fair to say that the 6-Watch project became the tipping point for the acceptance of the DC as a viable innovation initiative because its outcome – a smartwatch – not only won a Thales Innovation Award but also received considerable attention in the leading French trade show for security. This first public success story played a pivotal role and served as a reference when illustrating the benefits of the design thinking approach to other divisions.

How the 6-Watch Project Made a Difference

The 6-Watch project was launched for a business unit that specialized in providing security and defense products and services to governments. The business unit leader was looking to diversify the product portfolio in the market segment related to the police, and the idea was to become much more proactive in identifying new concepts that would be useful for police officers.

At the same time, Didier was looking for how to promote the design thinking approach. Considering that Thales is a business-to-government (B2G) business, the team was looking for business units to get close to the end-user for testing purposes and to show the potential of design thinking to identify unmet needs. The DC presented design thinking to the sales and business development teams, which sponsored the launch of a six-month project targeting police officers. A core team that included Charles-Antoine, a design intern, and six individuals (marketing, sales, business developers, etc.) from the business unit was formed.

Following the DC framework, the first phase (inspiration) took three months and involved intensive user research with a focus on observing and understanding the activities of police officers in the field. At the same time, the team documented key technology trends and reviewed security models of major cities in different geographical contexts.

The first phase led to a series of sense-making workshops involving a multi-disciplinary team (including business development, marketing, research and technology) and representatives from several subsidiaries within the security business (e.g., Mexico, Singapore) where Thales had major police systems customers and presence. During these workshops, the data collected was displayed and discussed through shared synthetic inspiration boards.

Several interesting and surprising insights about police officers' activities, actions, and decision-making emerged from these sessions. For example, the team found that police officers rely on intuition in analyzing situations. Intuitions are based on experience and on patterns of behavior. Another insight was that sharing information when officers are in the field without revealing their location is critical and, when they can't share information, they rely on routines that have been developed based on pattern matching. Yet another key insight from the officers was that routines are dangerous and, that under pressure, they rely on past situations and are unable to apprehend new elements.

These insights led the team to reframe the project challenge and organize several ideation workshops that included thirty people from Thales staff coming from Europe, Mexico, and Singapore. Hundreds of ideas and twelve initial concepts emerged from the ideation sessions. After a period of low-fidelity prototyping (including rough business model exploration), the team selected three concepts: augmented reality glasses, a connected smartwatch, and a smart bullet-proof jacket. After inputs from the users, the team converged on the development of the connected smartwatch (a product that had just begun to enter the market). The idea entered the product design phase, which lasted another six months (see figure 9.1).

The Design Center Network Is Born

During these first twelve months of the initiative, another story unfolded. The DC stimulated a lot of interest among innovation teams throughout the organization (different countries, global and local business units). This happened mainly through word of mouth. People from across the organization (London, Glasgow, Bordeaux, and Singapore, for example) started reaching out and asked whether they too could use the design thinking material the DC had developed as well as its branding and identity.

This immediate traction with innovation peers surprised the DC team. It was not Thales businesses asking the DC to facilitate its own projects but people (intrapreneurs) belonging to different innovation teams within the firm who were curious about the potential of design thinking and interested in exploring it on their own.

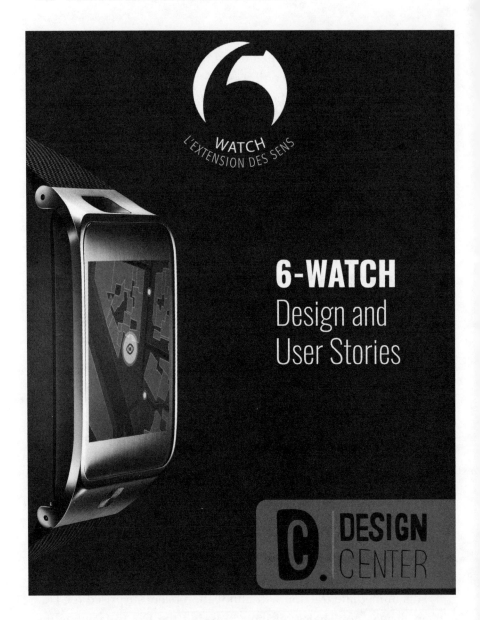

Figure 9.1. The 6-Watch project

After the early success of the 6-Watch project, there was a second inflection point because the team realized that the DC could become more than a single local agency based in the university. An alternative growth channel opened with a larger scope and impact. The DC team realized that beyond the training offered through the university, workshops, and projects facilitated for the business units, design thinking could scale through its adoption by other innovation teams spread within the firm at a global level.

As a result, Didier suggested positioning the DC so that it could respond better to the needs of the locally decentralized innovation teams. This was an opportunity for the DC that could not be missed and that required a specific development: the Design Center had turned into an innovation franchise. In the weeks that followed, Didier and his team started to formalize further the identity and value proposition of the DC, its methodologies and tools. The team created a complete program for accelerating and enabling new Design Centers, the DC Leadership and Enablement Package. Over time, this package has been continuously enriched. It has become the DC OPS and is being delivered by multiple Design Centers in a crowd-sourced, community-driven manner. By the end of 2013, only one year after the launch of the first DC, two new centers were launched in Glasgow and Singapore, and two other new centers opened in 2014 in London and Bordeaux.

The Growth Years (2014 and 2015)

Over the following two years, the internal traction that Didier had observed in 2013 continued. The growth of design thinking activity across the organization allowed him to recruit two new team members. Among them was Antonin, who was one of the first design thinking pioneers in Thales and had worked as the project coordinator in the ME310 collaboration with Stanford's d.school. The

DC team in Paris had grown to four full-time staff and two design interns.

At this point more than half of the project requests from the business units were related to business or strategic challenges. Mostly these were one of three kinds: (1) turning a product business into a service business, (2) exploring diversification opportunities, and (3) analyzing and developing complete product value propositions.

Didier realized that these challenges were not traditional product designs or development projects like the 6-Watch project had been. These briefs were much more strategic, and they were proposed by the marketing and business development managers of various business units. What became clear was that managers across the organization had increasingly started to consider the DC to address problems or situations that they could not address with traditional innovation tools.

To respond to more strategic briefs, the DC team adapted its approach and enriched the design thinking toolkit with more marketing and strategy tools. Progressively, they established themselves as a center of competence for business model innovation and value proposition design.

But more importantly, the evolution from dealing with product innovation to dealing with strategic innovation was the third inflection point in the development of the initiative. By diversifying the types of projects it would work on, the DC had expanded not only the audience it was serving but also the scope of its activities.

Over the following months, projects, both in size and number, continued to grow to achieve 30 per cent of the overall activity portfolio, the others dedicated to training and workshops (see figure 9.2). This was possible in part because the DC team was able to re-use previous project outcomes such as the 6-Watch to evangelize and create a "snowball effect."

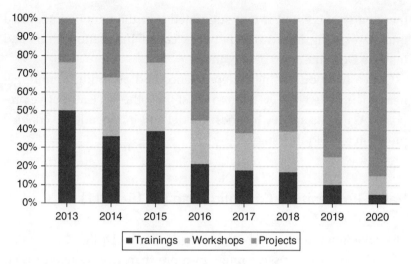

Figure 9.2. Evolution of DC activities

The team seized every opportunity to communicate information about its projects and design-led approach through numerous internal conventions, at conferences and management meetings. Design thinking also became more integrated into Thales leadership programs, where participants were asked to deliver a strategic innovation project over several months using design thinking and using the DC as their base camp. In 2014 and 2015, more than 200 managers went through these programs and practiced design thinking.

In 2015, a sixth DC was launched in Stuttgart. Like previous centers, the new center in Germany operated independently with its own business model. It is interesting to note that most of the new centers were not set up as "agencies" but rather as internal design thinking centers that were fully funded by the business unit to which they belonged.

Also in 2015, the Design Center of Paris won the Thales Innovation Award for customer engagement and, as such, was the first major recognition from the Thales Innovation Directorate. Following these early successes, it was suggested that the DCs be integrated into an existing innovation network called Innovation Hubs and that the Design Center be rebranded.

Concerns about losing independence and adopting a more generic identity led the DC team to resist this otherwise attractive proposal. Again, its agency business model and independence enabled the team to hold that stance.

Value Proposition Consolidation (2016–2017)

Over the first four years of operation, the Thales Design Center staff worked on an impressive range of more than twenty-five projects in its Paris location alone. The projects supported a growing value proposition by diversifying the projects facilitated, including product design, service design, business model design, transformation projects, venture design, and user experience (UX) projects.

The complete project portfolio of the Design Centers spans three key categories: product and service development (30 per cent), business and strategy development (50 per cent), and disruptive technology development (20 per cent). In 2017, projects represented 60 per cent of all the overall DC activities (see figure 9.2). The activity of DC Paris grew eightfold over five years and its team grew from one to six full-time employees (excluding interns).

Overall, the Design Center network counts in 2019 more than forty-five design thinking professionals ranging from strategic designers, industrial designers, UX designers, creative facilitators to engineers mirroring the variety of the projects facilitated. The DC team covers a range of skills and capabilities, meaning the majority fits a true hybrid profile. In 2017 two additional Design Centers were created in Brest, France, and Quebec City, Canada. The first DC in Paris moved into a brand-new facility, which coincided with the move of Thales Corporate University to a new campus and its rebranding to Thales Learning Hub.

The Digital Transformation Boost (2017–2021)

In 2017, Thales significantly accelerated its digital strategy and made several significant investments. It created a Digital Factory composed of more than 250 people in three locations (Paris, Montreal, and Singapore). The Digital Factory has had a profound impact on Thales by accelerating the injection of a new digital culture, technologies, and product development approaches (MVP, entrepreneurship, DevOps, UX, design, data) into the company. The Digital Factory became, in less than two years, a powerhouse for developing new digital products and platforms.

After one year of intense collaboration with the Thales Digital Factory, the Design Center Paris was integrated into the Digital Factory to reinforce its innovation impact and pave the way for great digital products (MVPs). This move has had a considerable impact on the DC profile, which is recognized as being instrumental and strategic in the new digital ecosystem. The collateral effect was the opening of four new Design Centers during this period.

Beyond the Digital Factory, a group-wide digital transformation plan was launched in 2018 that covered seven critical digital work streams. The first of these work streams was fully dedicated to UX design. Recognizing his pivotal role in bringing design-driven innovation into Thales, the company chose Didier to lead this work stream. The scope of the UX design transformation was to cover the entire user-centered continuum from research to innovation, engineering, and services. Consequently, it also included the Design Center Network. Design Centers became de facto instruments and assets in the larger design transformation.

Impact (2012–2021)

After nine years of operation, the thirteen Thales Design Centers have collectively delivered more than 1,000 workshops, supported more than eighty projects, and have trained more than 3,000 managers and engineers. The most successful DC projects have led to new and disruptive solutions for the police, military and civil radar technicians, inflight entertainment, multi-modular drones, Thales employee experience, collaborative consoles, rail traffic management, new vehicle designs, airport security, maritime surveillance, future cities, autonomous systems, and many more. Beyond these achievements, the Design Centers have also become a key platform for attracting design and creative talents into the company.

The Next Chapter (2021–2025)

What will the next five to ten years look like for the Design Centers? Didier considers that two forces will shape the second Design Center decade.

The first one is related to a stronger Design Center Network. The Design Center Network with its thirteen centers must further increase its impact by better tying together its centers, reinforcing their value propositions, developing new global offers (prospective design, strategic foresight), and combining the forces of multiple Design Centers on the same projects. As such, it will represent a unique distribution of innovation capabilities in Thales.

The second force is linked to the Thales digital transformation. This group-wide transformation has triggered a collateral design transformation leading to the creation of Thales Design in 2021 and the appointment of Didier as its first chief design officer.

Thales Design covers the full design spectrum from research and innovation, engineering, customer experience and services. It has the ambition to transform Thales into a design leader in the coming years. Design Centers are, of course, meant to play a pivotal role in that strategy as a platform for design-driven innovation and human-centered design.

Finally, the Design Center Network will most likely continue to grow with (hopefully) more strategic intent, this time mapping the Thales international footprint, strategic accounts, and markets more consistently. And Didier is beginning his journey towards fulfilling his next dream: "Realizing a more profound design revolution within this amazing company."

Lessons Learned

- A low-cost and low-risk "underdog" strategy as well as the positioning of the Design Centers within the Thales Corporate University enabled an independent existence and distancing from a strong technology-bias culture in the Thales research and technology organization.
- The internal consultancy business model was key to preserving the integrity and protecting the early independence of the project. It also enabled the diversification of the activities (projects, workshops, and training) and the types of projects by adapting the design thinking methods to accommodate the different nature of the briefs received (B2B, B2G, techno-driven, business model, etc.). This enabled the DC to show results and outcomes rather than evangelizing and advocating for a method.
- The Design Center "franchise" model was critical to disseminating the DC model to other innovation teams, leveraging a network effect, and achieving a critical mass rather than being the lone design thinking agent lost in a large firm.
- Design Center was a catalyst for projects rather than an owner. The Design Center co-designed with the internal customers (the business unit owner of the project). Therefore, the teams within the business units were active and took part in all the phases of the project (exploration, sense-making, ideation, concepts development, prototyping, and experimentation). They

continued working on the project after the collaboration with the Design Centers ended and were ultimately responsible for the destiny of the design thinking projects explored and their outcomes.

- As the Design Centers are now part of a larger design transformation, it is critical to develop their future positioning in both the innovation ecosystem and design ecosystem. In the Thales case, the notion of Design Continuum allowed positioning various design teams in regards to the product life cycle and the associated design disciplines: design thinking, design research, UX/UI, industrial design, service design.

Timeline

- 2009: Thirty high potential VP-level employees, including the VP strategy, VP professional development, and corporate university general manager, go on a learning expedition and discover design thinking.
- 2012: Start of a three-year partnership and collaboration with the Stanford University d.school ME310 program; Didier Boulet secures a physical space and budget for the Thales Corporate University.
- 2013: Launch of the first Design Center with two employees and two design interns providing agency-like services, including training, workshop facilitation, and innovation projects.
- 2014: Two hundred employees are trained in design thinking, several projects are underway, and regular workshops being offered; Design Centers are now established in Glasgow, Singapore, London, and Bordeaux; franchise model established.
- 2015: Team grows to four employees and two design interns; design thinking is introduced into the leadership program for managers and top executives; Stuttgart Design Center opens.

- 2016: Further growth of project activities; team grows to six employees; two additional Design Centers start in Brest and Quebec City; Design Center of Paris wins the Thales Innovation Award.
- 2017–18: Integration of Design Centers in Thales Factory; now twelve Design Centers worldwide established and forty-five design thinking resources established.
- 2019: A digital transformation plan, including seven work streams, is announced, with one dedicated to user-experience design.

CHAPTER TEN

An Army of One – How One Person Set Off a Grassroots Movement at the US Department of Labor

VIRGINIA HAMILTON AND LISA CARLGREN

In 2014, the **US Department of Labor (DOL)** was tasked with implementing the Workforce Innovation and Opportunity Act (WIOA). At this time, DOL was widely perceived as an agency focused on ensuring compliance with laws, but not the creation of innovative services. But this time a new approach was needed, and a human-centered design (HCD) movement was created from the bottom up. Over time, human centricity became part of the fabric of the new law through guidelines, deliberate communication, and working with internal stakeholders. Other critical factors included building relationships with the right people, communicating wisely, and being somewhat shielded from Washington's bureaucracy. Since 2019, hundreds more workforce professionals have attended in-depth HCD sessions, including training sponsored by state governments around the country. Many of them have used new methods and tools to improve government services. The WIOA now requires government agencies to collaborate, where they have previously been siloed and didn't work together. HCD gave the DOL and many not-for-profit workers a renewed sense of purpose, connection with the government's mission, joy in the workplace, and appreciation for their work.

In 2012, 4.7 million people in the United States had been unemployed for more than six months,[1] and many were coming into government-run American Job Centers (AJCs) for help finding jobs. These older workers were skilled, most had been in the same job for many years, and they didn't know how to look for work. Staff at the AJCs didn't have experience with helping the long-term unemployed and didn't know how to provide the support that was desperately needed.

In July 2014, then US President Barack Obama signed a bipartisan bill called the Workforce Innovation and Opportunity Act (WIOA), which funded Workforce Development Boards that operated over 2,500 AJCs across the United States. The US Department of Labor (DOL) was tasked with implementing the law. Many states and local government agencies perceived DOL as an agency that was focused on ensuring compliance with laws, not the implementation of innovative job services. The usual practice when implementing a new law was to work with lawyers and experts to write and issue regulations, provide guidance to states and local governments, and provide training on the provisions of the law. This situation was different, and some people believed an innovative approach to the implementation of WIOA was needed. This case study will tell you how Virginia Hamilton – the West Coast regional administrator at the DOL – built a human-centered design (HCD) movement, starting as a zero-budget one-woman band.

The **US Department of Labor (DOL)** is a cabinet-level department of the US federal government responsible for occupational safety and health, wage and hour standards, unemployment benefits, reemployment services, and occasionally, economic statistics. The US Secretary of Labor heads the DOL. The department's purpose is to foster, promote, and develop the well-being of the wage earners, job seekers, and retirees of the United States; improve working conditions; advance opportunities for profitable employment; and assure work-related benefits and rights. In carrying out this mission, the DOL applies and enforces more than 180 federal laws and thousands of federal regulations. These mandates and the regulations that implement them cover many workplace activities for about 10 million employers and 125 million workers.

Through a series of carefully planned and serendipitous events, Virginia managed to give implementing agencies both the permission and the tools to experiment. By building relationships with the right people, communicating wisely, and being somewhat shielded from Washington's bureaucracy, she managed to build an HCD movement bottom-up. Since 2019, hundreds more workforce professionals have attended in-depth HCD sessions, including training sponsored by state governments around the country. Many of them have gone on to take other design classes such as advanced human-centered design, prototyping and testing, and design classes from other sources, and have used HCD to improve government services. The consequences of these initiatives are impressive. The WIOA now requires government agencies to collaborate, where they had previously been siloed and did not have to work together. Applying an HCD approach provided agencies with the structure and opportunity to engage with each other. The use of HCD also gave the government and not-for-profit workers a renewed sense of purpose, connection with the government's mission, joy in the workplace, and appreciation for their work.

A Different Demographic That Called for New Mindsets and Tools

Eight months into her new job as head of the San Francisco Regional Office for the US Department of Labor's Employment and Training Administration (ETA), Virginia became aware of a problem that needed solving. She had started reading about how almost anyone who was unemployed for over six months was experiencing discrimination when applying for jobs and was unlikely to find a job quickly. In fact, many didn't succeed in securing new employment for eight months to a year. These people were typically over forty years old and highly skilled, they had stable work histories, but had lost their jobs during the Great Recession.

In her role as a regional administrator, Virginia had oversight of the public workforce system in eight states on the West Coast of the United States, which included federally funded career centers where people who were looking for work came to get help. The typical customer had never worked or had low skill levels and was looking for an entry-level job. The new group of unemployed people who were entering the system was different. Many were desperate; they were living on their savings and their Unemployment Insurance that would run out eventually. Many had expectations that their work experience and skills would be desirable to employers. But they were not finding jobs. Virginia had heard from several colleagues that this new group of customers was coming into the AJCs in unprecedented numbers. No one knew how to help them. While her colleagues at the job centers wanted to improve services to help these long-term unemployed, they didn't have the knowledge, tools, or even the mandate to do things differently. Her agency, like many other government bodies, had often been characterized by a compliance mindset, inhibiting innovation and risk avoidance.

At DOL, regional administrators are responsible for several states across the United States. Their job is to be stewards of the public dollar, to monitor and provide oversight for the state agencies in their geographical area. They are often perceived as the bad guys – states and local government agencies get nervous when DOL monitors visit, look at their files, and write a report of everything that is wrong or not working. Virginia looked upon her role differently: by developing good relationships with people, she hoped that they would ask for help rather than hide. She wondered if she could also empower them and give them the tools to innovate their services.

Early Interactions with IDEO to Try HCD

Before Virginia came to DOL, she had met a designer from IDEO, a global design and innovation company, who was giving a speech before her at a transit conference. She was intrigued with the idea of using HCD as an approach to design services in the workforce arena. In early 2013, she asked her assistant, Diane, to contact the IDEO office in San Francisco to set up a meeting. Six weeks and four meetings later, equipped with $30,000 of technical assistance funding she had in her budget, DOL and IDEO shook hands on a two-week contract to tackle the issue of how to design job seeking and employment services for the long-term unemployed.

IDEO's senior director for public sector work convened a team of designers to do initial research. They talked to directors of workforce programs around the country and interviewed some long-term unemployed. Virginia invited a group of workforce development leaders to attend a two-day design workshop at the San Francisco IDEO office. In April 2013, twenty-five state workforce development leaders from Washington and California, along with local government workforce development directors from both states, showed up at IDEO. Virginia chose people she knew, whom she knew would have an appetite to learn about HCD methods and would be keen to try them out.

During the workshop, participants learned and started to employ HCD methods to find ways to help long-term unemployed get back to work. Specifically, they learned how to observe and interview customers and how to brainstorm and develop "How Might We" questions. Ideas for prototypes emerged from key insights about the emotional state of unemployed people. It turned out that one's emotional state mattered significantly when long-term unemployed came into AJCs. Someone who was about to lose their house or car didn't need to learn how to network or write a résumé. They were panicked and needed money. Those who were panicked were different from those who were discouraged after submitting hundreds of résumés to faceless companies over the Internet. The team concluded that the customer experience needed to be much more personalized and tuned into people's states of mind.

Participants in the workshop were on fire. They were flattered to have been chosen to come to the event, thrilled to be in such an interesting creative physical space that was far different from their own government offices, and they saw the possibility of a new way of thinking about designing services. Local workforce managers developed intriguing prototypes to test, ranging from completely rethinking an office remodel that was about to happen in Washington state, changing the front end of services from a one-size-fits-all orientation workshop to a "speed dating" approach in Sacramento, in which customers had short visits with staff who focused on different needs and triaged their services. People caught the HCD bug and started to think about how to create incentives for their local workforce boards to also learn about HCD and start experimenting.

As a result, the DOL Regional Office used the additional funding to engage IDEO two more times over the course of five months. The second engagement with IDEO in late 2013 focused on improving services to customers in the AJCs in Oregon. Again, Virginia chose sites where she knew the managers and knew they would be open and interested in learning about HCD. A team from IDEO went to Oregon and prototyped small ways to improve customer experience, ranging from new ways to display information about upcoming events, changing signage to make it friendlier, using a set of visual cards to describe barriers to getting jobs, and many more (see figure 10.1).

One small example is that customers used to get a schedule of workshops that were provided only on the day they came to the center. They prototyped a large calendar that was placed on the wall and that displayed workshops for the whole month, so customers could better schedule attending workshops at times that were more convenient for them. They took pictures and developed a compelling slide deck to describe their work and the benefits that came from it. They learned that every small detail sends a message to customers, and that added together, the customer felt like they were treated with dignity and respect. In turn, those customers felt more confident in the likelihood that this professional agency could provide the help they needed.

From Auditing to Giving Permission to Experiment

The IDEO workshops and mini-projects were significant in the sense that Virginia, as the DOL regional administrator, was giving people permission and encouragement to innovate. For decades, DOL had been perceived as a regulator; an oversight agency that was focused on compliance and auditing, ensuring states and locals were following the rules of the law. It was a far cry from catalyzing new ways of thinking and experimentation. Many state and local government workers were skeptical, saying things like, "This is all well and good, but what about when the auditors come?" It turned out that public permission to take risks was an important component of scaling HCD. Here, Virginia describes one action she took

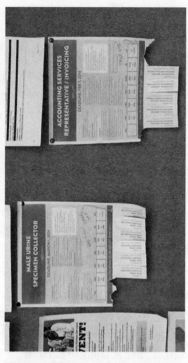

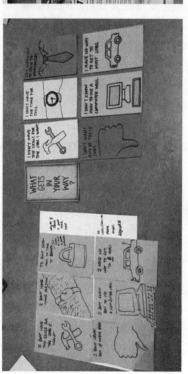

Figure 10.1. Examples of project outputs

in this regard: "Of course, you don't experiment with fiscal systems and of course we want to make sure organizations are following the law. But at one large workforce conference, I came out from behind the podium and said 'My name is Virginia Hamilton. I am a regional administrator for the US DOL. You have my permission to experiment with customer experience.' People literally stood up and clapped their hands; it gave them agency."

This change in attitude became a key component in shifting mindsets over the next three years. But it wasn't only the mindsets of AJC employees that needed to be shifted. At one point, the senior director for IDEO's public sector practice wanted to talk to senior DOL leaders in DC. Virginia asked them not to. Since her grassroots bottom-up initiative wasn't sponsored politically, she did not want to risk being able to do the work she believed mattered most: focusing on customers to improve services. Working in San Francisco was far enough from DC headquarters so that she could launch small projects using a little funding without headquarter scrutiny. She had realized that being far away from central power allowed her to keep projects "under the radar" until there was sufficient interest, buy-in, and success stories to tell.

Getting Buy-In from the New Secretary of Labor

In July 2013, President Barack Obama appointed Tom Perez as the new Secretary of Labor. From the beginning, Tom was a strong advocate for DOL's mission to help people learn skills and get jobs. He traveled around the country meeting people, visiting AJCs and job training programs, and increasing the visibility of the public workforce system to policymakers, elected officials, and members of Congress. Something that truly supported the rise of HCD from a small pilot to a national initiative was the confidence and support that Virginia gained from the secretary.

Tom's first trip as a DOL secretary was to visit an AJC in Nevada. Virginia helped to set up the visit. Like every other secretary, Tom had several loyal, political appointees. One of the secretary's representatives was Elmy; she and Virginia had become acquainted and whenever the secretary went to places within the region, Elmy would get Virginia invited. Virginia recalls, "Eventually the secretary got to know me and used to ask me to get in the car with him. He'd ask me questions and I gave him honest answers, for example on the effectiveness of the existing tools, which actually did not work very well." Appreciating her frankness, the secretary started to ask that Virginia accompany him on other visits. On one of these occasions, she gave Tom a handwritten note summarizing her views on the DOL's current state and desired future state. She also proposed three ways to get there, one of which was training people in HCD across government agencies. Tom was impressed that she did not come with a problem but analysis and a possible solution. He loved the idea, which gave Virginia huge (lower case p) political cover to work on this initiative without getting redirected back to oversight work by her own agency. She notes, "I was someone he thought was doing good work, which helped me get introduced to the White House. A regional administrator normally wouldn't be going to the White House – but with this relationship, it happened."

Piggybacking a New Law and Making Design Thinking Part of the Fabric

When the WIOA was enacted, Virginia saw the law, with the words "innovation" and "opportunity" in the title, as the perfect pretext to spread innovation methods, including HCD. She used it to legitimize the work she had done and make people take innovation seriously. Implementing a new law is hard enough for federal agencies and focusing on innovation would take time and resources. She argued that unless the DOL did something new and different in the implementation of the law, it would be nothing more than a minor tweak of the old law, and the "innovation" part of WIOA would never be realized. "I used it," she said, "to legitimize, to take innovation seriously so that my home agency couldn't tell me that innovation wasn't important. Without it, it would have been much harder, but now I was able to piggyback on it."

Virginia's office, along with five others around the country, were on the front lines of implementing the WIOA. Implementation of the new law had to be done by states, local government agencies, and nonprofits. The DOL had very little direct line authority over the process. Regional administrators worked directly with the states and local government agencies that had responsibility for implementation, and Virginia knew many key players had the appetite and willingness to try new things.

While the law helped legitimize the work, Virginia also realized that if she played it smart, she had the opportunity to make HCD part of the very fabric of how people looked at the WIOA. Once a law is passed by Congress, federal agencies in charge of its implementation write regulations. It was a big roll-out, and many federal agencies and staff were involved in the writing. During this period, Virginia did her best to add certain phrases into the regulations like "customer in the center" and "customer focus."

As the regional administrator, she was often asked to give speeches about all the new provisions of the WIOA, throughout her eight-state region. These speeches were given to administrators at the workforce development, adult education, welfare, food stamps, and other agencies and proved to be a great opportunity to gain interest and momentum for using HCD. Virginia would talk about the topic she was supposed to talk about for no more than ten minutes before she would pivot her speech to talk about HCD and how it was sparking innovation, improving relationships among local partner agencies, and bringing energy to the implementation of the WIOA. The documentation and photos from the early IDEO workshops and projects became important to draw people into understanding the experience of using HCD methods to innovate services.

At the same time, Tom was concerned about the annual employee survey of federal agencies. For the innovation and leadership categories, the DOL ranked only seventeen out of eighteen large federal agencies. The secretary created a task force to work on improving the organization in these areas. Around the same time, Virginia went to DC to teach a course in participatory facilitation. While there, she was asked to facilitate high-stakes meetings for the secretary's office. Given the success of these meetings, eventually one of the secretary's deputies asked her to spend 25 per cent of her time working for his office to assist with the improvement of innovation and leadership throughout the agency. Deputy Secretary Lu and others in the office loved the idea of using HCD to implement the WIOA. Now, Virginia was able to raise awareness about HCD at a whole new level and it was well-received throughout the organization. For example, she included several slides about HCD and "How Might We" questions when facilitating the secretary's senior leadership retreat for DOL.

Creating a Series of Challenge-Based Training: Round One and Round Two

By May 2015, Virginia had an opportunity to meet with appointees in the White House Office of Science and Technology Policy (OSTP) who were particularly interested in encouraging innovation at federal government levels. After they learned about her efforts of implementing HCD on the West Coast, and her success with the implementation of the WIOA, people got very excited and offered to help. Virginia had recently discovered a free seven-week online HCD class sponsored by IDEO and +Acumen and was thinking about ways she could create incentives for workforce professionals around the country to take the class.

In May 2015, she wrote an email to the OSTP officials:

> The main idea, and I may have mentioned this in our meeting, is to get our states and local governments to use human-centered design to implement the provisions of the law as a real opportunity (innovation and opportunity act, after all) rather than trying to do as little as possible to comply with the law and regulations.
>
> It seems like we have several issues in making this work. The first is just convincing people that this is important and will produce better customer experiences and outcomes and is worth the time that it will take. The second is getting people to stick to it – in the face of upper managers wanting to just get it done and having some perceived big bonus at the end. That's where you come in. By building in your presence at the launch webinar – just to say you are interested and this is important, and then at the end, with a Learning Exchange (or call it something cooler) at the White House, I think I have solved both of those problems. It is a huge coup to be acknowledged by the WH.

The online class seemed like the perfect way to scale teaching across the country, but it was very time-consuming, and to do it well, it would take the commitment of workforce agency employees and their community partners. The excitement in the White House, coupled with some brainstorming about how to use real-world challenges, led to the creation of Round One – a competition in which the winning teams were invited to the White House for a Celebration and Learning Exchange.

Several key leaders in the Employment and Training Administration (ETA) in DC were starting to see the value in HCD, including Assistant Secretary Portia Wu. She authorized the use of $200,000 to hire coaches who helped teams take the online class and complete applications for the White House Celebration and Learning Exchange. The coaches were consultants who knew workforce development and were already doing work for DOL. They didn't know anything about HCD but were a group of willing learners, who committed to taking the HCD class along with the local teams and would go on to play an important role in the initiative. Their coaching kept teams motivated, connected to each other, and participating in the training.

Only two months later, in July 2015, DOL launched the first webinar that introduced HCD concepts, gave examples of local innovation, issued three challenges, and announced the prize of going to the White House. Virginia had invited two key champions – Dan Correa and Jake Brewer – from the OSTP to participate in the webinar. This was to demonstrate the interest of the White House and confirm that the prize of going to the White House was legitimate. The audience for a DOL webinar typically ranged from 50 to 100 people. Over 800 people signed up to watch this webinar in real-time, and by the end of the next couple of months, there were over 10,000 viewings of the recorded webinar.

Virginia had been working with the coaches to set up schedules and resources for supporting teams that were going to sign up. Everyone thought that there would be no more than twelve teams willing to commit to quite a rigorous schedule over seven weeks. But to everyone's surprise, eighty teams signed up to take the class. The coaches were in touch with all the teams every week providing support and cheerleading, issuing electronic badges to teams that were very creative, or completing their homework on time, or sharing their stories with other teams. Using coaches was a surprisingly successful way of keeping participants motivated and engaged.

By November 2015, Virginia and a small team of ETA managers in DC selected ten teams to visit the White House in February 2016. Megan Smith, head of President Barack Obama's Technology Office, and other White House dignitaries attended, gave speeches, and listened to the stories of the new HCD converts. Participants were excited to be at the White House but equally thrilled to meet each other, tell stories, and share information about their projects.

By March 2016, enthusiasm had grown even further, and stories of the White House event had spread across state and local government agencies. Virginia had now gathered more than fifty success stories about using HCD to improve government services. She had also given a keynote speech at a major DOL-sponsored conference in January, where teams of workforce leaders from every state listened to local champions talk about the enthusiasm of staff and managers in system redesign. She launched Round Two of the Customer Centered Design initiative, and this time, 120 teams from around the country signed up to participate.

Additionally, Code for America, a well-respected innovative tech startup (focused on using technology for government to work better for people who need it most), had found out what they were doing and signed up to help on the project. Code for America gave webinars, convened teams, and focused attention on this initiative at its annual summit. Because Code for America had such a good brand, and provided pro bono staff to work with DOL, its participation gave the initiative more cachet and support from the White House.

By September 2016, it was time for a second celebration at the White House, and this time fifteen teams were selected: again, a resounding success. Apart from the celebration at the White House, teams were invited to an event at DOL where they told their stories to staff who were not ordinarily in contact with people at the front lines of service delivery. The idea was to use the excitement and energy of the teams to demonstrate to administrators how powerful the HCD methods were in making services better and moving forward in an engaging way to implement the WIOA.

Implementation Phase: Spreading the Methods

Between the launch of Rounds One and Two between July 2015 and October 2016, some other state administrations got engaged in the process. California began by investing $500,000 of the governor's workforce funding in both, supporting the teams who participated in Round One by providing resources to implement their prototypes, and in supporting participation in Round Two. A series of Accelerator Grants were established. These were small grants to be used to experiment with new ideas and services. The mindset that these grants were aiming to instill was aligned with HCD in that they promoted "trying something and, if it doesn't work, you have learned something. Take a risk."

The State of Washington, too, invested in HCD by funding the enrollment of almost 900 state workforce professionals in a two-day HCD class taught by the Luma Institute. The Luma Institute has trained people in over seventy-eight countries, with the mission of helping everyone to start thinking and working like a designer so they can solve problems faster, with better results. With a new mindset, knowledge, and tools, these staff started redesigning services for their customers across the state. Within eight months, the state agency redesigned the way Unemployment Insurance claimants learn about and receive services to get them back to work more quickly. The take-up rates had been low, despite penalties if people didn't show up at the AJCs, but after the redesign, people who weren't required to participate were lobbying to get into the program.

At this point, there were close to thirty local teams across the country that were very successful in using HCD. They began to give their own workshops at conferences and to spread the word with their colleagues in industry association meetings and other events. The initiative was now well underway, and Virginia continued to evangelize wherever she could – presenting keynote speeches at conferences, facilitating workshops, and holding meetings with other agencies.

As more and more people began to implement HCD, Virginia was approached at every meeting and conference she attended by people saying the same thing over and over: learning and practicing HCD was reconnecting people to the passion they had for their work, which they had lost along the way. One AJC manager from Wisconsin wrote her an email in 2016 and said: "I was so focused on paperwork and data systems and administrative work that I forgot that I came to this job because I wanted to help people. HCD put me back in contact with our customers, and now I love my job again." Virginia heard this same sentiment everywhere she went; new staff engagement, renewed energy, and a reminder of their mission.

Examples of how HCD was being used ranged far and wide. In Denver, Colorado, they rebranded their programs for out-of-school youth after spending time listening to the young people they were targeting. They learned that twenty-two-year-olds don't want to go to a "Youth Program." The Workforce Development Board in Santa Barbara, California, told DOL staff that they used HCD to redesign what happens when formerly incarcerated people leave jail and begin looking for jobs. They learned that many people in these circumstances go back into old environments and use drugs. One of their insights was that if people leaving jail had Narcan, the drug that can reverse an overdose, they could help save lives. The State of California gave them a grant to buy Narcan to include in the kits they received when leaving jail. In Long Beach, California, they redesigned the physical space so homeless job seekers had a safe place to leave their belongings while they talked to career advisors.

From Experimentation to Scaling: Round Three and Round Four

Round Three was launched in February 2017, but by now the political landscape had radically changed. The new President, Donald Trump, and his administration had moved into the White House, there was no longer a Secretary of Labor, and most federal agencies were being run by career leadership.[2] Innovation at DOL had become a very low priority for the new administration, and career staff,[3] including Virginia, no longer had access to political appointees at the White House. Therefore, the incentive of being invited to the White House for winning teams no longer existed. However, instead, a Learning Exchange at the DOL was proposed. Twenty teams signed up for Round Three. This was a clear signal that the Obama White House incentive had been powerful. Rushed for time, Round Four was launched soon thereafter, with another twenty teams signing up.

Throughout the spring of 2017, Virginia gave keynote speeches on HCD at three DOL regional convenings where she had local practitioners tell their stories. This led to state leadership expressing interest in designing projects that would allow state-level teams to participate.

In October 2017, the combined winners of Rounds Three and Four were invited to the DOL for the Learning Exchange event. At this event, Virginia wanted to reach people at a policy level of the DOL. Therefore, policy staff attended the event to listen to each team giving a short presentation of their work. During deep-dive sessions, they also gained a good understanding of how HCD had changed service delivery and could make connections back to the policy work they were engaged in.

Looking Back and Ahead

By 2018, over 2,000 workforce development professionals had participated in HCD training. Many of them have gone on to take other classes and use HCD to improve services for the unemployed, those coming out of the criminal justice system, and others who needed help in getting skills and jobs. Local government agencies and nonprofits developed new ways of working with the business community to help them find and keep skilled workers. There is anecdotal evidence that outcomes for customers were improving, which implementers hoped to quantify through more rigorous evaluation. Virginia said she got a phone call in March 2019 from one of her former staff who said, "If you had any doubt you made a difference, stop doubting! I went to a job office that used to be a hell hole. I walked in – it looked beautiful, the staff was enthusiastic, they treated people well, and they were super excited to contribute to reinventing services."

There continues to be an interest and appetite from local workforce boards and AJCs to participate in the online HCD class. Although Virginia believes that the White House was initially a necessary ingredient as an incentive for this initiative, there is now enough widespread knowledge about how using HCD can improve services and bring energy to local partnerships, and people want to learn and participate without this incentive.

Many American states are now interested in bringing in capacity-building opportunities for their staff so they can learn HCD. Other states want to use HCD to launch statewide projects with both state and local workforce agencies and their partners. For example, the governor of Indiana has developed a customer-focused state workforce plan by bringing in personas to the state's planning process, reminding them of who they were planning for. In Michigan, the City of Detroit has been using HCD to redesign its entire workforce system. Further, North Carolina funded three local workforce boards to redesign services in its AJCs. The National Governors Association sponsored several workshops at its annual meetings in 2019 and 2020 that were focused on how to use HCD to develop policies. The list goes on.

Some unintended consequences are equally significant. The WIOA required partnerships between government agencies, which are typically siloed and don't work together. Using HCD gave partners a structured approach and an opportunity to engage with each other to figure out how to work together, and not because the law says so. They have been partnering because they have a shared vision of the ways they can best serve their customers. Most unexpectedly, HCD gave the government agencies and nonprofit workers a new sense of purpose; a reconnection to the mission of their organization; and renewed energy, fun, and appreciation for their work. The project participants were delighted with the reconnection to the love of the work, and the true and authentic partnerships that were built.

Everything that HCD embodies – experimentation, taking risks, not knowing, being comfortable with ambiguity – all these features are difficult, uncomfortable, and usually impossible in most government organizations. By their nature, bureaucracies strive for consistent, risk-averse, and stable working conditions. And DOL, whose mission is in part to oversee laws, has a strong culture and mindset of compliance. But Virginia was able to do what she did despite how the DOL was perceived by the public and other government agencies, and doing so by working within the culture of DOL. According to Virginia, using HCD is the right way to accomplish the mission of workforce organizations – to help people find skills and jobs, and to help employers find the talent they need. HCD helps by understanding what those customers' needs and motivations are and by encouraging them to achieve their own goals. "Using HCD," she says, "is carrying out the work in the organization in a better way. It's really a virtuous cycle."

What started as a small snowball, pushed by Virginia, is growing in size and is definitely in motion. The spread of HCD has gained such traction and legitimacy that the movement seems unstoppable, pushed forward by an ever-growing army of enthusiastic employees and managers convinced of the benefits of the HCD approach. Virginia keeps getting signals from the grassroots, with constant updates and testimonials of projects that have had a large impact on the lives of fellow Americans and, in some instances, even saving lives.

Virginia left DOL at the end of 2017. In her consulting practice, she continues to be an evangelist for HCD. She has worked with several cities, states, local workforce boards, the National Governors Association, and non-profit organizations to help build their capacity to use HCD to redesign programs, services, and policies. She has also been working to build HCD into adult education programs in California. In December 2019, one of the Detroit Design team members with whom she is working sent her an email that said, "Why would we ever design a new program, remodel office space, or think about new marketing materials without having customers in the room to design with us?"

Lessons Learned

- Giving government agencies explicit permission to experiment and redesign services to customers was a key in scaling innovation.
- Leveraging personal relationships with people in decision-making positions in state and local governments created an immediate group of champions and willing implementers.
- Deliberately seeking reduced visibility to avoid scrutiny from headquarters before the initiative was anchored politically was a good step. Being far from central power and keeping projects under the radar until there was sufficient interest, buy-in, and stories to take public was done by using informal ways of communicating, voluntarism, and creative use of existing funds that gave the freedom to explore.
- Interpreting HCD as the way to enact a new law provided legitimacy and internal support. HCD was made part of the fabric of that law through written guidelines, deliberate communications, and working internals to get support. Planned events to communicate about the new law were piggybacked to spread knowledge about HCD.
- Online courses lowered the barriers to entry and learning. Once employees engaged in course projects, they fell in love with the

methodology that secured further use and helped the snowball gain momentum.

- At the very beginning, the combination of a challenge structure and the incentive of a potential visit to the Obama White House was enough to generate surprisingly substantial participation. With a later change in administration, the incentive was lost but a movement had already been created, and internal examples were enough to create interest and spread.
- Having someone who was obsessed with HCD and uses every opportunity to talk about it and tell stories, capitalized on personal relationships with people who had influence and who took on HCD implementation at scale as her mission was key to the success of this initiative.

Timeline

- 2013: Virginia Hamilton contacted IDEO followed by a joint design session and works with IDEO in Oregon; Tom Perez becomes Secretary of Labor in the Obama administration.
- 2014: The WIOA signed into law by President Obama.
- 2015: Virginia meets with staff in the White House; DOL launches first HCD challenge webinar; eleven teams selected to visit White House; Virginia speaks at a DOL-sponsored conference about HCD; White House hosts first Learning Exchange and Celebration.
- 2016: DOL launches second HCD challenge webinar; White House hosts second Learning Exchange and Celebration.
- 2017: DOL launches third and fourth HCD challenge webinar; Virginia speaks at three DOL regional conferences about HCD; DOL hosts Learning Exchange and Celebration.

CHAPTER ELEVEN

Veteran-Centered Healthcare – Navigating Change at the US Department of Veterans Affairs

AARON STIENSTRA, AMBER SCHLEUNING,
VERONICA X. VELA, AND JARYN MILLER

At the **US Department of Veterans Affairs (VA)**, design thinking evolved in a large governmental healthcare organization. It began with the establishment of the Veterans Affairs Center for Innovation and the Veterans Experience Office. Both units invested substantial resources in user research to develop a deeper understanding of veterans' experiences with current services and operations. This research proved invaluable when working on issues like mental health services for veterans. In addition, the department introduced new forms of collaboration with the Office of Personnel and Management, and it managed to overcome the resistance to change that is so typical for large government organizations. The team realized a human-centered approach in an environment where substantial high-level political forces are at work.

This is a story about how the US Department of Veterans Affairs (VA) adopted design thinking to build better services, care, and experiences for the people it serves. It is also a story about how design thinking spurred a culture change from one that is system-centered to one that is user-centered. And finally, it is a story about innovators and designers at VA who have managed to stay the course amid tides of change. The story will primarily follow two organizations within VA that led design thinking efforts starting in 2010 and continues to this day.

Every presidential administration change carries a shift in priorities and strategies across the federal government. Shortly after January 2017, VA embodied these shifts. At the time, many people in VA were familiar with the concepts of design thinking and human-centered design (HCD). This was the result of successful projects and exemplary work practices. They had a positive impact on veterans, VA employees, and the VA culture at large. In the previous administration, many in leadership, including the VA's secretary, the head of the agency, saw the benefits of design-led practices and supported them. Some of this support carried forward into 2017. At the same time, a new perspective emerged that questioned previous approaches to select and adapt them to new priorities as well as a new political landscape.

The **US Department of Veterans Affairs (VA)** is a cabinet-level executive branch department of the federal government charged with integrating life-long healthcare services to eligible military veterans at the 1,700 VA medical centers and outpatient clinics located throughout the United States. Non-healthcare benefits include disability compensation, vocational rehabilitation, education assistance, home loans, and life insurance; benefits also provide burial and memorial services for eligible veterans and family members at 135 national cemeteries. As of 2020, the VA employs 412,892 people at hundreds of Veterans Affairs medical facilities,

clinics, benefits offices, and cemeteries. In 2016 net program costs for the department were US$273 billion. The
agency is led by the secretary of Veterans Affairs, who, as a
cabinet member, is selected by the US President.

VA Is Massive and Complex

The Department of Veteran Affairs serves 9 million customers out
of a population of 20 million veterans. It is the federal agency with
the second-largest budget (US$180 billion in 2017) after the Depart-
ment of Defense. The agency has approximately 400,000 employees.
VA's primary service is healthcare for veterans and family members.
The Veterans Health Administration (VHA) provides care at more
than 1,200 facilities across the nation. VHA is the largest integrated
healthcare system in the United States and is often regarded as the
most complex. It must be responsive to battlefield injuries as well
as changing healthcare needs of an aging population of veterans. It
must also offer care everywhere veterans live. This broad responsibility and the bureaucracy of a government agency complicates
service design and execution. Gaps in processes, training, or culture can prevent employees from delivering excellent service. VA
employees often perceive this complexity as a system that does not
work for or with them. As a result of these challenges, the system
may not always work to the benefit of veterans. Bureaucracy and
"red tape" can often win out.

Prior to 2014, VA healthcare was systems-centered and rules-
based and thus employees were often risk-averse. This culture bred
unproductive behaviors within the system that led to fateful consequences for veterans. However, within these challenges, there was
an opportunity for VA leaders to work with fellow staff, veterans,
advocates, and a larger healthcare community to improve and raise

the standard of care. Leaders at VA viewed design as a novel approach to address new and ongoing challenges in service and use design where it mattered most.

Design Where It Matters Most

At VA, design thinking is often referred to as human-centered design (HCD). The purpose and approach are the same. The adopted term puts people first and it aligns with the agency's ethos. The human-centered mindset and approach matter most in areas where people are sensitive and vulnerable. Healthcare is one such area.

A Human Story and Motivation

Army Sergeant Brenda Reed was twenty-two years old when she joined the military and participated in the Army's first coed basic training class.[1] Like all soldiers who joined in the 1970s, the Army issued Reed standard men's combat boots.[2] Shortly after enlisting and while serving in Germany, she injured her foot and sought treatment by a provider on base.[3] She reported that the military provider dismissed her injury, advising her to "shake it off." After an additional three months of severe pain, she received an X-ray, which revealed that her foot was broken in four places.

Reed's initial fractures would result in a series of recurring injuries that would lead to a foot amputation thirty-five years later at a VA Medical Center (VAMC). While the initial surgery was a success, the oversized prosthesis Reed received from VA was woefully inadequate. Like the combat boots Reed used over thirty years ago, the prosthesis she received did not fit into her shoes. To address the ill-fitting limb, Reed's provider cut off the toes of her prosthetic to allow the artificial limb to fit into her shoe. Reed spent the next two and a half years demanding a well-fitting prosthesis. After repeatedly contacting the secretary of VA, Reed finally received a prosthesis designed for women from the VAMC in Tampa, Florida.

While Reed's injury and her experiences seeking care represent one journey in the military and her subsequent care from VA, it illustrates the limited capacity and attunement of VA to meet the healthcare needs of the veterans they serve. Reed spent a great deal of time and energy and elevated her issue to the highest level of decision-making authority in VA, the agency's secretary, to receive a prosthetic suitable for her injury and body. Stories like Reed's demonstrate the urgency for VA to reorient its care around the needs of its patients.

A First Attempt in Patient-Centered Healthcare

Patient-centered healthcare is a holistic approach to healthcare, where the patient is actively involved in the care provided and the system orients its service around patient needs. Kaiser Permanente started adopting a patient-centered care approach in the mid-1980s.[4] In 2010, VA began infusing patient-centered care through the design of the patient-centered medical home (PCMH). However, enterprise changes in a big, bureaucratic system, such as healthcare at VA, happen slowly, if at all. To support the transition to patient-centeredness, the national office allocated funding for local VA healthcare systems to implement medical homes. However, local systems were not held accountable for how they used the funds. Thus, a shift to patient-centeredness was optional and not implemented universally across all VA healthcare systems. The concept was there, but it failed to catch on without consistent strategic direction.

Design as a Way to Innovate

An early sign of VA's integration of design was a focus on innovation. In late 2010, VA Secretary Eric Shinseki and one of his senior advisors set out to develop an initiative that would foster improvements through innovation. This was an early example of VA leadership recognizing a design-related approach and supporting it as a strategy.

The initial effort, the VA Innovation Initiative (VAi2), explored what it meant to be innovative in the federal government; the small team invested in promising ideas for enabling healthful lives for veterans. After two years, this initiative became the standing VA Center for Innovation (VACI) and its operating model continued to mature.

In 2013, the VACI's deputy director, a military veteran who served in Iraq, led the center to expound upon the stories she heard from fellow veterans about their struggles engaging with the VA system. To do so, she created an exploratory team and placed at the helm a service designer from the Presidential Innovation Fellows program. Next, she directed the group to investigate the misalignment of VA intent and veteran satisfaction through the application of HCD.

The team developed two main goals for the effort: (1) pilot design research methods within VA to gauge feasibility and opportunities to scale, and (2) identify high-level user needs and characterize trends in veterans' experiences interacting with VA as a start for designing more effective services.

In early 2014, the team began the investigation and traveled across the country, interviewing veterans in the context of their lives. They recruited participants through personal networks, local businesses, and chapter offices of Veterans of Foreign Wars (VFW), American Legion Halls, and Team Red White and Blue. They spoke with veterans in their homes, coffee shops, and workplaces to better understand their values, beliefs, and needs. This approach generated deep qualitative insights that gave VA a more holistic understanding of its primary customers. The effort catalyzed a perspective shift that would spread across the department from one that prioritizes the system to one that focuses on customer needs.

While VACI explored how HCD could improve services, VA endured a high-profile scandal at VA medical centers that broke the trust between VA and veterans, their families, and the American public.

In 2014, over forty veterans died waiting for care at the VA in Phoenix, Arizona.[5] Investigations by the VA inspector general revealed widespread neglect of veterans waiting for medical care across the country. It found that employees at all levels manipulated the scheduling system. They adjusted appointments to make it appear that veterans were seen promptly, when in fact they were languishing without care.

VA Rises from Phoenix

In response to VA's neglect, Congress established an independent group to assess VA's ability to meet the health needs of veterans.[6] It found that administrative silos, isolated views of problems, and an unnecessarily complex health system made it difficult to prioritize issues and align actions and resources. Eric Shinseki accepted responsibility for the scandal and resigned as secretary. Shortly after, Congress confirmed the President's selection for the next secretary of VA, former CEO for Procter & Gamble, Bob McDonald. He pledged to rebuild integrity and trust in VA. He promised that veterans would inform how VA delivers benefits and healthcare services.[7] Secretary McDonald developed twelve breakthrough agency priorities, with the first one to improve the veterans' experiences. Among the first major actions in 2014, was hiring a chief veterans experience officer and establishing the Veterans Experience Office

(VEO)[8] to follow through on his promise. VA's response to the scandal demonstrated a posture to react and respond to a challenge with a vision for change and a strategy to get there. Based on his experience at P&G, McDonald envisioned that customer experience would play a key role in this strategy.

Be Number One in Customer Experience

The VACI continued to operate and mature in the healthcare space at VA. Separately, it supplied the newly formed VEO with its initial research findings.[9] It also gave the VEO two Presidential Innovation Fellows, originally assigned to VACI. The fellows were experienced in HCD and had participated in VACI's listening tours. In 2015, these two individuals became founding members of the Veterans Experience Office, and worked with VEO's chief experience officer and team to set directions for the office.

Building off McDonald's promise, the inaugural goal of VEO was to be the number one customer experience office in the federal government. To start, VEO conducted a broad qualitative research project to gain a picture of veterans' life journeys. The project would explore veterans' situations, needs, behaviors, and aspirations. One of the key artifacts from that work, the Journey of Veterans Map, became transformational for the office and for VA. It represented a shift in viewpoint from being system-centered to being user-centered. Designers used the map in discovery and prototyping workshops. VEO leadership shared the map with VA's secretary and other elected officials. For the first time, internal and external individuals, departments, and organizations had a bird's-eye view of veterans' life stages and needs and the corresponding VA supports in place to meet those needs. Veterans saw elements of their own journey in the map; it communicated empathy and helped build trust in the VA. The map quickly became emblematic for a new perspective on veterans' experiences. The map also earned credibility for VEO and its HCD approach.

A Human Capital Experiment

Encouraged by the results of the Journey of Veterans Map and with new demands for design-led research and problem solving, VEO established a design team, called Insight and Design. The design manager wanted to quickly hire talented designers to build the team. However, the new organization did not have an internal process for recruiting, hiring, and onboarding designers. After a year of investigating internal options, the director of the Insight and Design team decided to explore other avenues. She developed a partnership with the Office of Personnel and Management (OPM). The interagency partnership established an experimental fellowship that allowed VEO to bring on ten designers from the private sector. The Human Innovation Fellowship (HIF) gave designers a two to four term to work with VA through OPM's Innovation Lab. The partnership was itself innovative and exploratory. The Lab's managing director called it a human capital experiment. The Insight and Design team was staffed with HIF fellows by August of 2016.

This time was a high point in design-led approaches at VA. The work product and positive impact on veterans and VA employees started to validate the approach. Leadership was excited by it and they were open and eager to see more of it. VACI and VEO were two organizations that helped pioneer and promote a human- and veterans-centered approach to the design of VA services and products. There were others. Innovators and doers from within the VA Digital Services team, Chief Technology Office, Veterans Engineering Resource Center (VERC), VA Innovators Network, and Diffusion of Excellence are some of the key groups who used HCD to address the challenges that both veterans and VA employees faced.

Move Fast and Make Things

"If you're seeing a veteran, nine times out of ten it's because they have to. We want to get to them before a crisis."

– VA mental healthcare provider

One of the key themes in earlier research that also received growing attention was veterans' mental healthcare. In response, the VA Center for Innovation initiated an in-depth effort to map veterans' experiences in early 2016. As shown in figure 11.2, veterans undertake a broad journey when seeking mental healthcare. The team aimed to focus their efforts on two major phases of the journey: Turning Point and Seeking Care. The investigation focused on veterans and their attempts to access behavioral health services. The team partnered with VA mental health teams and an external service design team to deepen the VA's understanding of this unique subset of veterans.

Employing HCD methods, they spoke with healthcare and nonprofit providers, academics, and, importantly, family members and supporters. They accessed openly available quantitative VA data regarding the prevalence of mental healthcare use, suicide statistics, and veteran populations across geographies to determine where they would go to conduct interviews. Recruiting was much more difficult than previous efforts had been, given the sensitive subject matter and associated stigma; the team relied heavily on veteran networks, local VA clinics, local government veteran offices, and in-person drop-ins at the Veteran Service Organization (VSO) chapter offices and lodges.[10]

Synthesized data from the interviews enabled VA teams at headquarters and in hospitals across the country to co-develop prototypes of operational innovation. The teams tested prototypes within the context of VA processes and policies and documented where the innovations bumped up against existing regulations and habits of

MILITARY SERVICE	TURNING POINT	SEEKING CARE	GETTING CARE
HOW DOES MILITARY SERVICE SHAPE PEOPLE'S PERCEPTIONS OF MENTAL HEALTHCARE AND THEIR PATHWAYS TO SEEKING IT?	WHAT CAUSES THE TURNING POINT WHERE PEOPLE DECIDE TO GET MENTAL HEALTHCARE?	WHAT HAPPENS WHEN PEOPLE SEEK MENTAL HEALTHCARE FROM THE VA OR OTHER PROVIDERS?	HOW DOES THE NATURE OF SOMEONE'S TURNING POINT AND PATHWAY TO CARE INFLUENCE THEIR EXPERIENCE RECEIVING CARE?

Figure 11.1. Veterans' journey in seeking mental healthcare

process. They advocated for changes to those deemed archaic or counterproductive.

Each co-designed prototype became an in-depth project unto itself, requiring significant time, planning, and resources. The VACI team partnered externally to invite outside perspectives. One such project, "Space Standards," leaned on bright graduate students from the New York University Wagner School of Public Policy. The students were tasked with thinking about how to alter existing physical space to improve uptake of mental healthcare services. In another effort, the VA Innovators Network (a collection of innovators at VA medical centers across the country) ran a Design-A-Thon to redesign a post-traumatic stress disorder (PTSD) disability claims form (VA Form 21-0781) to one that felt respectful and non-triggering (see figure 11.2).

A partnership between the VACI's lead designer and a psychologist from the VA hospital in Jackson, Mississippi, led to the pilot of a universal symbol that sought to help veterans navigate complex clinical settings and keep non-emergent patients out of the Emergency Room.

These efforts were developed using HCD methods to improve appropriate access to mental healthcare at VA so that it is meaningful to veterans and their families. Mental healthcare is an issue that many VA employees continue to tackle. While VACI was leading HCD

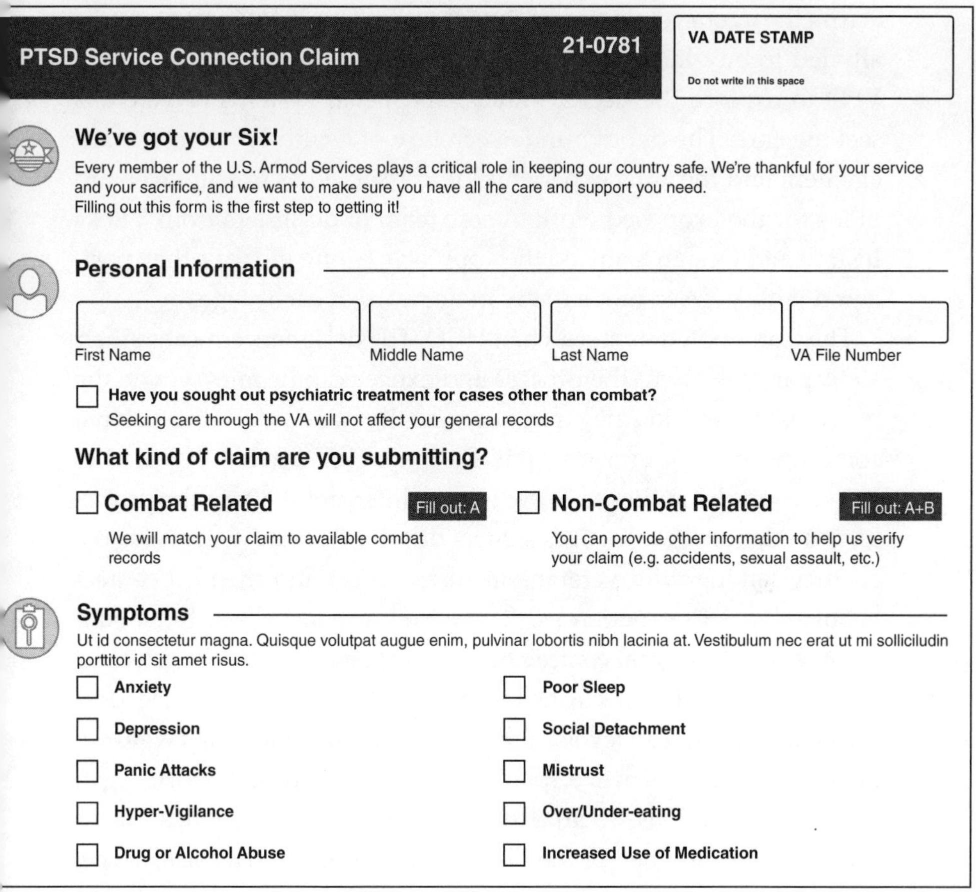

PTSD Service Connection Claim 21-0781

VA DATE STAMP
Do not write in this space

We've got your Six!

Every member of the U.S. Armod Services plays a critical role in keeping our country safe. We're thankful for your service and your sacrifice, and we want to make sure you have all the care and support you need.
Filling out this form is the first step to getting it!

Personal Information

First Name | Middle Name | Last Name | VA File Number

☐ **Have you sought out psychiatric treatment for cases other than combat?**
Seeking care through the VA will not affect your general records

What kind of claim are you submitting?

☐ **Combat Related** Fill out: A
We will match your claim to available combat records

☐ **Non-Combat Related** Fill out: A+B
You can provide other information to help us verify your claim (e.g. accidents, sexual assault, etc.)

Symptoms

Ut id consectetur magna. Quisque volutpat augue enim, pulvinar lobortis nibh lacinia at. Vestibulum nec erat ut mi solliciludin porttitor id sit amet risus.

☐ **Anxiety**
☐ **Poor Sleep**
☐ **Depression**
☐ **Social Detachment**
☐ **Panic Attacks**
☐ **Mistrust**
☐ **Hyper-Vigilance**
☐ **Over/Under-eating**
☐ **Drug or Alcohol Abuse**
☐ **Increased Use of Medication**

Figure 11.2. PTSD claim form[11]

work, leadership at the Veterans Experience Office was looking to expand HCD into a patient-centered care program across the VA.

Rekindling Patient-Centered Healthcare at VA

The VEO spent 2016 proposing, initiating, and socializing with the aim of understanding how veterans experience their healthcare. The success of the Journey of Veterans Map and relationship building across the agency helped initiate the talks. The 2016 efforts eventually led to buy-in from VHA leaders. They agreed to partner with VEO to explore the needs, values, and belief systems of veterans seeking care. The deputy undersecretary of health operations management and the chief experience officer served as executive champions for the proposed work. A core team of designers from VEO's Insight and Design team led the approach. Along the way, they partnered with VHA to move the work forward at each stage.

The team rooted its research in HCD. The designers educated their VHA partners about the process and expected outcomes. Given the previous success, journey maps became the standard for the internal communication of user research. Designers knew what they had to deliver, and the audience knew how to interpret it. Once the project kicked off, a small team of designers developed plans to traverse the country talking with veterans in their homes and medical centers about their care experiences. It required a team of nearly 80 staff members and external contractors to interview close to 100 veterans. The process required securing buy-in from the broader office, leaders across the VA, and all levels of the organization. Nine teams were deployed to nine cities over a span of three weeks. The fieldwork began in late October, a week before the 2016 presidential election, and was set for completion before the Thanksgiving holiday. The size, scope, and timeframe resulted in one of the largest human-centered design undertakings at the VA and in the federal government at the time.

After the completion of ethnographic field research, the project team met in person with the extended field research team and VA stakeholders to synthesize the findings. The results of the synthesis led to a shared understanding of the healthcare experiences of veterans across the country. The design team summarized the findings, creating two important artifacts: the Patient Experience (PX) Journey Map and an accompanying project storybook.

The PX Journey Map represents a common set of outpatient care experiences of veterans at VA healthcare. The map identifies bright spots and pain points. It also summarizes the moments that matter most to veterans. The storybook provided a deeper understanding of the parts of the journey and the opportunities to improve it. These artifacts were instrumental in helping the VHA, VEO's client, identify areas to innovate and improve the patient experience.

Following the discovery research, VEO established a patient experience team and strategic focus. The team continued to work with members of the VHA to build an operational patient experience program. Again, leadership invited designers and the HCD approach into the development process. The VEO PX team deployed five interventions to improve and create a more consistent care experience across the country. These interventions, best practices borrowed from the private sector and adapted to the VA environment, were designed by VEO's Insight and Design team and were rolled out by VEO's PX implementation and training teams. These implementation and training teams are responsible for working with local VA healthcare systems to incorporate the interventions into the system's operations.

Shortly after the office began planning for implementation, medical directors of VA healthcare systems noted the need to help leaders and staff understand the transformation toward a more veteran and patient-centered healthcare system. In order to move toward a more patient-centered healthcare system, health system staff would need to understand their role and how they could contribute to the transformation.

The Insight and Design team, with members of the PX leadership team, were invited to develop and design a tool to facilitate a greater understanding of the transformation. The team underwent three months of research and design with medical center leaders and staff to understand how to successfully deploy, integrate, and maintain the PX initiative across the VA's 152 healthcare systems. The office wanted to avoid the initiative being perceived as another short-term initiative, mocked internally as a "flavor of the month." This led the design team to investigate past initiatives and factors that determined their success or failure. The research resulted in four design opportunities prioritized by leaders and staff in VA facilities. The users prioritized the need for a visual roadmap to describe VA's patient experience path to excellence. The PX Roadmap to Excellence is in use and is an integral part of all five interventions (see figure 11.3).

The discovery work that began in 2016 led to a transformation within VA. By 2020, veteran trust scores surpassed 90 per cent, for the first time ever. The VA also began outpacing the private sector in patient satisfaction scores. Today, VA's approach to improving the patient experience is routinely seen as a national best practice among healthcare systems. It all started with design.

Nurturing Culture Change

Once an obscure term in government, human-centered design (HCD) is now understood as an effective means for improving veteran experiences at VA. Today, teams at VA apply HCD to do creative, user-centered work when it might not otherwise be understood or supported. Leaders use these approaches in areas beyond healthcare, including assisting veterans to access other VA benefits. As new agendas and priorities are developed by leadership, a mission focus continues to be on improving veterans' experiences with VA broadly and specifically in healthcare. There's a lot to do but with the tools of design thinking and HCD, cross-sector partnerships, and empowering an already dedicated VA staff, the opportunity to improve the VA is a real and tangible one.

The Transformation Was about Momentum and Not a Moment

Organizational culture change is a project in itself. In our case, culture change and the HCD work is happening in tandem, both

VETERANS EXPERIENCE OFFICE

Developed and designed by:
Veterans Experience Office

VA PATIENT EXPERIENCE ROADMAP TO EXCELLENCE

"One thing that stood out in my visit with UCLA was that their unwavering focus was not simply realized through a list of disconnected initiatives … They worked hard to establish and sustain an extensive framework, aligning purpose with people and performance management that provided the structures for success and the measurement to continuously track the path to improvement."

– Jason A. Wolf, PhD, CPXP
President of the Beryl Institute

Learning facility
A facility that is just starting to think about PX will start here

1. UNDERSTAND PATIENT EXPERIENCE

→ Know the definition of patient experience (PX)
→ Establish what PX means to you, your unit, and your health care system
→ Address how interactions, culture, perceptions, and environment influence the patient experience journey at your health care system
→ Discuss what you hear Veterans say about their health care journeys.
→ Give your staff and leaders dedicated time to discuss these concepts
→ Assess your health care system's PX maturity

"Patient experience is not just about patient happiness…it is delivering clinical care that reduces patient suffering."

– Press Ganey

3x Satisfied patients are three times more likely to return to a provider they've seen before.
McKinsey & Company

"It feels like a whole city helped me get back together."
– Veteran Patient, Las Vegas NV

2. BUILD PX STRUCTURE

→ Identify a dedicated PX leader, who directly reports to Medical Center Director, to spearhead all things PX
→ Evaluate each service in your org chart to determine how their core functions enhance the patient experience
→ Foster a culture that encompasses teamwork integration, good communication, and an environment of continuous learning
→ Value staff by listening and integrating their feedback in decisions

→ Dive into the PX domains to establish which ones require attention
→ Create and nurture a just culture
→ Instill a sense of responsibility and accountability among leaders and staff
→ Engage key stakeholders in your PX development and design
  ▫ Veteran Advisory Council
  ▫ Patient Experience Steering Committee

80% of organizations have a dedicated patient experience leader.
Beryl Institute

"Leadership is a must in patient experience and not simply as a figure-head or as a slice of an executive's already stretched responsibilities."
– Beryl Institute

3. ALIGN & EXECUTE PX STRATEGY

→ Develop your PX strategy and integrate the PX domains
→ Incorporate expected communication behaviors and key service principles and standards (The VA Way)
→ Implement VEO PX solutions

→ Incorporate WECARE rounding
→ Ensure infrastructure initiatives in these areas support the PX strategy
  ▫ Communications Strategy
  ▫ Training & Education
  ▫ Hiring & Performance
  ▫ Budget Allocation
  ▫ IT Transformation

82% of organizations place patient experience as one of their top three priorities.
Beryl Institute

Transforming facility
A facility with a strong foundation might work to align its strategy

4. MEASURE & ANALYZE

→ Discuss the value of PX scores and their relationship with quality measures among all work units
→ Promote transparency by making PX scores available to all staff
→ Facilitate discussions on the PX scores within each work unit
→ Look beyond PX scores to identify other meaningful indicators for experience
→ Conduct listening sessions to gather the voice of the Veteran

→ Review the PX Journey Map and Storybook to identify possible explanations for experience at your health care system
→ Integrate the voice of the Veteran with your PX indicators to establish priority areas for improvement
→ Brainstorm and gather feedback from team members on how to improve PX indicators
→ Incorporate priority areas in your PX strategic plan

50% of disengaged employees plan to leave their organization.
Dr. Graham Lowe, Researcher

Leading facility
A facility which embraces PX and is evident in its operations may focus on sustainment

5. RECOGNIZE & SUSTAIN

→ Demonstrate leadership commitment by actively leading WECARE rounds
→ Inspire and celebrate teams through patient stories and recognizing meaningful contributions by staff
→ Use data to drive system redesign efforts and adjust your PX strategy
→ Practice Lean methods by embracing constructive energy from staff to solve problems within their work network
→ Develop concrete plans of action with desired outcomes for improvement projects

→ Give staff the freedom to evaluate and test new ideas
→ Track progress and determine the impact of changes
→ Communicate lessons learned and successes for systemic improvement
→ Exchange best practices across your teams, VHA healthcare affiliates, and local community network
→ Expand your PX knowledge and invest in PX professional development for all staff, including clinicians

The Patient Experience Domains guide the necessary actions at every stage to ensure a well-grounded operating system.

Align purpose with people and performance management to establish structures for success. Measure and continuously track the path to excellence.

1 UNDERSTAND **2 BUILD** **3 ALIGN** **4 MEASURE** **5 SUSTAIN**

Figure 11.3. PX Roadmap to Excellence *(cont.)*

VA PATIENT EXPERIENCE ROADMAP TO EXCELLENCE

Charting the course towards PX excellence

The VEO Patient Experience (PX) and the VEO Insight & Design teams designed this artifact in partnership with the Veterans Health Administration. This roadmap integrates ideas from VA facility leaders with best practices from the best in class private sector health systems. This roadmap is uniquely designed for VHA.

We invite you to use this roadmap as your operating model towards PX excellence. It builds upon the VA Patient Experience Domains, providing an adaptable approach based on five key action-oriented stages. Start and maintain the dialogue about patient experience. Follow suit by taking deliberate actions towards your journey to PX excellence.

A special thank you to VHA subject matter experts who shared their experiences launching and leading initiatives at their facilities. Clinical and administrative leaders shared the triumphs and failures of creating change within their health care systems. This project would not be possible without their sincerity, candor and desire of to make VA the best place for Veterans to get care. Contributors: Boston, East Orange, Indianapolis, Las Vegas, Los Angeles, Palo Alto, Reno, Roseburg, and San Francisco.

For questions and resources:
vapxprogramleadership@VA.gov
https://www.vapulse.net/groups/vha-patient-experience

> *"Operating a truly patient-centered organization isn't a program; it's a way of life."*
>
> – James I. Merlino and Ananth Raman
> Cleveland Clinic

VA health care living up to the best care anywhere.

DEFINITION
The sum of all interactions, shaped by the organization's culture, that influence Veterans and their families' perceptions along their healthcare journey.

VISION
Veterans and their families are at the center of everything we do, and our system ensures that every Veteran has a consistent, exceptional experience no matter where they go for care.

MISSION
To provide a consistent, exceptional experience that strengthens trust and confidence with the Veterans, their families and caregivers.

Three dimensions of Veterans' customer experience

EFFECTIVENESS
"It was easy to get the services I needed."
Understand and Respond to Needs
"I got the services I needed."

EASE
Guide the Journey

EMOTION
Connect and Care
"I felt like a valued customer."

The VA Way

VALUES
- **I** INTEGRITY
- **C** COMMITMENT
- **A** ADVOCACY
- **R** RESPECT
- **E** EXCELLENCE

BEHAVIORS
- **W** WELCOME
- **E** EXPLAIN
- **C** CONNECT
- **A** ACTIVELY LISTEN
- **R** RESPECT
- **E** EXPRESS GRATITUDE

SERVICE RECOVERY
- **S** SAY HELLO
- **A** APOLOGIZE
- **L** LISTEN
- **U** UNDERSTAND
- **T** TAKE ACTION
- **E** EXPRESS GRATITUDE

PATIENT EXPERIENCE DOMAINS

(Domains shown: LEADERSHIP, PATIENT COMMUNICATION, ENVIRONMENT, MEASUREMENT & IMPROVEMENT, EMPLOYEE ENGAGEMENT, VOICE OF THE VETERAN, CULTURE — surrounding EMPLOYEE EXPERIENCE and VETERANS EXPERIENCE)

LEADERSHIP
Leaders are visible, engaged, and set the tone of patient experience. Leaders empower employees and build an organization committed to patient experience.

PATIENT COMMUNICATION
Veterans know what to expect from their health care. Communications with Veterans are consistent, use plain language, and invite engagement. Veterans feel confident that they are being listened to and heard.

ENVIRONMENT
Veterans and their families feel welcomed and supported in an environment that is clean and safe that exudes healing and mitigates anxiety.

MEASUREMENT & IMPROVEMENT
The organization uses meaningful, contextual, and real-time insight to gain better understanding.

EMPLOYEE ENGAGEMENT
Employees feel passionate about serving Veterans, are committed and accountable to the organization and each other, and are empowered by leadership to solve meaningful problems that improve the patient experience. Employees understand their role and embody the philosophy behind the patient experience.

VOICE OF THE VETERAN
The organization proactively gathers and utilizes Veteran feedback and perspectives to make decisions and solve issues that matter most to Veterans and their families.

CULTURE
A culture of kindness, collaboration, innovation, transparency and accountability impacts how we treat each other and Veterans who come seeking care. Veterans feel welcomed and cared for when they sense a supportive environment.

informing and influencing each other. We learn through every project that, in turn, shapes the scope of the HCD work we do next. With that, the transformation of the VA and the use of HCD is evolving, without a ceremony or strategy, based on organizational and veterans' needs. This is a place of empowerment and frustration, a position to lead change, but also subject to the pains that go with it. The work that we do does positively influence people, outcomes, and strategy. The changes are incremental and sometimes fleeting. Many factors beyond our ability to manage or influence are at play. Sometimes we are aware of them and often we are not. Leadership changes, politics, strategy, funding, congressional or public attention are unpredictable tides that shift strategy and operations. For a slow-moving bureaucracy, strategic shifts seem to come upon us quickly. We have found that in these shifts, the organization can change its perception and value of approaches, like HCD. We find ourselves again and again in a position to pitch, explain, and defend what we do.

But we stay, persist, and continue to steward HCD at the agency because it is within our ability to influence the culture and the care at the VA, help sustain established innovations, and do human-centered work. We are seeing the benefits, and these continue to motivate us. For example, a 2018 memo from VA Secretary Peter O'Rourke stated: "Ensure that every veteran's experience with their care and benefits services is effective, easy, and emotionally resonant, when in-person, by phone, online, or by mail – to promote trust." The three Es – effective, easy, and emotionally resonant – are based on a Forrester model that was championed by the VEO when first setting up the office. It took time but that change is now supported by leadership and working its way toward being embedded in the culture. With the adoption of this purpose, the stage is set to effectively continue doing HCD into the future.

Lessons Learned

- Teach through collaboration and demonstration. Showing concrete results also helps people see the connection between the process and the outcome. In the case of VA, a steady stream of incoming diverse projects and strategic shifts led to an ever-changing set of stakeholders and perspectives. Add to this, fluctuating understanding and interpretation of HCD. This situation requires that we explain how we work, pitch the value-add, and advocate for why our team should be involved. Even when we're invited to work on projects, we still must advocate for the integrity of the method and why the details matter.
- Interest in design thinking efforts within an organization can ebb and flow. As a design leader, it's your job to channel the enthusiasm when it's present and cultivate when it is low. At VA, the momentum for HCD projects fluctuates, depending on how the current administration and leadership views our approaches. Interest sometimes comes because of pitching, advocating, and teaching. It may be that people want to replicate something good we did in the past. Motivation may also originate from something outside of our control, such as a reaction to a crisis or a new priority from senior leaders. We tune into this momentum and use it to shape the projects. When momentum is low, we look for ways to build it back up again. We seek out unmet needs. We bring attention back to people at the center of unmet needs.
- Build relationships with like-minded people and organizations. It's also important to share your innovations and advancements. This will build a community of practice. The idea is to show leaders and decision-makers that design thinking works. We do this within the VA and external to it. We look to see

where others have figured out how to do something before we have. An early example of this at VEO was looking to the LAB at OPM to learn about hiring designers in the agency. Another example is looking at how other offices and groups are carrying user-centered design forward. Case studies, maps, reports, and even anecdotes of success are extremely valuable for this purpose.

- Carefully choose the right tools for the context and do not cut corners: success in winning over critics requires a deep understanding of the appropriateness of tools and methods for the situation. The power of communicating insights throughout the large organization with the right visual tools (journey maps, storybooks) is particularly important. Be sure to execute the finished tool with quality and care to reach its full potential. We have noticed at VA that quality work leads to positive outcomes. Unfortunately, in some projects, "good enough" becomes the standard. Check the box. Get a quick win. Short-term progress is prioritized over long-term ability to inspire action or have a lasting impact. For example, the original ask for what would become the PX Roadmap to Excellence (see figure 11.3), was to make a simple guidebook. We could have made a good-looking book but we know now in retrospect that would have been the wrong tool. We quickly learned in our field research with VHA staff that guidebooks get emailed around all the time – each one a new flavor of the month. They asked for something different and better. We heard them and produced the map. It's a solution that they favored over other prototypes we shared with them. The map was different and helped to change the perception of the program.
- Build a tight-knit team and internal community. This will help you navigate change and stay aligned with your purpose. Change is constant at the VA. In early 2017, the outgoing

director of the Insight and Design team urged the team to *always* support each other. We listened. We navigated this period of uncertainty together. After the administration change, there was a period when the Insight and Design team and the VEO leadership were being reacquainted. At times we felt wayward, unsure of what the future projects would be and what our role would be. During that time, we found ways to stay united and positive. We collectively defined our beliefs and values – we called it our rudder. We used it to steer us to where we are today – together.

Timeline

- 2010: VA began infusing patient-centered care through the design of the Patient-Centered Medical Home (PCMH); VA Secretary Eric Shinseki and one of his senior advisors set out to develop an initiative that would foster improvements through innovation; the VA Innovation Initiative (VAi2) was developed to bring innovation to VA.
- 2012: After two years, this initiative became the standing VA Center for Innovation (VACI).
- 2013: VACI's deputy director led the center to expound upon the stories she heard from fellow veterans about their struggles engaging with the VA system.
- 2014: Over forty veterans died waiting for care at the VA in Phoenix, Arizona. Secretary Shinseki resigned and Bob McDonald became the new VA secretary; the VACI interviewed veterans in the context of their lives. One of the key themes in previous research that received growing attention is veterans' mental healthcare; VA Secretary Bob McDonald established the Veterans Experience Office and hired the agency's first chief customer experience officer.

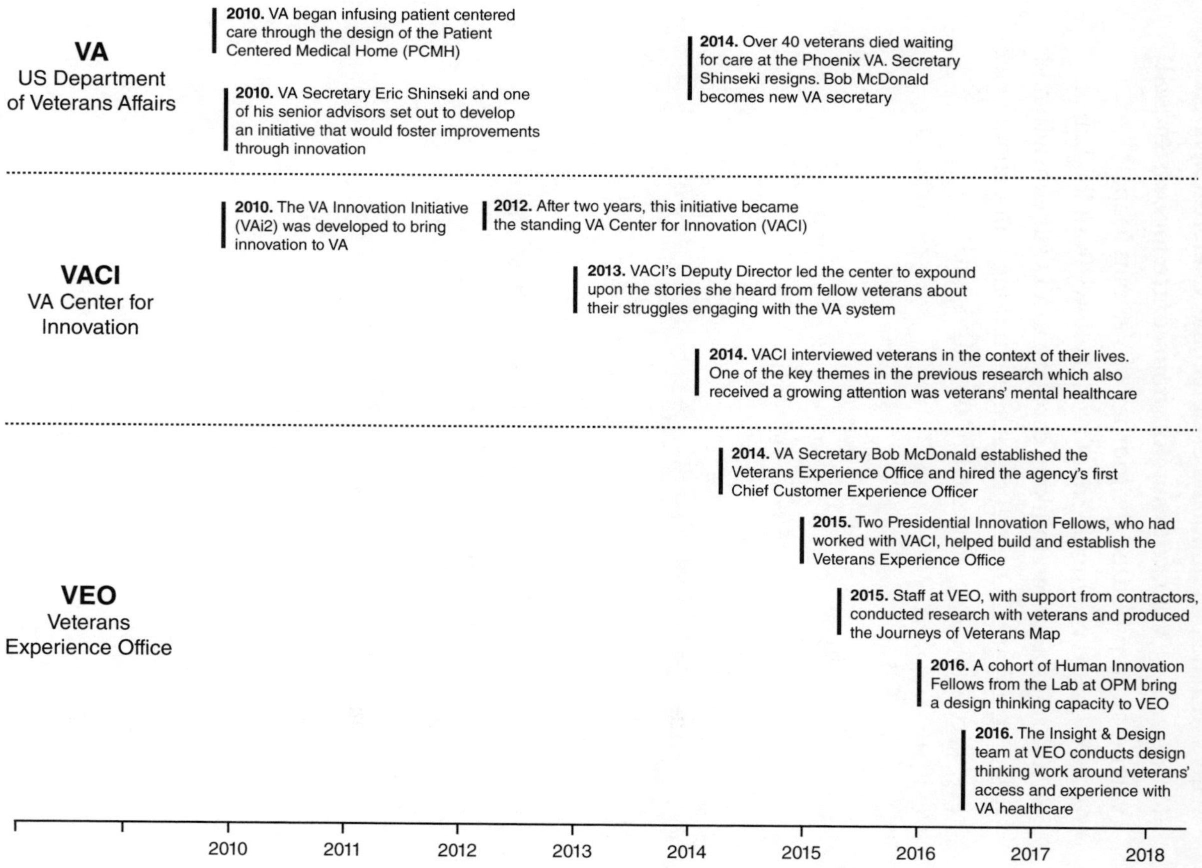

VA
US Department
of Veterans Affairs

2010. VA began infusing patient centered care through the design of the Patient Centered Medical Home (PCMH)

2010. VA Secretary Eric Shinseki and one of his senior advisors set out to develop an initiative that would foster improvements through innovation

2014. Over 40 veterans died waiting for care at the Phoenix VA. Secretary Shinseki resigns. Bob McDonald becomes new VA secretary

VACI
VA Center for
Innovation

2010. The VA Innovation Initiative (VAi2) was developed to bring innovation to VA

2012. After two years, this initiative became the standing VA Center for Innovation (VACI)

2013. VACI's Deputy Director led the center to expound upon the stories she heard from fellow veterans about their struggles engaging with the VA system

2014. VACI interviewed veterans in the context of their lives. One of the key themes in the previous research which also received a growing attention was veterans' mental healthcare

VEO
Veterans
Experience Office

2014. VA Secretary Bob McDonald established the Veterans Experience Office and hired the agency's first Chief Customer Experience Officer

2015. Two Presidential Innovation Fellows, who had worked with VACI, helped build and establish the Veterans Experience Office

2015. Staff at VEO, with support from contractors, conducted research with veterans and produced the Journeys of Veterans Map

2016. A cohort of Human Innovation Fellows from the Lab at OPM bring a design thinking capacity to VEO

2016. The Insight & Design team at VEO conducts design thinking work around veterans' access and experience with VA healthcare

2010   2011   2012   2013   2014   2015   2016   2017   2018

Figure 11.4. VA timeline

- 2015: Two Presidential Innovation Fellows, who had worked with VACI, helped build and establish the Veterans Experience Office; staff at VEO, with support from contractors, researched veterans and produced the Journey of Veterans Map.
- 2016: A cohort of Human Innovation Fellows from the Lab at OPM brings a design thinking capacity to VEO; the insight and design team at VEO conducts design thinking work about veterans' access and experience with VA healthcare.

CHAPTER TWELVE

Transform with Design in Seven Lessons

JOCHEN SCHWEITZER, SIHEM BENMAHMOUD-JOUINI,
AND SEBASTIAN FIXSON

The comparative analysis of the design thinking implementation and organizational transformation case studies revealed some interesting similarities, managerial patterns, success factors, and barriers to achieving innovation and transformation through design. In our analysis of the long-term data, we identified what managers do to achieve the desired outcomes; hence, we focus on the practices of adopting and adapting design thinking. Here we highlight seven key lessons for executives and managers who find themselves in the situation of starting and developing an organizational innovation initiative and want to leverage design thinking as a driver for organizational transformation. While each lesson draws from more than one case, it is important to note that despite sharing these commonalities, each case organization crafted its own approach and ended up having a distinct transformation journey.

The first four lessons take an external focus relative to the change agents, that is, the design team. These lessons focus on acquiring support from above (top management), outside (external stakeholders), and below (employees), and how education and training programs can be used to multiply this support. The last three lessons remind the design team of the challenges that the change process asks of themselves: to keep an open mind to flexibly adapt design thinking tools and methods to the situation at hand, to commit to the patience and persistence that pursuing a long-term change requires, and to develop the habit of measuring and communicating progress.

1. Build the Business Case Top-Down

Almost all the cases show that receiving and maintaining top leadership support is one of the most critical factors for success. For example, as discussed in the Blue Cross Blue Shield case, members of the C-suite gave crucial backing, communicated with a sense of power and influence, and ensured the necessary resourcing for design thinking activities. To this end, adopting design thinking is not unlike other change agendas that are foreign to an organization's usual practices. Hence, it requires someone in an executive leadership position to be the sponsor and explain to the organization's members why change is needed and how it affects everyone.

Yet, as seen in the cases of Mirvac, Intuit, and Kaiser Permanente, there are advantages beyond recognizing the purpose and the value of design by senior leaders if they are trained and know how to apply design thinking tools and approaches. When executives understand the nature of the work required and appreciate the challenges involved with achieving strategic innovation objectives, they have a much better perspective on balancing the needs to meet financial targets, manage risks and reputation, and foster strategic innovation. And, as seen in the case of Thales, the leadership team's training in design thinking resulted not only in their continued support but found its way into strategic conversations and problem-solving workshops.

But how to obtain and sustain such a level of support? Unless a design initiative originates at the top of the organization, as in the case of Mirvac, the innovation team needs to identify the key people in the larger leadership group that can assist in convincing others.

Such purposeful involvement of senior leadership in the decisions of the innovation team highlights how any of these deliberations must be part of a more significant change effort. Knowing who the influencers are and making them a partner is an essential job of the innovation team.

In other cases, the top management team discovered design thinking and its potential through learning expeditions and exposure to emblematic situations, which convinced them of its potential value to their strategy and organization. As seen in the case of the US Department of Labor, once the initiative had genuine leadership support, it meant not only adequate provision of resources but the mandate to experiment and learn through design thinking. But when leadership changes, as shown in the case of Kaiser Permanente, it can leave innovation teams in a very vulnerable position, which makes it even more critical to engage with top leadership broadly.

2. Leverage External Stakeholders and Resources to Get Things Moving

Another lesson we can learn from our case studies is the value of external stakeholders in getting crucial traction for design-led innovation initiatives in an organization. Even with top executive sponsorship, we have seen that it is critical to leverage various stakeholders and relationships to gain and sustain broad support inside the organization and demonstrate early achievements.

Many organizations begin with the help of consultants, who can bring much-needed resources, as can be seen in the cases of Swisscom and Mirvac, or as in the case of Danone, where consultants supported specific projects. Involving consultants also means benefiting from their experience and exposure to other organizations that have gone down the same or similar paths. However, organizations benefit from developing their internal design thinking and innovation capability in the long term. Consulting companies can introduce best practices and help implement programs and processes and lend legitimacy to an innovation initiative internally. But eventually, an organization must assume ownership of the initiative and let go of consultants. It is what Mirvac referred to as "the ripple effect."

Other relevant external stakeholders who provide much-needed support, particularly in public services, are decision-makers at different levels of government. As seen in the case of MindLab and the US Department of Labor, leveraging the relationships with key decision-makers in state and local government created an immediate group of champions and willing implementers. Similarly, and as seen in the case of Kaiser Permanente, positive media coverage that features successes and praises innovation outcomes helps legitimize the work internally and may even enthuse shareholders.

3. Build Momentum and Culture from the Bottom-Up

Beyond ensuring leadership support and involving external stakeholders, the cases show the importance of developing momentum in the organization and growing an innovation culture from the bottom-up. In the case of MindLab, the team progressively expanded its engagement with government employees as the initiative evolved and organizational change started to transpire. But team members also frequently spoke publicly on innovation and design and saw it as an essential part of their role as innovation leaders. Besides, guests and speakers came to visit, and doctoral students joined a research program, which helped the team remain open to new perspectives.

Purposely creating and supporting an innovation culture also produced momentum in the US Department of Labor. For example, the incentive to visit the White House and meet with the US President was enough to generate strong participation amongst public servants in innovation activities. It helped to inspire a movement, which later enabled and sustained reform. Similarly, at the US Department of Veterans Affairs, the tight-knit innovation team and community of public servants navigated change and stayed aligned to the purpose of the innovation agenda. Teamwork, identity, and trusting relationships helped the team find ways to define their values and remain positive in challenging times. Such factors contributed to cultivating the conditions for innovation to happen from the bottom-up.

A related lesson is that of *building relationships with like-minded people* in other parts of the larger organization. Again, in the case of the US Department of Veterans Affairs, the team broadly shared their innovations and advancements to create a community of practice. The idea is to demonstrate to internal decision-makers that design thinking works and to show external parties, including those on a similar journey, what successful design innovation looks like.

As seen in the Kaiser Permanente and Swisscom cases, growing momentum and building an innovation culture is an upstream battle against existing work practices. Yet what worked was to back the small groups of facilitators, change agents, and innovation coaches to promote new methods, facilitate awareness for the work being done, and help create a human-centered work ethic.

In addition, successful design innovation teams find ways to *initiate and incentivize good design thinking behavior*. At Danone, the team looked for opportunities to apply design thinking in several projects and closely manage and support the project teams. At Mirvac, incentives related to key performance indicators were tied into existing rewards systems to recognize and reward innovative behavior. This allowed employees across the organization to contribute to innovation initiatives broadly. At Thales, the variety and diversity of activities involving design (training, facilitating workshops, and supporting projects) played a crucial role in developing such a culture.

From the Intuit case, we learn that when shifting toward more innovative work practices through design, the innovation team required a good deal of *freedom to experiment* (and possibly fail) as they found ways to work with the organization's current culture. To this end, new work practices should appear like a natural extension of what people already do.

The last aspect of this lesson about building momentum and innovation culture recognizes middle managers' central role. Winning their support was critical at Mirvac, the US Department of Labor, and Blue Cross Blue Shield. Often middle managers are most directly experiencing the tensions of achieving short-term business objectives and long-term innovation plans of the organizations, which puts them in a challenging but critical position. At Blue Cross Blue Shield, the innovation team took extra care to work with middle managers collaboratively and gain their commitment to adopt a new process and method. At the US Department of Labor, some middle managers grew very passionate about the potential of design for innovation and became influential advocates who leveraged their relationships and connections to support the innovation initiative.

4. Train an Army of Advocates, Tackle Internal Challenges, and Find Allies

All case organizations engaged in a training or education program to develop design innovation skills and provide opportunities to practice the newly acquired capabilities in real-life project contexts. These programs were enhanced, for example, at Kaiser Permanente and Mirvac, by integrating a mentorship and coaching framework that would see already more experienced practitioners working with the new learners and innovations champions (or executive sponsors) supporting the training programs early on.

In the case of Danone, the team benefited from being trained by the same provider and thereby creating an equally skilled group of internal design innovation specialists. At Swisscom, a similar outcome was achieved by collaborating with the in-house leadership academy, while the US Department of Labor produced online courses that lowered the barriers for people to learning and engagement.

The result of these training efforts was the same: Once people got involved in real-life projects, applying design methods and tools, they enjoyed the approach, which not only helped its adaptation but led to its wider spread within the organization. Because design thinking has such a contagious nature, learners turn to advocates and champions with innovative ideas that bring them and others along.

As an effective way to increase such organizational support, our case organizations let design advocates practice their new skills by tackling internal challenges and involving others as "internal" customers. Indeed, while the human centricity of design thinking is generally associated with end-users (usually meaning the customers), employees should be included in this human-centered perspective, too. Involving them broadly from the beginning builds acceptance and understanding of what design thinking can do for them. In the case of MindLab, the team worked closely with the bureaucracy it was destined to change. This engagement entailed facilitating kickoff workshops, involving ministry staff in fieldwork, analyzing and evaluating results, and ultimately engaging with ministries in project implementation. The Swisscom case shows that both internal and external customers, when viewed as co-creators, played an essential role due to their ability to use design methods and demonstrate their value.

The overall objective, especially in the early days of a design innovation program, is finding and leveraging accolades that help obtain further internal support and get things moving faster. It can be achieved through engagement and collaboration inside the organization and outside the immediate sphere of the design initiative or unit/department that supports it. In the case of Danone, it was a collaboration with the corporate marketing group that provided significant exposure across the entire organization.

This lesson stresses the significance of education and training for organizational change in the pursuit of design innovation and points to the benefits of collaboration with other parts of the larger organization, particularly when the initiative focuses on only one part of the organization.

5. Apply New Methods and Tools with an Open Mind

While our analysis of cases suggests it is important to establish a foundation of knowledge about design-led approaches, it is equally important to keep flexibility with how those are applied and how the organization may simultaneously adopt other practical ways and strategies to drive innovation.

Design methods are not very difficult to learn, yet it's essential not to cut corners when applying them. From the US Department of Veterans Affairs case, we understand that winning over critics requires a deep understanding of how suitable tools and methods are for a given situation. Carefully selecting the right tools for the job and leveraging the power of, for example, communicating insights with the right visual tools like journey maps or storybooks contributes to gaining acceptance for design thinking. Especially when starting, it is vital to deliver quality work leading to positive outcomes that will advance the innovation agenda.

At Intuit, the team understood that they needed to mix and match methods to accommodate emerging approaches and leverage best practices from other fields, including agile project management, service design, lean management, and entrepreneurship. At Danone, this testing and experimenting with innovation, change, and transformation led to fast learning and ultimately a version of design thinking that the firm truly owned and appreciated. At Thales, the design thinking approach was progressively applied in many projects beyond the traditional product or service development to design innovative business models and strategies. The internal innovation consultants of the Thales Design Center adapted their tools and approach to the requirements of each business unit they worked with.

Creating effective organizational structures that support the innovation initiative complements the development of an approach. At Mirvac, Intuit, and others, roles such as champions, catalysts, or project sponsors helped clarify responsibilities in the innovation process and keep everyone involved. Swisscom formed a whole department dedicated to providing shared design innovation services. At Danone, a dedicated team pursued a mission of encouraging experimentation and making design-led innovation relevant across the organization. Structures and roles can also inspire employees to learn and take on more or different responsibilities in the innovation effort. Ultimately the aim is for the design thinking projects explored and their outcomes.

Establishing structures for innovation also includes creating a physical space for innovation. Many firms, including Blue Cross Blue Shield, MindLab, and Mirvac, created purposefully built spaces to foster collaboration and discovery. A room for innovation serves as a physical display of where and how innovation happens. While the long-term goal is for innovation to occur throughout the organization, there are benefits in assigning a space to these activities when starting an initiative. It allows employees, leaders, and innovators to engage with each other, participate in project work, learn and share. It is important, however, to make this space accessible to broad portions of the employees. Otherwise, it risks being seen as an exclusive perk to a select few, undermining broad support for the design transformation activities.

The MindLab, located centrally in Copenhagen, was housed in a separate office that looked and felt very different from other Danish government facilities. While the ministries that sponsored the project wanted the innovation outcomes, they found it challenging to fit such space within the government departments preoccupied with day-to-day policy-making. At Blue Cross Blue Shield, the early presence of an innovation space supported the leadership's decision to invest in a much larger-scale corporate center for innovation that now houses a whole range of innovation efforts.

Finally, it matters what the innovation effort is called. As seen at Blue Cross Blue Shield, the team used the term "design thinking" only for early exposure activities but used "design doing" for project work to clarify how these are more than thought experiments. In other instances, the team avoided terms like "consultant" and "facilitating" as those clashed with organizational history. The shift from using the word "design thinking" to "human-centered design" made the method more immediately relevant for all consumer-facing activities. Interestingly, some organizations avoided the term "design" altogether, which resulted in perceived broader acceptance levels across the organization.

6. Brace Yourself, Buckle Down, and Have a Model for Growth

In all cases we were able to study the role of design over several years. We found that each case exemplifies how the adoption of design is not a short-term play but a continuous process of small steps, some wins, and many failures, that over time and little by little, shift people's mindsets. Over time, the resilience and perseverance of the innovation team and their sustained efforts to influence behavioral and attitudinal changes through practicing new tools and techniques allow the organization to develop an innovation mindset. This shift goes hand in hand with creating a supportive work environment where employees feel safe sharing ideas and taking risks.

However, as seen at the US Department of Veterans Affairs, organization-wide engagement with design innovation can sway. Sometimes other strategic initiatives take center stage, and people get busy or distracted. The role of the innovation team is to sense those shifts and channel the enthusiasm when it's present while cultivating it at other times. Innovation leaders tune in to the momentum that develops in one part of the organization to develop opportunities for design innovation while building it up again in other parts of the organization where it may have faded.

Yet, as seen at Intuit and Blue Cross Blue Shield, scaling efforts may disappoint if they are built on momentum alone. So, bracing yourself, buckling down, and taking a long-term perspective is about avoiding complacency and continually emphasizing that developing new competencies takes time and effort. This lesson applies to large corporate organizations, where inertia can be the usual modus operandi.

So, start small but have a model for growth. Successful organizations in our review understood the importance of allowing an emerging innovation initiative to discover what works by experimenting with new ways of working while planning and developing a path to scale.

At Kaiser Permanente, starting with a few focused activities and working on not-overly complicated efforts gave the team a chance to learn how design methods work, how people could use them, and how the organization responds. Activities increasingly involved more people, different units, and more complex and strategic challenges from those relatively modest trials. Both patience and persistence are critical for the innovation team and the executives who sponsor the initiative.

Humble beginnings also mean the innovation team does not need to worry about getting everyone's endorsement; they can fly "under the radar" for a while, learn quickly, yet prove value to the organization. A tested and proven approach run by a small group of passionate people on a small scale has better potential to scale than an extensive and possibly over-publicized program; the former was precisely the approach that the team at Thales took.

Building innovation capacity progressively and anchoring it within the organization is more important for achieving long-term growth than short-term exposure and quick wins. At Thales, an internal consultancy approach was an excellent path to growth. Their *franchise* model for scaling design innovation was critical for spreading it globally to every part of the organization. It preserved the integrity and independence of the project and enabled tangible outcomes rather than evangelizing and advocating for a method.

At Kaiser Permanente, the innovation team worked with specific growth targets and goals in mind, knowing that if they could get a reasonable portion of the innovation projects to translate into tangible benefits for the business, the initiative would sustain itself.

7. Measure Everything, Communicate Deliberately, and Know When to Stop

How to communicate the impact of design thinking? The key to effectively convey the potential of new solutions or already achieved outcomes is to measure every aspect of it in every way possible. While some accuse design thinking of being inexplicit or based on intuition and gut feeling, design practitioners understand this could not be further from the truth.

Deep insights that emerge through a discovery phase or the feedback gathered when prototyping and testing are invaluable for creating better solutions and serve as the indisputable evidence that supports the innovation initiative and keeps people engaged and supportive. Accumulating this information means measuring, which may be as easy as counting the number of projects, people involved, innovations brought to market, as seen in the case of Danone, or it may be a new KPI like the Customer Centricity Score in the case of Swisscom.

What is measured can be communicated, so what works is speaking deliberately and extensively to all stakeholder groups using various channels. At the US Department of Labor, this involved events like roadshows; elsewhere, as in the case of Thales, communication was embedded in a learning strategy via the corporate university. As seen at the US Department of Veterans Affairs, it is helpful to communicate tangible results that allow people to understand the relationship between the new design-led process and the innovative outcomes.

More generally, organizational circumstances usually require the innovation team to explain how they work, demonstrate their value, advocate for the integrity of the method, and justify why they should be involved. What the cases also showed is that sometimes it is better to hold back on communication efforts. Deliberate communication means being conscious about when to seek organizational visibility and when to avoid it. While at Swisscom and Intuit, the teams communicated broadly to ensure management buy-in and general awareness through visibility, at the US Department of Labor, the innovation team deliberately sought reduced visibility to avoid scrutiny from headquarters before the initiative was anchored politically.

Finally, measuring outcomes, documenting achievements, and communicating results help establish and assess the value that design innovation has brought to the organization. MindLab, which without doubt, made its mark as a thought leader in design-based innovation for government services, was in the end replaced by something else. It had fulfilled its purpose and delivered the expected outcomes. Ultimately, design-driven innovation initiatives are but one means of an organization's broader strategy and can be vulnerable to changes in prevailing power structures, competitive environments, or other constraints.

Notes

1 Why Implementing Design Thinking Remains a Challenge

1 See, for example, Knight, E., et al. (2020). "Design-Led Strategy: How to Bring Design Thinking into the Art of Strategic Management." *California Management Review 62*(2): 30–52; Elsbach, K.D., and Stigliani, I. (2018). "Design Thinking and Organizational Culture: A Review and Framework for Future Research." *Journal of Management 44*(6): 2274–306; Liedtka, J. (2018). "Why Design Thinking Works." *Harvard Business Review 96*(5): 72–9; and Verganti, R. (2009). *Design-Driven Innovation: Changing the Rules of Competition by Radically Innovating What Things Mean.* Boston: Harvard Business Review Press.

2 See Simon, H.A. (1969). *Sciences of the Artificial.* Cambridge, MA: MIT Press; and Buchanan, R. (1992). "Wicked Problems in Design Thinking." *Design Issues 8*(2): 5–21.

3 See Brown, T. (2009). *Change by Design.* New York: HarperCollins; Verganti, R., and Dell'Era, C. (2014). "Design-Driven Innovation: Meaning as a Source of Innovation." In M. Dodgson (Ed.), *The Oxford Handbook of Innovation Management*, 139–62. New York: Oxford Academic; Seidel, V.P., and Fixson, S.K. (2013). "Adopting Design Thinking in Novice Multidisciplinary Teams: The Application and Limits of Design Methods and Reflexive Practices." *Journal of Product Innovation Management 30*(S1): 19–33; Martin, R.L. (2009). *The Design of Business: Why Design Thinking Is the Next Competitive Advantage.* Boston, MA: Harvard Business Press; Liedtka, J., and Kaplan, S. (2019). "How Design Thinking Opens New Frontiers for Strategy Development." *Strategy & Leadership 47*(2): 3–10.

4 See Carlgren, L., et al. (2014). "Design Thinking: Exploring Values and Effects from an Innovation Capability Perspective." *The Design Journal 17*(3):

403–23; Micheli, P., et al. (2019). "Doing Design Thinking: Conceptual Review, Synthesis, and Research Agenda." *Journal of Product Innovation Management* 36(2): 124–48; Carlgren, L., et al. (2016). "Framing Design Thinking: The Concept in Idea and Enactment." *Creativity and Innovation Management* 25(1): 38–57; and Mahmoud-Jouini, S.B., et al. (2019). "Making Design Thinking Work: Adapting an Innovation Approach to Fit a Large Technology-Driven Firm." *Research-Technology Management* 62(5): 50–8.

5 See Csaszar, F.A. (2013). "An Efficient Frontier in Organization Design: Organizational Structure as a Determinant of Exploration and Exploitation." *Organization Science* 24(4): 1083–101; Elsbach, K.D., and Stigliani, I. (2018). "Design Thinking and Organizational Culture: A Review and Framework for Future Research." *Journal of Management* 44(6): 2274–306; Walters, H. (2011, March 24). "'Design Thinking' Isn't a Miracle Cure, but Here's How It Helps." *Fast Company*. https://www.fastcompany .com/90186356/design-thinking-isnt-a-miracle-cure-but-heres-how -it-helps.

6 For a detailed overview of relevant tools and methods, see Seidel and Fixson (2013). "Adopting Design Thinking in Novice Multidisciplinary Teams." For a description of phases, see Liedtka, J. (2014). "Innovative Ways Companies Are Using Design Thinking." *Strategy & Leadership* 42(2): 40–5.

7 For a more detailed discussion of the design thinking mindset, see Schweitzer, J., et al. (2016). "The Design Thinking Mindset: An Assessment of What We Know and What We See in Practice." *Journal of Design, Business & Society* 2(1): 71–94; Beverland, M.B., et al. (2016). "Resourceful Sensemaking: Overcoming Barriers between Marketing and Design in NPD." *Journal of Product Innovation Management* 33(5): 628–48; and Carlgren et al., (2016), "Framing Design Thinking."

8 You can find out more about the Design Thinking Exchange (DTX) conferences at http://dt-exchange.com/.

2 Reimagining Healthcare

1 The predominantly private nature of the U.S. health insurance market notwithstanding, there are major exceptions. Examples for government-administered and tax-funded programs are Medicare (for the elderly), MedicAid (for the poor), and Veterans Affairs (for military veterans).

2 Blue Cross Blue Shield Association. "About." Accessed 9 January 2023. https://www.bcbs.com/about-us/the-blue-cross-blue-shield-system. "Members" in the BCBS systems are the insured individuals.

3   Blue Cross Blue Shield of Massachusetts. (2019). *2019 Annual Report: The Power of Partnerships.* https://aboutus.bluecrossma.com/sites/g /files/csphws1376/files/acquiadam-assets/2019%20Anual%20Report .pdf.

4   Blue Cross Blue Shield of Massachusetts. (n.d.). "Our Company at a Glance." Newsroom. Accessed 9 January 2023. http://newsroom .bluecrossma.com/fact-sheets.

5   Amadeo, K. (2019). "The Rising Cost of Healthcare by Year and Its Causes." The Balance. Last Updated 21 October 2022. https:// www.thebalance.com/causes-of-rising-healthcare-costs-4064878.

6   Cutler, D. (2020). "The World's Costliest Health Care … and What America Might Do about It." *Harvard Magazine,* May-June 2020. https:// www.harvardmagazine.com/2020/05/feature-forum-costliest-health -care.

7   The model is also known as the "four levels of teaching" or the "four stages of learning any new skill." See "Four Stages of Competence." Wikipedia. Accessed 9 January 2023, https://en.wikipedia.org/wiki/Four _stages_of_competence.

8   "How to Kick Off a Crash Course." d.school at Stanford University. Accessed 9 January 2023. https://dschool.stanford.edu/resources/gear -up-how-to-kick-off-a-crash-course.

9   Carlgren, Lisa, Rauth, I., and Elmquist, M. (2016). "Framing Design Thinking: The Concept in Idea and Enactment." *Creativity and Innovation Management 25*(1): 38–57.

10 See the timeline at the end of this chapter.

11 Griffin, S. (2018, October 30). "South Shore Hospital, Blue Cross Pilot Aims to Reduce Total Medical Expenses." South Shore Health. https:// www.southshorehealth.org/about-us/news-media/news/south-shore -hospital-blue-cross-pilot-aims-reduce-total-medical-expenses.

12 See Silverberg, B. (2019, June 17). "The Blending of Industry & Academia: How Wentworth Is Leading the Way with the Idea of the Embedded Classroom." *Wit Magazine.* https://wit.edu/news/how-wentworth -leading-way-idea-embedded-classroom.

13 See Freyer, F.J. (2018, October 3). "Many People Don't Know How to Administer Overdose-Reversing Drugs. Blue Cross Is Trying to Change That." *Boston Globe.* https://www.bostonglobe.com/metro/2018/10/03 /worker-overdosed-would-you-know-what/p94RYpQqYtXtvFBuL- QLpyN/story.html.

14 Norman, D.A. (2016, August 24). "Design Doing with Don Norman." *UX Podcast.* Search Medium. https://medium.com/@uxpodcast/design -doing-with-don-norman-6434b022831b.

3 Design Thinking Recipe in a Food Company

1 Comex is Danone's Executive Committee, a key governance body of the organization.
2 The Hasso Plattner Institute (HPI) is a German information technology institute with faculty at the University of Potsdam. Teaching and research of HPI is focused on "IT-Systems Engineering" and includes a specialized design thinking training for students and professionals. It belongs to the worldwide d.school network, including the d.school at Stanford University, California.
3 In 2015, Danone had five business divisions: Dairy, Waters and Beverages, Early Life, Medical, and African. Typically, a research and innovation (R&I) director and marketing director were responsible for innovation within each division. The R&I department maintained local teams in key Country Business Units per region, and global teams contributing specific expertise.
4 General managers of Danone Country Business Units have the power to launch and execute innovation and renovation projects. R&I and marketing directors are responsible for innovation management.
5 See Cultured Snacking Company, https://www.culturedsnackingco.com.
6 See "Research and Innovation." (n.d.). Danone. Accessed 14 March 2023. https://flytedrink.com.
7 See "Mizone." (n.d.). Danone. Accessed 14 March 2023. https://www.danone.com/brands/waters/mizone.html.
8 At that time, Danone chose to open a corporate team dedicated to innovation outside existing divisions of the company.
9 La Petite Fabrique is an incubator for disruptive innovation around the Bledina brand.
10 See "Hayat ice tea : une nouveaut(h)é sur le marché turc." (2019, March 3). Danone. https://www.danone.com/fr/stories/articles-list/hayat-tea.html.
11 The choice of the name was motivated by the capitalization of a marketing event that happened in December 2018 called People Powered Brand. The objective was to engage the marketing teams with a human-centered approach of managing brands.
12 See Martin, R.L. (2009). *The Design of Business: Why Design Thinking Is the Next Competitive Advantage.* Boston, MA: Harvard Business Press.

4 Keeping the Momentum

1 The CCD team was a central organization that included designers and researchers who worked on strategic future-work, cross-business efforts, cascaded best practices, and so on. The XD Leadership team was made up

of XD directors and the XD community was a "community" that included anyone who worked in a user-experience function. Members worked across Intuit. It was not a formal group. CCD, however, "led" the group.

2 You can find out more about The Wallet Exercise at https://www.ideo.com /blog/build-your-creative-confidence-the-wallet-exercise.

3 Customer-driven innovation (CDI) is an approach to developing products that Intuit embraced to innovate.

4 See Martin, R.L. (2011). "The Innovation Catalysts." *Harvard Business Review 89*(6): 82–7.

5 The Strategy Group at Intuit was classically trained with years of management consulting experience. The team provided in-house services for Intuit, using rigorous research to identify future directions and predict market size and opportunities.

6 See Ries, E. (2011). *The Lean Startup: How Today's Entrepreneurs Use Continuous Innovation to Create Radically Successful Businesses*. New York: Crown Business.

7 See Intuit. "Our Values." Accessed 13 January 2023. https://www.intuit .com/content/dam/intuit/intuitcom/company/images/intuit -operating-values.png.

5 Design for Joy

1 Zuber, C., and Moody, L. (2016). "Learning from the Best: Unpacking the Journey of Organizational Design Thinking Leaders." Paper presented at the 21st DMI Academic Design Management Conference, Boston, MA, 28–9 July; Zuber, C.D., Alterescu, V., and Chow, M.P. (2005). "Fail Often to Succeed Sooner: Adventures in Innovation." *The Permanente Journal 9*(4): 44.

2 Marilyn Chow, personal interview with authors, 20 August 2012.

3 Chris McCarthy, personal interview with authors, August 2011.

4 McCreary, L. (2010). "Kaiser Permanente's Innovation on the Front Lines." *Harvard Business Review 88*(9): 92–4.

5 See Innovation Learning Network. "About." Accessed 15 March 2023. https://iln.org.

6 See Kaiser Permanente. "Garfield Innovation Center." Accessed 16 January 2023. https://garfieldcenter.kaiserpermanente.org.

7 Christi Zuber Chow, personal interview with Lisa Carlgren, 23 August 2012.

6 Throwing a Hand Grenade at the Bureaucracy

1 Nissen, C.J. (2006). Presentation of External Evaluation of MindLab. Open Futures Consortium Meeting, Warsaw, October.

2 Christian Bason, interview with author, 22 August 2014.
3 See "MindLab: The Evolution of a Public Innovation Lab." (2016). TheGovLab. Accessed 6 August 2021. http://thegovlab.org/mindlab-the -evolution-of-a-public-innovation-lab.
4 Carstensen, H.V., and Bason, C. (2012). "Powering Collaborative Policy Innovation: Can Innovation Labs Help?" *The Innovation Journal: The Public Sector Innovation Journal*, 17(1): 18.
5 Christian Bason, interview.
6 Christian Bason, interview.
7 Dunne, D. (2011). "User-centered Design and Design-centred Business Schools." In R. Cooper, S. Junginger, and T. Lockwood (Eds.), *The Handbook of Design Management*, 128–43. London: Bloomsbury Academic.
8 Jakob Schjørring, interview with author, 22 August 2014.
9 Christian Bason, interview.
10 Boland Jr., R., and Collopy, F. (2004). "Design Matters for Management." In R. Boland Jr. and F. Collopy (Eds.), *Managing as Designing*, 4. Stanford, CA: Stanford Business Books.
11 Jakob Schjørring, interview.
12 Bason, C. (2018). *Leading Public Sector Innovation: Co-creating for a Better Society*. Bristol: Policy Press.
13 McClory, J., and Andersson, E.N. (2011). "North Stars – Nordic." *Monocle Magazine*, 14(5): 121–4.
14 Carstensen and Bason. (2012). "Power Collaborative Policy Innovation," 20.
15 "The Journey of MindLab." (2015). InnovaGov. https://redeinovagov .blogspot.com/2015/12/the-journey-of-mindlab-parte-12.html.
16 "Mindlab 2.0: Denmark Establishes Its Next-Generation Innovation Lab." (2018). Apolitical. https://apolitical.co/solution-articles/en/mindlab -2-0-denmark-establishes-its-next-generation-innovation-lab.
17 Such a problem arises in experimenting with new drugs for hitherto incurable diseases, as seen in the case of Ebola in 2014. Cohen, J. (2014, October 16). "Issues Continue to Dog the Testing of Ebola Drugs and Vaccines." *Science*. http://news.sciencemag.org/health/2014/10/issues-continue -dog-testing-ebola-drugs-and-vaccines.
18 National Audit Office. (2006). "Achieving Innovation in Central Government Organisations." https://www.nao.org.uk/report/achieving -innovation-in-central-government-organisations/.
19 Carstensen and Bason. (2012). "Power Collaborative Policy Innovation," 19.
20 Carstensen and Bason. (2012). "Power Collaborative Policy Innovation," 20.

21 For a more detailed version of this timeline, see the Design for Europe website, http://www.designforeurope.eu/sites/default/files/asset/document/mindlab_thejourney_final.pdf.
22 "How Public Design? A Conference at Mindlab." (2013). Putting People First. https://blog.experientia.com/how-public-design-a-conference-at-mindlab/.
23 See European Commission, Research and Innovation. (2013). *Powering European Public Sector Innovation: Towards a New Architecture Report of the Expert Group on Public Sector Innovation*. https://ec.europa.eu/futurium/en/system/files/ged/42-public_sector_innovation_-_towards_a_new_architecture.pdf.

7 The Making of a Design-Led Innovation Strategy

1 The quotes presented in this chapter are drawn from over thirty interviews that the authors conducted with Mirvac staff between 2016 and 2020.
2 "Chook" is Australian for hen/chicken.
3 See Mirvac. (2019). "Mirvac No.1 Innovative Property Company." https://www.mirvac.com/about/news-and-media/mirvac-no1-innovative-property-company.
4 See Mirvac. (2019). "Mirvac Group FY Results – 30 June 2019." https://www.mirvac.com/about/news-and-media/mirvac-group-fy-results---30-june-2019.

8 From Department to Consultancy

1 See Swisscom. (n.d.). "About Us." Accessed 23 January 2023. https://www.swisscom.ch/en/about.html.
2 The NPS indicates the degree to which customers are willing to recommend Swisscom, its products, and services.
3 Taylor, C. (2018). *Oops! Innovation Is No Accident*. Bern: Editions Weblaw.

10 An Army of One

1 See Mitchell, J. (2013). "Who Are the Long-Term Unemployed?" Washington, DC: The Urban Institute. https://www.urban.org/sites/default/files/publication/23911/412885-Who-Are-the-Long-Term-Unemployed-.PDF.
2 Career leadership refers to the process of taking charge of one's career by actively developing and implementing strategies to achieve career goals. It involves taking ownership of one's professional development and making deliberate choices to pursue career advancement opportunities.

3 Career staff refers to employees who work in a particular field or industry and have made a long-term commitment to building their career in that area. These individuals typically have a high level of expertise and experience in their field and are committed to continuous learning and professional development.

11 Veteran-Centered Healthcare

1 Chapman, A.W. (2008). *Mixed-Gender Basic Training: The US Army Experience, 1973–2004*. Washington, DC: U.S. Government Printing Office. https://www.tradoc.army.mil/wp-content/uploads/2020/10/Mixed-Gender-Basic-Training.-The-US-Army-Experience-Anne-W.-Chapman.pdf.
2 See Hefling, K. (2011, April 22). "They're Not Guys: New Gear to Fit Female Soldiers." *The Seattle Times*. https://www.seattletimes.com/nation-world/theyre-not-guys-new-gear-to-fit-female-soldiers/. See also Bensel, C.K., and Kish, R.N. (1983). "Lower Extremity Disorders among Men and Women in Army Basic Training and Effects of Two Types of Boots." Natick, MA: Natick Research and Development Laboratories. https://apps.dtic.mil/sti/citations/ADA133002.
3 See Wax-Thibodeaux, E. (2015, September 5). "One Female Veteran's Epic Quest for a 'Foot That Fits.'" *The Washington Post*. https://www.washingtonpost.com/politics/one-female-veterans-epic-quest-for-a-foot-that-fits/2015/09/05/b0e226c4-4ff5-11e5-8c19-0b6825aa4a3a_story.html.
4 See Kaiser Permanente. (n.d.). "About." Accessed 25 January 2023. https://about.kaiserpermanente.org/our-story/our-care/trust-me-im-the-patient.
5 VA Office of Inspector General. (2014). *Veterans Health Administration: Review of Alleged Patient Deaths, Patient Wait Times, and Scheduling Practices at the Phoenix VA Health Care System*. https://www.va.gov/oig/pubs/VAOIG-14-02603-267.pdf.
6 Commission on Care. (2016). *Final Report of the Commission on Care*. https://psnet.ahrq.gov/issue/final-report-commission-care.
7 Brooks, S. (2016). "Customer Experience at Veterans Affairs." *Design Management Review* 27(1): 28–34.
8 Konkel, F.R. (2016). "Improving the Veteran Experience is (Literally) the Top Priority at VA." Nextgov. http://www.nextgov.com/cio-briefing/2016/03/improving-Veteran-experience-literally-top-priority-va/126897/.
9 VA Center for Innovation and Public Policy Lab. (2016). "Veteran Access to Mental Health Services: Current Experiences and Future Design

Opportunities to Better Serve Veterans and Front-line Providers." https://static1.squarespace.com/static/52cc7007e4b0a71de057df1e/t/5bbe37c608 52299a1c68d6aa/1539192778778/VeteranAccessToMentalHealthServices. pdf.

10 VA Center for Innovation and Public Policy Lab. (2016). "Veteran Access to Mental Health Services: Current Experiences and Future Design Opportunities to Better Serve Veterans and Front-line Providers." https://static1 .squarespace.com/static/52cc7007e4b0a71de057df1e/t/5bbe37c60852299a 1c68d6aa/1539192778778/VeteranAccessToMentalHealthServices.pdf.

11 Example prototype (not in use) of redesigned VA Form that seeks to use relatable language, feel supportive, and not trigger mental health-related symptoms while a veteran is outside the care of a professional. The prototype is one of many developed by teams of VA employees, non-VA designers, and veterans.

Index

Page numbers in **bold** denote figures and tables